For Mary Sprifke
a delightful
fellow + traveller!

Forgotten War
Forgiven Guilt

David A. Witts

David A. Witts
July 05

Cover painting by
Bill Neale

YUCCA TREE PRESS
LAS CRUCES, NEW MEXICO

Yucca Tree Press
an imprint of
Barbed Wire Publishing
270 Avenida de Mesilla
Las Cruces, New Mexico 88005 USA

Cover painting by Bill Neale
Book and cover design by Vicki Ligon
Fonts used in this book are
Horley Old Style and ITC Legacy Sans

First printing: July 2003
Printed in the United States of America.

ISBN #1-881325-71-7

1   2   3   4   5

Dedication

To those two angels
whose wings touched the earth
during my lifetime—

My wife Jean

and

My daughter Elane

Commentaries

"A highly personal and passionate commentary on the 13th Air Force by someone who was there. Opinionated and shocking, and also highly readable." –Milton Friedman, Nobel Laureate

"*Forgotten War, Forgiven Guilt* will open your eyes! For the great war, the epic war the war that saved the nation and humanity itself to be just ancient history to today's youngsters is a tragedy - but trying to rewrite it to prove ourselves guilty is a crime!" –David Nevin, Author of *Dream West, 1812, Treason*

"The epic campaigns of the U.S. Army Air Force during World War II have never been adequately chronicled. The irrepressible David Witts - a veteran survivor of those campaigns - undertakes in the pages of *Forgotten War, Forgiven Guilt* to redress this historic neglect. Readers of his fascinating and well-informed pages will agree that he has succeeded admirably." –Keith E. Eiler, Historian - Hoover Institution on War, Peace and Revolution and author of *Wedemeyer On War and Peace*

"First, your book is a magnificent achievement. I was totally enthralled with the description of missions, the hop-scotching tactics, and your ability to describe the events and people. To say that it is a meritorious work is a great understatement." –Roger Mansell, Publisher

"Power-packed with little known wartime data. Excellent review of the Japanese enemy few understood. Great writing, great reading about the short-changed Pacific War." –Mauro J. Messina, Editor and Historian, 13th Air Force Veterans Association

"A must read book for its historical value and honest recording of wartime events. David Witts lived this story night and day, flying over uncharted land and water, rescuing down crews, POWs and the war's wounded, plus flying many secret missions for the War Department. *Forgotten War, Forgiven Guilt* is a tribute to the Americans and Allied soldiers who fought, lived and died in the Pacific conflict to save their nation and homeland." –Bill Harris [Editor's Note: Bill Harris is the greatest living Ace of the 13th Air Force]

"A well written account of a small air force achieving great successes. It brings back many memories of air combat I experienced from Guadalcanal to Rabaul. I am appreciative that David Witts has done such a masterful job of writing this history of the 13th Air Force." –George T. Chandler, P-38 Fighter Ace, 339th Fighter Squadron.

The Cover

The cover painting for this book was done by Bill Neale, a world renowned artist who specializes in automobiles and airplanes. Bill is a founding member of the prestigious Automotive Fine Arts Society (AFAS) and a contributing artist to *Car and Driver*, *Cavallino*, and *Automobile* magazines. He is best known for his beautiful, private commissions of automobiles, both new and old. Mr. Neale resides in Dallas, Texas with his wife of fifty-one years, Nelda.

Table of Contents

David A. Witts

Foreword

Card carrying historians will say this book lacks scholarly composition since it is not tethered to chronology or to statistics—and they would be right. Each chapter tells an independent story. The book is episodic because that is the nature of war.

The 13th Air Force was a small, gutsy bunch of men and their planes, forged together during the darkest days of Guadalcanal, whose remarkable exploits have gone unreported. They rose daily to fight the massive Japanese air armada when merely taking to the air was often a death warrant. Flying the war's longest missions through tumultuous weather, they hemorrhaged the enemy and shot down its military icon, Admiral Yamamoto, after which Japan never won another battle. It is unlikely we shall see their likes again.

The reader will also discover the Hidden Holocaust of torture, suicide bombers, hell ships and slave labor, which inexplicably have been forgiven and forgotten. War criminals in Germany, however, were punished by the thousands.

A generation which earned its right to be authoritative and judgmental now sings its swan song. It should be heeded.

Preface

I. Missing Air Force

It all started so simply. I donated to the Hoover Institution at Stanford University my World War II collection of maps, photographs, flying equipment, Japanese battle flags and paraphernalia collected during a fifty-mission tour with the 13th Air Force in the South Pacific. The Hoover Archivist asked if I could provide a history to accompany the items. To my disbelief no history of the 13th Air Force and its remarkable accomplishments existed.

How could an entire air force be missing? Trying to find its history graduated into an emotional narrative spanning half a century. What emerged four years later was a book of unusual architecture founded on personal memories recalled with humor and remorse, buttressed with first-hand experiences of others, and laced with dark and savage deeds scrolled across the immense tableau of the Pacific. Connecting tissue for the book is formed by people and events in which I was personally involved or in the blast area. Shorn of proper literary protocol, it is a maverick book.

The 13th Air Force is now our largest air force. I asked the Official Historian of 13th Air Force on Guam for its history. It came back. A total of thirteen pages, three pages devoted to its Commanding General. World War II was graced with ten lines. Neither my own squadron nor our renowned plane, the Catalina PBY patrol bomber, was mentioned.

The Pacific War 1941-1945 by John Costello, "The comprehensive account of World War II in the Pacific," never mentions the 13th Air Force. *The American Heritage Picture History Of World War II* by C. L. Sulzberger, the inclusive history of the War, ignores the 13th. Edward Jablonski's *Pictorial History Of World War II* discusses every air force except the 13th.

Michael John Claringbould, Publisher of *Aerothentic Publications* in Australia, is the authority on South Pacific air war. I asked him about the Pacific slight. His reply was quick and bold: "I agree with everything you say. The 13th Air Force story has not been told. Furthermore, nearly everything on it printed to date is completely inaccurate. The 13th produced some of the most interesting military aviation ever. It was certainly more interesting than the aerial trench warfare which characterized the European Theater."

I confronted the Chief of the Air Force Historical Research Agency with the paucity of the 13th's history, and the outrageous omission of my own squadron. Although "puzzled" by the omissions, he stonewalled with cavalier disregard: "We regret the omissions, but obviously cannot reverse a thirty year old decision." Thus, there are explanations for the omission. There are no excuses.

Mauro Messina was in the 13th Air Force on Guadalcanal, and now publishes the *13th Air Force Veterans Bulletin*. Doggedly tracking down why the 13th Air Force lacks a written history, he found the air war was reported through communiques of army and navy field commanders. These communiques sourced the *Official History of Air War in the Pacific* written years later by Craven and Cates. They presented history through the eyes of the major commanders, not the actual combat reports. They focused on the 5th Air Force to the virtual exclusion of the 13th.

When MacArthur was ordered to Australia in April 1942, he was a general without an army or an air force. As the army reorganized in Australia, its first air force was the 5th Air Force, commanded by the vigorous General Kenney. Pacific communiques originated with General Kenney, who favored his 5th Air Force in all reports. MacArthur's headquarters were a fiefdom in which the newborn 13th Air Force had no knights at the communique table. Kenney's influence surfaces in Craven's confession that "official history" was based on communiques of field commanders: "The 5th Air Force operated with the advantage of more favorable command relations than any other air force in the war with Japan. If the 5th Air Force receives an undue share of attention, no slight is intended for organizations less fortunate in their resources."

But that's only part of the story. During its first year, the 13th was under navy command COMAIRSOL-SOPAC (Command Air Solomons South Pacific). Inter-service rivalry was an ugly fact of life in the Pacific. Innate jealousy with the army and endemic hostility to MacArthur left the navy with little inclination to report accomplishments of army units under its command.

One Of Our Planes Is Missing, the popular World War II ballad, is a cameo of the small, gutsy bunch of flyers and their planes, cobbled together in the darkest days of the Pacific War. Living in jungles, always advancing, always fighting, it was called "The Jungle Air Force." Without a home, its base was 'just one damn island after another'.

The 13th Air Force flew the greatest distances and longest missions of the war. Its missions were all over water. Its maps were vague Australian and Dutch charts, some areas being identified as "unexplored." There was no such thing as reserve fuel. Every mission was a stretch across the unearthly architecture of the sky. Planes often ditched, unable to make it back to base. Flying through formidable weather along the equator, boiling black clouds constantly erupted, forming a tumultuous barrier that could be neither climbed nor skirted. Groping through schizophrenic weather brought down as many planes as enemy fire. Going down was always behind enemy lines—in the vastness of the ocean or suffocation of the jungle. Parachuting flyers were strafed by Japanese planes. Capture meant torture and death. The Presidential Citation awarded my squadron cited that not one of its planes ever turned back from a mission.

The 13th's theater was 4,000,000 square miles. Starting at Guadalcanal, it knifed north through the Solomons and Admiralties, hopscotched the 1,500 mile length of New Guinea, hit every major island in the Philippines, fought in Borneo, Celebes, Marianas, Ryukyus, and struck distant targets in Indonesia, Java, Malaya, Indo China and Formosa. It flew in fourteen campaigns: Guadalcanal, Solomons, Bismarck Archipelago, Eastern Mandates, Central Pacific, Western Pacific, New Guinea, Southern Philippines, Luzon, China, Borneo, Ryukyus, China-Burma-India, and Japan. It ended the war over Okinawa, Formosa, China and Japan.

Rendering the 13th's history unique is not only its immense geographical sweep, but its performance against an appalling mosaic of distance and deprivation, torture and execution. The 13th lived in a jungle prison with no escape from heat, humidity and disease; trucks, tents and men mired in mud; no fresh water or fresh food. Dysentery, jungle rot, salt pills and Atabrine tablets were its daily diet. Animals and insects crawled and crept, slithered and bit. They all loved white meat.

Unknown islands and endless seas are the final resting place for which these men fought. There are no cemeteries in the sky. Some sleep forever on sand, some float in water, but they don't know where, for they are dead. Incredibly, the saga of those men and their planes is missing from official history.

II. Forgotten War

Baffled and resentful of history's neglect of the Pacific, I turned to Milton Friedman, my candidate for the smartest man on earth, and asked: "Why are books and movies, newspaper and TV stories so obsessed with the European side of World War II? Why is the Pacific, where war began for America and ended for the world, over-looked?"

Milton Friedman replied: "You make a very strong case indeed for the Eurocentric character of the reporting on World War II... You are clear-ly right that something is needed, and you are clearly the person to provide it. Your letter showed both an extraor-dinary grasp of the history of the 13th Air Force and an expository ability that is quite exceptional. The two together would make a splendid book. By all means, it seems to me, you ought to undertake to write such a book... Perhaps you can get the air force to contract for a historian to

My friend, Milton Friedman

write a history of the 13th Air Force... but it would not have the force, immediacy, the passion that you would give to such a book. By all means take it on."

Thus encouraged, I replied, quoting John Connally's comment to the Senate considering him for Secretary of the Navy: "I'm vain enough to believe it, and foolish enough to try it!"

So I set pen to paper. Without official records, the product is part memoir, part history and part meditation on history, sometimes sketchy, sometimes vivid. Lacking the accuracy of a historian or the eloquence of

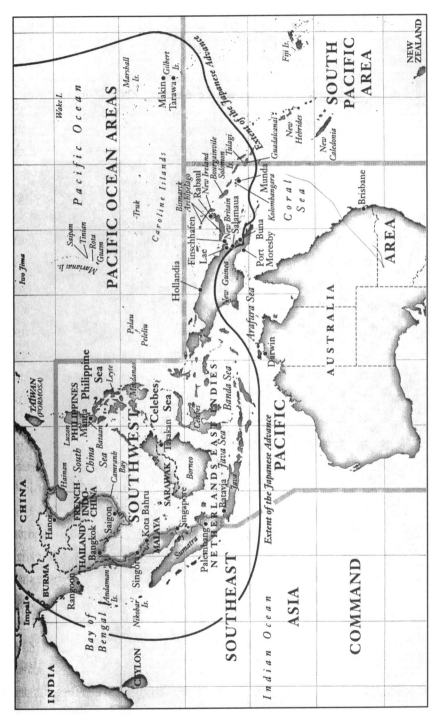

Japanese influence 1942

a novelist, it is a tapestry of events swirling in that distant part of the world where history was being made. A project of preservation, I write about what I did, what I saw and what I know. It is a maverick book without pretension or protocol, recalling past events and their current consequences. Professional writers report in statistical detail and cultured prose. But that is not the history I wish to tell. The powerful humanistic story of the Pacific air war is a story that has never been told.

The "great war" was many wars in many places. One war was across the Atlantic—it was Europe's war. The other was in and across the Pacific—it was our war, it was the neglected war. Unfathomable distances, primitive jungles and trackless oceans, its tangled skein of brutality and death merged in a cauldron of misery, shielded from public view. America's airmen were singled out for torture and atrocities so bestial they numb the mind. Instances reported here are not judgmental, but rather to record barbarism that confronted the Army Air Forces. Historian John W. Dower wrote: "There was an obsession with extermination on both sides—it was a war without mercy."

T he Pacific is the oldest and greatest of oceans. Its endless waters roll in from the west on America, and from the east on Japan's rocky shores. Covering a third of the globe, it is vaster than all world land area combined. It is studded with thousands of wild jungles and desolate islands. Its temperature ranges from tropical to frigid. Its waters face white, black, brown and yellow races. Its civilizations range from aboriginal to advanced. I saw cannibals in New Guinea, head hunters in Borneo and pygmies in the Philippines. Balboa named it Pacifica for peaceful. Was he ever wrong!

The Pacific War produced tectonic shifts in geography and politics. Japan, a warring nation which had not known defeat in a thousand years, was vanquished by a rain of fire from above. Empires 400 years in the building disappeared. Colonies became nations. China became one nation and then two. Korea bifurcated. The Pacific became an American lake.

Fought in the shadow of Eurocentrism, the Pacific war suffered a paucity of news coverage. Correspondents like Ernest Hemingway and John Steinbeck, and commentators like Edward R. Murrow covered the European War from hotels in London and Paris, rather than Pacific jungles and foxholes. News coverage was further unbalanced by saturated navy and marine reporting. The army and its air force dropped into a black hole of history, despite their being in forty-four months of uninterrupted, unrelieved combat. Their casualties were greater than those of the navy and marines combined. In the public mind, the war took place at

Pearl Harbor and Midway, Iwo Jima and Okinawa, all navy shows. Yet the army and air force campaigns in the Philippines alone produced more Japanese casualties than Iwo Jima and Okinawa combined. Japanese General Yamashita's army was viciously fighting at war's end. He did not surrender until ordered by the Emperor. I know. My plane picked up Yamashita in Northern Luzon and flew him in to surrender.

We destroyed a savage enemy in a type of war never fought before. It was an amphibious war fought across islands scattered over millions of square miles from the Equator to the Arctic. There were no cities, no factories, no roads, no airdromes. The terrain was a montage of beaches and jungles, mountains and coral reefs, heat and humidity, distance and disease. Battles raged on islands with unpronounceable names that couldn't be found on a map. Much territory was unexplored. Natives spoke no recognizable language. Many had never seen a white man.

We entered Europe's war at times and places of our choosing. The Pacific war came to us. The December 7, 1941 headline read: "Japs Bomb Pearl Harbor." At that moment America changed forever. Outraged, we left plows standing in the field in a rush to enlist. We lusted for revenge against an enemy that stabbed us in the back. Volunteers stood in lines to join up. Women worked in factories. Mothers planted victory gardens. Children collected tin cans. Armies first clashed in hand-to-hand combat 5,000 miles away on a peninsula in the Philippines called Bataan and on a rock named Corregidor.

The Japanese tsunami swept across the Pacific from Siberia to Singapore. In its wake our battleships lay in Pearl Harbor mud, our planes smashed on runways. British and Dutch navies were destroyed. Japanese forces controlled a third of the earth. Only the Americans on Bataan and Corregidor fought on, holding out for five grim months. Aid was promised, but it never came. The 100,000 man American and Filipino army, starving and abandoned, surrendered in the greatest defeat ever suffered by American arms. Survivors were herded off to prison camps in a parade of brutality. Ten thousand died in the Bataan Death March. A news blackout fell. The Pacific was moved to the back of the bus, yet the bitter Pacific War raged in obscurity for almost three years before D-Day in Europe in battles for inches and five hundred mile leaps. It received scant attention then, and even less today.

Europe seized center stage. MacArthur, beleaguered in Australia, was told he could not have one plane, one ship or one man needed in Europe. North Africa, Sicily, Italy and France were all invaded before we returned to the Philippines.

Soon after Pearl Harbor, Japan began constructing an airfield on an unknown island with an improbable name, Guadalcanal, whose air base would sever our lifeline to Australia. That shocked the Chiefs of Staff out of their European myopia. The marines were rushed in like a volunteer fire department. During landing operations in August 1942, the navy suffered its worst defeat in history. Losing four cruisers in ten minutes, Admiral Fletcher spooked and withdrew his ships, stranding the marines with only what they carried ashore. Marines viewed his abrupt departure as desertion.

In a place nobody planned, the battle line was drawn. Japan controlled the land, sea and air around Guadalcanal. But the marines and a handful of fighter planes doggedly held on. Guadalcanal became a six-month Bastogne. Several disastrous sea battles whittled the navy down to one carrier, which it withdrew. An oddball assortment of planes and pilots from the army, navy and marines were spooned on to a short, mean jungle airstrip, code named "Cactus." That polyglot was known as the "Cactus Air Force," from which embattled nest the 13th Air Force hatched.

Outnumbered, the 13th Air Force honed its skills flying inferior planes against a swaggering enemy. Hanging on against shelling from sea, bombing from air and attack from land, it grew up fast and hard. Within a year, it helped splash the enemy air force so thoroughly that Japan, for the first time, fell back. In the most significant mission, a 13th Air Force pilot, Lt. Rex Barber in his P-38, shot down Japan's military icon, Admiral Yamamoto. This marked the high water mark of Japanese conquest, after which Japan never won another battle. The loss was so devastating it was withheld from the Japanese public for months. COMGENSOPAC Millard Harmon wired congratulations: "The 13th Air Force, born January 13, 1943, is now almost a year old and what a year! You have fought and sweated through mud and heat, malaria, dangers and hardships. You helped break forever the myth of Jap invincibility and to blast him from Guadalcanal, the Russels, Munda, New Georgia and now, Treasury and Bougainville."

The remarkable story of the 13th Air Force has never been told. In a huge, remote theater of operations avoided by war correspondents, the army air war in the Pacific is a four-year black hole. At the end of a 10,000 mile line, the 13th Air Force was the runt of the supply litter. Navy got first pick. Marines stole what they wanted, leaving the Army Air Force to scratch. European air forces were popularized in movies like Memphis Belle, Twelve O'Clock High and Hogan's Heroes, with crews sauntering into Piccadilly on days off. The Pacific was a sentence without parole— "Golden Gate in Forty Eight."

III. Forgiven Guilt

Japanese atrocities were more bestial, of longer duration and more widespread than those of Germany. German atrocities left survivors and a vengeful constituency. Japan's crimes left few survivors and no constituency. German atrocities were planned and persistent—Japan's were episodic and personal. Germany's Holocaust left photographs and memoirs—Japan's left none. Unlike Germany, which apologized, prosecuted its criminals and compensated its victims, Japan remains in smug and resolute denial. Its criminals marched seamlessly into post-war government and industry. Japanese war crimes were forgotten and forgiven. Unknown at the time and buried beneath mountains of denial, an enormous crime against humanity festers—the "Hidden Holocaust." The Japanese, individually polite, collectively become very aggressive. Descriptions of barbarism, some first-hand, some never before told, are so repulsive the reader may turn away. They are included, not to pass judgment, but as stark reality of the Pacific War.

Pacific veterans are victimized by a double standard. America's greatest defeat was at Corregidor, where 40,000 soldiers surrendered. Forced into a Death March, 10,000 perished. Others went to prison camps, where almost fifty percent died from torture and starvation. Some went as slave labor to work in factories and mines for Mitsubishi, et al. The U.S. government ordered its POWs never to discuss their treatment by Japan. Survivors who came home were paid $1.00 per day for the term of their captivity, subject to an IRS haircut when paid.

Those forced to work in German factories were recently awarded $5 billion for past wages. Clinton cheered the payment saying: "this was payment of a debt long overdue." In the proceeding filed by slave laborers in Japan, the U.S. State Department intervened, asking that the case be dismissed. A federal judge obliged. Piling on, the Justice Department persuaded the Judiciary to ban such future claims from the courts.

The Holocaust is discussed more today than when it happened. Japan's "Hidden Holocaust" remains obscure. American flyers were designated "special war criminals." Tortured and executed, their survival rate approached zero. The emperor was neither indicted nor tried. Japanese books ignore the Rape of Nanking, thousands of women enslaved to "comfort" their troops, sacking Manila and waging germ warfare. During its decade of aggression, Japan looted treasures like the Nazis stripped Europe. Unlike German loot which ended up in private caches and Swiss banks, Asian booty was siphoned to the Imperial Palace. Japan's war criminals are enshrined at Yasakuni Shrine where they are regularly honored by the emperor and government officials. Japan's germ warfare program is only now being exposed. Survivors of prison camps finally find voice. America's slave labor victims, seeking compensatory wages from Japanese "keiretsu," like Kawasaki and Mitsui, now find their cause blocked by the U.S. State and Justice Departments.

These stories will disappear with the actors, but much can be learned from them. There is nothing new about crashing airplanes into targets. We suffered thousands of such attacks. Kamikazes at Okinawa alone inflicted thousands of casualties and destroyed countless ships. Today's terrorists give intense relevance to the Pacific War. Robert Conquest, the eminent historian of the Hoover Institution, wrote: "It is now clear that Americans have had an insufficient knowledge about the mental world of those outside America, and, in particular, about the mental world of the enemies of the democratic way of life."

A decade of rapacious aggression and plunder was fought and defeated in a war of sheer hatred by men locked in a four year struggle of brutality and death. When they came home, they brought the sounds of war with them, except for a hundred thousand Americans who sleep with the Pacific on their chest. But all has been forgiven and forgotten, lingering only in a few memories and spoken of during whispered goodbyes.

Acknowledgements

Some authors string a long list of people for recognition. This is a short list. There were few helpers. They were significant.

Rex Barber. The quiet, unassuming pilot who flew his P-38 into the formation of two bombers and six fighters escorting Admiral Yamamoto to Bougainville. His bravery matched his skill as he shot down Yamamoto's plane. Although another pilot claimed credit, later events, including Japanese testimony, proved that victory belonged to Rex Barber. He personally critiqued the chapter "Sayonara—Yamamoto."

Emile Beauregard. A quiet fellow penned up in Massachusetts. He has constantly encouraged this project. In addition, he solicited many bits of the personalized history found in the book. He closed every handwritten letter to me with "God Bless You and What You Are Doing."

Doug Canning. A P-38 pilot who flew on the "Killer Flight" of the Yamamoto Mission, provided significant and personal insights of the Guadalcanal days.

George Chandler. Another 13th Air Force Ace who survived the crush of Guadalcanal. He formed the Second Yamamoto Association in order to correct the implanted confusion of the Yamamoto mission and to seek proper recognition for Major John Mitchell who planned the mission, and for Lt. Rex Barber who made the kill. From day one, George was encouraging and enthusiastic.

Milton Friedman of the Hoover Institution at Stanford, who encouraged me to write the story and then patiently critiqued it.

Bill Harris. The greatest living Ace of the 13th Air Force, whose skill, courage and devotion were so remarkable, a book was written about him. His contributions appear throughout this book and his encouragement supported it.

Michael Mead. A computer whiz who took many war weary photos I had made in real time with a 98¢ Brownie Kodak, and nourished them back to vitality.

Mauro Messina, publisher of the 13th Air Force Veterans Association Bulletin. He published the 13th Air Force newspaper on Guadalcanal. He was the first to challenge the bureaucracy to correct the historical hiatus. He critiqued and corrected many chapters.

Deon "Dee" Short. With special appreciation for her long-suffering assistance and for being my severest critic.

Emergency kits carried by David Witts, author of Forgotten War—Forgiven Guilt. *The originals are in the Hoover Archives.*

Section I

THE DOGS OF WAR

December 4, 1941, three days before Pearl Harbor, Navy Secretary Frank Knox predicted that "war with Japan could start any minute. It will be a Navy show and we are ready for them. It will be over in six months." The Pearl Harbor attack caused Hitler to exult: "Now it is impossible for us to lose. We have an ally which has never been vanquished in 3,000 years."

Japan, an insular nation, was not self-sufficient in raw materials, nor could it ever be. Their solution was simple—take what they needed from their neighbors. On November 25, 1941, Japan launched attack forces in five different directions simultaneously. Even in a world already pregnant with war, this was brash and brazen aggression without precedent.

The Great East Asian Co-Prosperity Sphere was long in planning. Meticulous espionage identified the precise location of each ship in Pearl Harbor, anchored and helpless. Singapore, the Gibraltar of the Far East, suffered the humiliation of surrender to an invading army one-third its own size. The French handed over Indo-China. When the onslaught ended, Japan achieved what five great powers, Spain, Holland, Britain, France and Russia had attempted, but failed to master—all the lands surrounding the seas of China.

When that tsunami came to rest, the Rising Sun controlled the entire western Pacific, Southeast Asia, much of China, and was poised to attack India and Australia. During that rampage the U.S., British and Dutch fleets were sunk without Japan's losing a single battleship. That's the scenario America faced as it went to war in the Pacific.

CHAPTER ONE

How Now Book?

I'm proud of my generation. We survived a great depression and fought a great war. The last voice of that generation speaks. It talks of then and now. When the time comes, as it surely will, when America once again is attacked, will that moment be met with resolution? That generation watches and worries.

We lived through the most interesting period in history. Travel escalated from horse and wagon to space, the atom was split, genes altered, and men walked on the moon. When we grew up, obedience was automatic. Values were respected. Thousands of small towns comprised the world of Norman Rockwell. Families lived in real neighborhoods where people knew each other. Family recreation was checkers, parlor games and jigsaw puzzles. Going to Grandma's house for Thanksgiving Dinner was as ritualistic as the Christmas Tree. Parades, patriotism and parents were the norm. God and country were revered. I was so patriotic I'd salute a mail box. School prayer was routine. School days began with the Pledge of Allegiance.

Author David Witts, with new wings.

Bibles did not have to be smuggled into classrooms. Hard work was the norm. Good guys won. Cowboys kissed the horse instead of the girl. Our values were galvanized by parents, school and church. We were unhyphenated Americans, anxious to do good and one day be rich. America was the Promised Land where blessings were earned from personal achievement.

Then, students actually studied history. World War I hung fresh, what with Armistice Day parades and July 4th celebrations. Then, the kid next door was Audie Murphy. He lived a few miles away, one of nine children of tenant farmers Emmett and Josie Murphy:

"Audie was in the 4th grade when his daddy run off, and he quit school to take care of his family. At eleven he was the breadwinner for his mother and eight brothers and sisters. They didn't have enough to eat. His family was living in a box-car. He kept his head up. He kept himself neat and clean, and he wasn't afraid of anything.

"He was 5 ft. 7 and weighed 130 pounds when he entered the Army, a baby-faced buck private. He returned three years later, a First Lieutenant and the most honored soldier in American history. He received a battlefield commission and 33 awards including the Congressional Medal of Honor and every medal for valor the U.S. can bestow. He received the highest awards from France and from Belgium. He was wounded three times. When he came home, he was 20 years old."

When the War ended, we came home, went back to school and work. We were so busy trying to make up for those four lost years, we had no inclination to talk about our experiences. Our conduct was not original. It was traditional. It was a deeply shared national experience. There was no sneaking off to Oxford. Roosevelt's four sons served in uniform. We dropped into the Memory Hole, still married to our first wives. But now, half a century later, there is a fascination about that War, its people, their agony and their ecstasy. Today's interest in the War comes as a surprise to those who fought it. It's good to know some people do care, realizing who paid the butcher's bill for the prosperity they blissfully enjoy. Now that others want to hear our stories, they come as wistful goodbyes.

We didn't discuss our experiences. Our families would not understand the love of men for men, born in danger. We shared what Hemingway called "the steely voiced call to battle into a world where death, destruction, sacrifice and valor were the norm. Their universally shared purpose welded them as one." Our war is over—we walk slowly into history. The setting sun casts long shadows across our path. None of us would ever get over it.

An intensity still burns in our hearts for fallen comrades. It is seen in interviews as tears roll down wrinkled cheeks and voices falter. Bob

Greene, in his book *Duty*, described a reunion of his father's squadron. "When Carol sang *Where or When* and *I'll Be Seeing You*, she looked out into the eyes of the men and women in her small audience and she saw emotions so intense she had to look away." These figures so quickly slipping into the shadows are the praetorians of the Twentieth Century, the ones who turned back Hitler, Hirohito and Stalin. "Duty, Honor and Country" is our legacy.

Tom Brokaw says Americans who came of age in the Great Depression, and who fought in World War II were "the greatest generation." I think of others as the greatest. First, the Founding Fathers who risked "their lives, their fortunes and their sacred honor" to be free from oppressive taxation. Later came those wagon tracks across endless prairies, rutted by families trudging blindly westward, everything they owned in a wagon pulled by oxen and fired by hope of freedom and opportunity. They were the Greatest Generations!

Stephen Ambrose in his book *Citizen Soldiers* implores recognition of their deeds before all the voices fall silent:

"The World War II generation was a special breed. I was teaching a course on World War II to 350 students. They were dumbstruck by responsibilities of soldiers as young as they. They wondered if they could have done it—and even more, they wondered how anybody could have done it."

With World War II vets dying at the rate of 1,500 a day, it's time to reflect. Years close in quickly. Most are now gone. Some move in wheelchairs. Some cannot move at all. Each day they fight the one enemy they never defeated. I'm now the only member of my flight crew still alive.

When we pass from the scene our history will disappear because it is not taught. Youth want to be inspired, but they receive neither encouragement nor opportunity to study our history. It is not taught on campuses, which have become nurseries of hostility to the military that insures their freedom to be ungrateful. The miracle that is America can be understood when viewed through the prism of our history. Everything we have and are were fashioned by history. There's no secret to making history come alive. Historian Barbara Tuchman distilled it in two words— "tell stories."

Our story has not ended. The Pacific War lives on. Many who fought the Rising Sun still suffer its burn. They are those who survived Japanese prison camps, those who labored like zombies in Japanese mines and factories, the victims of germ warfare, and those tortured into an abbreviated life. Although forbidden by their government to discuss their hidden horrors, they brought war home with them. Suffering from savagery abroad and indifference at home, they pass away, rebuffed by their government and recused from history.

This war-time odyssey commenced on a quiet Sunday morning in a far off Pacific island when the greatest war in history engulfed America, stoking the slumbering giant into volcanic fury. In the rush for revenge, volunteers swamped enlistment offices, and men lied about their age to enlist. I walked straight from a law school class in Contracts to the Naval Air Corps Recruiting Station, savoring a vision of gold wings on white uniforms. Pre-war restrictions deemed my vision imperfect. Determined to get into the fight, I offered my skills to the FBI. Their 1941 perspective being superior to that of today, the Bureau hired me. Off to Washington I went in early 1942.

By October 1942, word flashed we were losing Guadalcanal in fighting that threatened to cut off our supply line to Australia and perhaps the whole Pacific. This was no drill. My grey flannel suit chafed ignobly and uncomfortably amidst a sea of uniforms. Off to the Army Air Corps I went, enlisting as an Aviation Cadet. Requirements for flyers were by this time less fastidious and I passed, visualizing silver wings on pinks and greens, topped by a "50 mission crush" cap. And so it came to pass. My progress through the Air Corps Training Command proceeded purposefully from Washington, D.C. to a training detachment at Martinsburg, West Virginia, basic training at Miami Beach, College Training Detachment at Spearfish, South Dakota, and Aviation Cadet Training at Santa Ana Army Air Base. Flight training was received at Ellington Field in Houston, capped by graduation, gold bars and silver wings.

The Army Air Corps, astutely recognizing talent, assigned me to instruct fledglings, a dream-posting. For a hot-shot second lieutenant instructor to be stationed in Houston, a lively, but under-militarized city was a passport to felicity. My stark habitat in the bachelor officers' quarters was soon upgraded to ad hoc accommodations at the luxurious Warwick Hotel, courtesy of a friendly occupant. The arrangement was too beatific not to have a downside. Flying Officers began their day at 0600 with a PT class. Making my way through Houston weather (New Guinea with concrete) to a sunrise rendezvous with a sadistic major conducting calisthenics on a cold concrete flight ramp disenchanted the inner man. Enthusiasm waned and attendance lagged. One day this pigheaded major jumped me hard before my peers, accusing me of slothful behavior. In a moment when reason abandoned me, I retaliated by allowing as how my cadets always topped their class, thereby contributing mightily to the war effort, and further reasoning aloud that my self-pro-claimed tutorial skills were in no way enhanced by his calisthenics class. Incapable of properly evaluating my worth, this Neanderthal ordered me to combat training at Keesler Field in Biloxi.

Painting of a PBY rescue mission

My sanity quickly returned. Ellington Field did not. My crew formed up and we went through naval flight training in a PBY. On graduation, those cheapies gave us little miniature gold wings and sent our crew to Hunter Field in Savannah to pick up our shiny new PBY. It and its suc-cessors shepherded me through an odyssey across 4,000,000 square miles of oceans, islands, jungles and mountains.

Before seeing Texas again, I would follow or lead the Pacific air war into far off places with strange names like Guadalcanal, Nadzab, Hollandia, Noemfoor, Biak, Sansapor, Morotai, Leyte, Zamboanga, Cebu, Palawan, Mindoro, Luzon, Balikpapan, Brunei, Tarakan, Celebes, Makassar, Munda, Bougainville, Ceram, Sarawak, Dobadura, Kadena and Hong Kong.

Never would I believe that I would come to know geography of the Philippines better than Texas or that I would join the Aussies to recapture the Borneo oil fields, or fly General Sir Thomas Blamey, Commanding General of the Australian Armed Forces into the invasion of Brunei Bay, or that I would be in the first plane to land at Balikpapan, or bear witness to Japanese atrocities so savage they numb the mind, or pick up General Yamashita when he walked out of the mountains of Luzon to surrender, or accidentally become the first American to set foot in Hong Kong since its capture in 1941, or be royally welcomed in Washington by

Congresswoman Clare Boothe Luce.

We were flying a Navy airplane in an Army squadron. The PBY5A's hermaphrodite body destined it to fly missions on land and sea, or lakes when supplying Moros in the highlands of Mindanao. Some were hairy scary missions like open sea landings on wind-driven swells in which rivets popped out of the hull sounding like firecrackers, or when the Japanese took great offense at our presence. Some were fun like dropping in on the submarine base at Cavite for ice cream, or the trip to Valhalla (rest leave in Sydney).

In retrospect this saga is implausible, particularly extending through fifty missions when you are actuarially dead at twenty-five. Since memories of that small, feisty 13th Air Force are in retrospect, so also should its actors be seen in their cameo appearances across the infinite stage of time.

REFERENCE

Bradley, James, *Flags of Our Fathers*, N.Y., Bantam, 2000

CHAPTER TWO

The Forgotten War— from There to Obscurity

The role of the 13th Air Force was shaped and scripted by the convoluted dynamics of the Pacific. No war in history has been like the Pacific War. Never was there a battlefield so vast. It was the first, and probably the last, war to be fought on such scale and stage. Never was the terrain so agonizing, nor the enemy so savage. Boundless water and endless sky covered an enormous area, much of it so hostile it was never explored. The enemy was viscerally hated, strange of culture and barbaric of mind. There were no highways, no cities, no buildings. Native people encountered were of a different color and civilization. Some were head-hunters who had never seen a white man; some were cannibals. It was for the most part a stone-age culture. Jungles were so debilitating, they inflicted more casualties than combat. Victims who fell into Japanese hands met with bizarre and bestial tortures. Both sides fought to the death. Few prisoners were taken. Even fewer survived. It was combat without quarter; none was asked, none was given.

There were three wars in the Pacific—a land war, a sea war and an air war. They commenced with the death of 2,500 Americans at Pearl Harbor at the very moment Japan's diplomats were in Washington talking peace (So sorry!). It ended with the most deadly air raid in history.

It began with appalling miscalculation on both sides. Japan thought we were so soft they could knock us out with a Pearl Harbor sucker punch. We ridiculed them as near-sighted, bandy-legged little people who couldn't copy straight. *Fortune Magazine* in February 1942 wrote: "these are comic opera people taking on a white giant. Our impression is a bowing, smirking little man who never invented anything, couldn't shoot or fly straight and whose war ships are top heavy and under-gunned." That they would never surrender, fight to the death, conquer Asia from Manchuria to Australia, subjugate 150 million people, and imprison 200,000 victims in ninety days was beyond our sense.

Convinced the U.S. lacked the fighting spirit of those sons of Nippon, Japan assumed we would supinely accept their conquests. The Greater

East Asian Co-prosperity Sphere envisioned Japan at its center as the Master Race. Other nations would be producer satellites. France had already handed over Indo-China, and China was occupied. Their conquest ran from Singapore, across Indonesia, to Australia. Inside this perimeter lay the oil of Borneo and the treasure trove of the Philippines. Protecting this core, lay a ring of island bases from Okinawa, running through Iwo Jima and the Marianas to Hawaii. Japan intended to fortify this outer wall and buttress it with the world's most powerful navy, an impenetrable barrier protecting the homeland. Like all Japanese plans, it looked good on paper. They underestimated the hatred erupting from Pearl Harbor.

Much of that brazen plan succeeded. At its high water mark, a tiny fraction of the world's population, squeezed onto less than one percent of the world's land, dominated twelve percent of the planet! That domain equated in area to all of North America, or South America times three. The Japanese domain was one-third larger than Hitler's, stretching 5,000 miles in every direction. A link between Germany and Japan in India appeared inevitable.

Why did the plan fail? It was a close thing, turning on a couple of "what ifs." America, insulated by oceans, was instinctively isolationist. Had Japan consolidated its hold and not struck Pearl Harbor, American isolationism would not likely have undertaken the enormous reach across the Pacific. If we had not broken the Japanese code, Japan would have taken Midway… if 13th Air Force P-38s had not shot down Yamamoto…

On December 7, 1941, "A Day That Will Live In Infamy," America's emotional volcano erupted with such force its hot ash covered the world. We went on the warpath against an enemy, alien in looks and language, culture and conscience. In the thirst for revenge Admiral Halsey predicted: "Japanese will be spoken only in hell. Our mission is to kill Japs, kill Japs and kill more Japs. The only good Japs are ones that have been dead six months." The *New York Times* wrote on February 13, 1942: "Even a dead Jap isn't a good Jap. A soldier stretched cold and dead beneath a palm concealed a booby trap. Such are the Nips in death, as in life, treacherous." General Holland Smith, the Marine commander, said: "The only way to fight Japs is to kill them all." Even songs bore titles such as *Play Taps on the Japs,* and *We're Gonna Slap The Dirty Jap.* Military analyst Major George Fielding Elliott declared "our aim must be the complete destruction of Japan's industry so that not one brick of any Japanese factory stands on another, so there shall not be one motor or chemical plant, nor a book which explains how these things are made."

Emotions were so raw, Japanese on the west coast were interned for their protection and for our national security. Ten thousand Japanese locals refused to take a loyalty oath to the United States. The Association of Japanese in America Obligated to Military Service had thousands of members. David Lohman's book *Magic* published instructions from Tokyo to their west coast agents. Thousands of Black Dragon Society members were trained in sabotage. Of 20,000 Japanese eligible for the draft less than 1,000 volunteered.

West Coast military installations were ringed with potential saboteurs. The 1941 Rose Bowl was transferred from Pasadena to North Carolina to avoid a Jap sub attack. Although not publicized for fear of civilian panic, enemy subs appeared off California, shelling oil fields and sinking ships. The West Coast was strung with barbed wire. Women were issued instructions, "How to Kill a Jap."

Internment centers were established. Internees were not harmed. No internee died from anything other than natural causes. They complained "although our plates were full of food, we had no private toilets; we waited in line at the beauty parlor." In 1943, all who swore allegiance to the U.S. were released. The liberal Supreme Court Justices, William O. Douglas and Hugo Black, affirmed the procedure, and the liberal editorial writer, Walter Lippman, supported internment as a national emergency.

Fifty years later, "feel good politics" overcame history and Congress gave $20,000 to any Japanese-American claiming to have been interned. The American Criminal Liberties Union rewrote history with its usual caterwaulings. Clinton apologized for a "sad day in American History." Japanese now hold a Day of Remembrance, even though they weren't alive at the time, giving Jesse Jackson a great idea.

The navy fiefdom dominated the Pacific, planning for its battleships to crush Japan's navy. The Army-Navy game divided the Pacific into zones, one commanded by General MacArthur and one by Admiral Nimitz. Pacific operations were in the hands of a committee. Eisenhower said "the navy wants to take all the islands in the Pacific, have them become bases for army planes, so the navy will have a safe place to sail its vessels." Pacific war news was navy news.

In war's first months, Bataan gripped the spotlight. After Corregidor fell, a news curtain dropped on the army and its air force. The media was embedded with the Navy. I never saw a news correspondent in the Pacific. The only one I ever heard of to come out was Ernie Pyle. He was killed by a sniper, but not before he told readers in 700 papers "European enemies were terrible, but out here the Japs are looked on as repulsive, the way people feel about cockroaches."

Japan believed Americans were "soft and effeminate." Four years later they confessed their mistake. On September 2, 1945, MacArthur, standing on the deck of the U.S.S. Missouri in Tokyo Bay, handed Foreign Minister Shigemitsu the "Instrument of Surrender." MacArthur barked: "Sutherland, show him where to sign!"

The 50th anniversary of D-Day in Europe was widely celebrated. Reunions were held, books written, films made, cemeteries visited. The President walked the Normandy beaches. America is fed World War II in European concepts—*Private Ryan*, *Battle of the Bulge*, *The Longest Day*, *Hogan's Heroes*, *Band of Brothers*. Its commanders were widely publicized—Eisenhower, Bradley, Patton, Montgomery. The Holocaust is constant news. What of the largest, longest and most brutal military campaign in American history? There are no pilgrimages, no monuments. Their only memorial is the Punch Bowl Cemetery on Oahu, the final resting place for 13,000 bodies, a place of bright tears, where the only sounds are American flags snapping in the breeze. America slipped into historical ignorance of the Pacific, the Forgotten War.

There is a mysterious disconnect between "unconditional surrender" in the Pacific and Europe. Why were atrocities forgiven in one and endlessly prosecuted in the other? Why was remorse demanded from one, and denial accepted from the other?

When Germany surrendered, a nation apologized. Its government was replaced, its leaders executed, its war criminals hunted to ground, reparations extracted, looted property returned, and slave laborers compensated. When Japan surrendered, its government remained intact with its Emperor enshrined. War trials were timorous and sparse. Few were convicted. War criminals spent less time behind bars than their victims. In 1958, the doors of Sugamo Prison were thrown open and its criminals marched out into the rising sun.

The Pacific War suffers a surly overhang. Its mercifully premature ending is portrayed as immoral by those who weren't there. Along with other Pacific veterans I bitterly resisted the Smithsonian Museum's efforts to celebrate the 50th Anniversary of V-J Day portraying Japan as victimized by the A-bomb. Maddening rationale a half century later included inane excuses as "other steps would have been less barbaric and less morally damaging to the U.S."; we should have "laid the ground work for international control of nuclear weapons before they were actually used," and blah, blah, blah.

Today's Japan perceives itself as victim, denies guilt, censors history and blames the bomb rather than those who produced the conditions that created it. A *New York Times* article describing Japan's new Museum of Military History recites: *"The museum is provocative, commemorating warriors and war criminals. It offers an unapologetic attitude about Japan's militaristic past. It is a totally unreconstructed regurgitation of their pre-1945 justifications, Japan always on the defensive, never the aggressor."*

From start to finish, it was a dirty war. It began in treachery and ended in deceit.

REFERENCES

Costello, John, *The Pacific War*, N.Y., Rawson Wade, 1981
Dower, John W., *War Without Mercy*, N.Y., Pantheon Books, 1986
Layton, Edwin T., *And I Was There*, N.Y., Wm. Morrow, 1985

CHAPTER THREE

Europe First

The war in Europe raged for two years before Pearl Harbor. Hitler scrupulously avoided conflict with the U.S. whose neutrality instinct hardened to strong sentiment against war with Germany. It's hard to hate a guy who isn't bothering you and whose cousin lives in New Braunfels.

Roosevelt sought to maneuver Japan into firing the first shot. Churchill quoted Roosevelt saying: "I shall not declare war, I shall make war." He commenced a series of provocations. Japan's assets in the U.S. were frozen and we embargoed oil, steel, and rubber. Japan went to war for raw materials. And so it came to pass the only war available was with Japan. References to the European war are made here, not for information since that subject is saturated, but to report how Europe's priority militated against the Pacific, which received only a fraction of our war resources.

Historian Keith Eiler of the Hoover Institution explains the difference between the Pacific and European wars:

"Not only was there disparity between two worlds, but also in the grand strategy of high command. Priority was placed on winning first in Europe. The Pacific was placed on 'strategic defensive.' They had to get along with the barest minimum."

"Europe First" was national policy. One month after Pearl Harbor, troops arrived in England. Roosevelt quickly sent an army to Africa. Africa Yes—Pacific No! In November 1942, Operation Torch launched a premature ejaculation of mushy green U.S. troops who tangled with Irwin Rommel's battle hardened Afrika Corps at Kasserine Pass. America suffered a disgraceful defeat, along with 7,000 casualties. The Pacific was on hold, and historically it remained in Europe's shadow.

The German army entered Paris unopposed. France saved serious fighting to use against Americans in North Africa. They shot our troop-carrying planes. The French battleship Bretagne attacked us and was sunk. French destroyers Mogador and Dunkerque were taught a like lesson. The "fighting French" did hold out for six more months—on Madagascar, off the east coast of Africa. American air crews in the South Pacific operating off French Islands Noumea and Efate astride the route to Australia found the French openly sympathetic to our enemies. Deja vu?

European peripheral campaigns proceeded in Sicily and Italy. The Italian Campaign had little value other than General Mark Clark's vainglorious walk in the Italian sun, after the German Army abandoned Rome. Napoleon likened Italy to a boot, to be entered only from the top. Our trudge up the Italian boot commenced at the toe in July 1943. Four months after landing troops at Anzio, we were clinging to a toe. Battles at Cassino and Rapido were bloody and ineffectual. Germans always on the high ground with their powerful 88mm guns shooting down on Americans. Virtually the entire 36th Texas Division was slaughtered at the Rapido, a Mark Clark disaster so reprehensible it sparked a congressional investigation. The Abbey at Cassino, built in 529 A.D., was bombed to rubble, yet it took three more months to capture. The Gustave Line in Italy buried divisions of American soldiers without ever tying up a significant portion of the Wehrmact. At War's end, we were still trudging up the Italian boot, without ever defeating Kesselring or ending Nazi occupation of Italy.

The Pacific played out as a sideshow. Historian John Keegan says reporting the war was heavily biased in favor of Europe. European air forces were popularized—Memphis Belle, Twelve O'clock High, The Mighty Eighth. Targets were household names—Berlin, Hamburg, Cologne, Dresden. Rivers and bridges were well known—Rhine and Rhone, Remagen and Arnhem. The European war was fought to conquer cities, cross rivers—places with names on a map. History richly records battlefields of Europe—Cherbourg, Normandy, Metz, Ardennes, Bastogne. But Balikpapan and Biak, Rabaul and Tassafaronga? These were places nobody ever heard of at the time and couldn't find on a map today. During four years of war in the Pacific, only one urban battle was fought. Manila, a lovely and gracious city, was sacked by the Japanese who raped, burned and massacred 100,000 citizens, and then fought to the last man. We built no prisoner of war camps in the Pacific. The reason was simple—we had no prisoners. The Pacific War was fought in unknown jungles and nameless skies. There are no flowers on those graves in the sky.

PACIFIC WAR

DECEMBER
Pearl Harbor attacked. December 7, 1941: Pacific Army Air Corps destroyed at Pearl Harbor. Philippines and Wake Island captured

FEBRUARY
Singapore surrenders

MARCH
Battle of Java Sea
British, Dutch, US Fleets destroyed

APRIL
Doolittle Raid on Toyko

MAY
Battle of Coral Sea:
U.S. loses two carriers
Japs land in New Guinea

JUNE
Battle of Midway:
Roosevelt shifts 2 carriers to the Atlantic

AUGUST
Marines land on Guadalcanal

SEPTEMBER
Army's first paratroop drop in New Guinea

OCTOBER
Marines and Army invade Bougainville

NOVEMBER
Marines invade Tarawa: 1,500 killed
Army Air Forces destroy Japanese Air Forces in New Guinea

FEBRUARY
Army and Marines land on Admiralties and Russells;
Munda captured

APRIL
Army air bases established in New Guinea

JUNE
Mariannas Campaign
Guam, Saipan, Tinian captured by Army and Marines

OCTOBER
Return to Philippines
Army lands on Leyte

JANUARY
MacArthur returns to Luzon and Mindano in the Philippines

FEBRUARY
Manilla retaken; Iwo Jima taken; U.S. flag raised on Suribachi

MARCH
Tokyo firebombed (80,000 killed)

APRIL
Okinawa Campaign

AUGUST
Atomic Bomb dropped on Hiroshima; Japan surrenders

WAR IN EUROPE

FEBRUARY
First U.S. troops sent to England

NOVEMBER
North Africa invaded

JULY
Invasion of Sicily

Continued buildup of U.S. troops in England

June 6th
D-Day in Normandy

DECEMBER
Battle of the Bulge

FEBRUARY
Patton crosses the Rhine

MAY
Germany surrenders

1941

1942

1943

1944

1945

REFERENCES

Carter, Kit C., *The Army Air Forces in World War II*, Office of Air Force History, Washington, D.C., 1974

Jablonski, Edward, *Air War*, N.Y., Doubleday, 1971

CHAPTER FOUR

Day of Deceit

The "surprise" attack on Pearl Harbor has been endlessly discussed. Speculation abounds as to what Roosevelt knew and when did he know it. Suspicion thickened through the years as secret documents were declassified. Undisputed is that critical information was kept from the army and navy commanders in Hawaii. The build up of facts rendered its verdict when Congress officially apologized and reinstated the ranks of Admiral Kimmel and General Short. Congress concluded: "The Hawaiian commanders were not given vital information available to defend Pearl Harbor. The blame should be widely shared."

In the1930s, a brilliant army cryptanalyst, Colonel William Freidman, performed the greatest feat of cryptanalysis in history. Through mathematical calculation, he produced a machine that could decipher a code based on millions of possible combinations. This enabled him to break Japan's code despite their changing the settings daily. We began reading their mail, a practice which continued throughout the War. Vast Pacific distances magnified the value of advance information about the enemy. Our field commanders were blindfolded at Pearl Harbor, despite the largest naval force in history having sailed from Japan on November 22, and for the next two weeks paraded across 3,000 miles of open ocean. This vital intelligence was denied the hapless Pearl Harbor commanders, who didn't even learn of the code-breaking machines until two years later.

December 22, two weeks after the Pearl Harbor attack, the Roberts Commission, appointed by Roosevelt, began closed door hearings. Led by Roosevelt's friend, Justice Roberts of the Supreme Court, it included Secretary of War Stimson, Secretary of Navy Knox, Admiral Stark and General Marshall. They met in private and reviewed unsworn and unrecorded interviews. One month later, the commission's report was handed to President Roosevelt, who requested it be published in Sunday newspapers. The report laid the responsibility for Pearl Harbor on Kimmel and Short, accusing them of dereliction of duty: "The Japanese attack was a complete surprise to the commanders, who failed to make suitable dispositions to meet such an attack. These errors of judgment were the causes for the success of the attack."

Code breaking in the Pacific was primarily the work of Capt. Joseph Rochefort, head of the cryptanalysis station at Honolulu. Nimitz recommended Rochefort for the Distinguished Service Medal. Washington nixed the award. In 1986, President Reagan awarded Rochefort the medal. Posthumously.

Day Of Deceit

Robert Stinnett, a naval officer, spent sixteen years researching 200,000 documents. He wrote an explosive book *Day of Deceit*, saying: *"The terrible truth is America would not have gone to war unless deliberately provoked at Pearl Harbor."*

REFERENCES

Prang, Gordon W., *At Dawn We Slept*, N.Y. McGraw-Hill, 1981

Toland, John, *Infamy*, N.Y., Doubleday, 1982

Toland, John, *But Not in Shame*, N.Y., Random House, 1961

Cohen, Stan, *East Wind Rain*, Missoula, Montana, Pictorial Histories, 1981

Stinnett, Robert, *Day Of Deceit*, N.Y., Free Press, 2000

CHAPTER FIVE

Over There—
England vs. New Guinea

Airmen in Europe didn't go overseas—they went abroad. Air crews stationed in England enjoyed wood floors, fresh food, booze and goodwill excursions to Piccadilly. England was a civilized and sanitary enclave, where disease and torture were unknown. Laughter and loving, however, were said to exist, eliciting complaints that "Americans were overpaid, over-sexed and over-here."

Citizen Soldiers, by Stephen Ambrose taunts the disparity: *"For England, living conditions were far better than those anywhere else. The airmen had beds, clean sheets, hot food, showers, clean clothes. They had easy access to London where a pack of cigarettes would pay for a woman and a night's worth of booze."*

England's Little America by Mike Nichols, brought tears to Pacific flyers living with mud, malaria and mosquitoes: *"During World War II, members of the 8th Air Force were stationed in East Anglia, a region of thatched cottages and stone churches near London. Each base was near a village, each village had its pub, and each pub had its 8th Air Force regulars. When the Americans came to town the pubs ran out of beer. All the girls were fascinated by the Americans in their uniforms. They had money to spend on chocolates, flowers and stockings. Village girls found themselves dancing cheek to check with American airmen."*

Pacific airmen jigged in jungle mud. Nocturnal excitement came from air raids and banzai charges. Social interface came from Tokyo Rose. I remember one night Tokyo Rose cooing (she had a soft voice): "We're going to get you boys down on Morotai tonight—I bet you don't know what your sweetheart back home is doing right now." She was right on both counts.

Our squadron log spins a 13th Air Force night-time story:

"29 July 1994. Message received to proceed to Lake Rombebai, Dutch New Guinea and evacuate ten wounded men on a lake in enemy territory. The PBY, piloted by Capt. Gerard F. Wientjes, proceeded to the area. They landed, launched the life raft and went ashore, finding ten soldiers, seven of whom were injured, and one wounded Jap. These ten men had been attacked by fifty Japanese soldiers who sneaked up on the guard, wounding him with knives. Then screaming 'Banzai', they attacked the sleeping men in their hammocks. The men fought the Japs with fists and clubs. One fired a signal flare, temporarily disconcerting the Japs. The Americans regrouped, seized their tommy guns and killed the Jap officer and two soldiers. The Jap force scattered, some were shot—fifteen of the enemy being accounted for in this manner. During the remainder of the night, the Japs kept attacking, but our three unwounded soldiers successfully held them off until the PBY rescue ship arrived and all personnel were taken aboard."

CHAPTER SIX

Anchors Away

The navy considered the Pacific its exclusive venue. However, the first two years following the Pearl Harbor debacle, navy performance, except for Midway, was not one for boasting.

The war opened with our battleships sunk in Pearl Harbor mud. Two months later, the Battle of Java Sea cost the navy its prize cruisers, U.S.S. Houston and Marblehead, the aircraft tender Langley, and destroyers Ford, Pope and Parrott. The U.S. Asiatic Fleet ceased to exist. British and Dutch fleets were sunk. Britain lost destroyers Exeter, Perth, Electra, Jupiter and Encounter. The Dutch lost cruisers DeRuyter, Java and Kortmorr, and destroyers Piet Hern and Evertsen. Britain's capital ships, Prince of Wales and Repulse, were sunk by planes off Singapore. In April 1942, Japan's navy rampaged through the Indian Ocean, sinking the British aircraft carrier Hermes, cruisers Cornwall and Dorsetshire and destroyers Vampire and Hollyhook. Banging on India's door, Japan planned to occupy Madagascar on Africa's east coast and link with Germany to choke off Britain's lifeline through the Suez Canal. Australia,

under attack and naked to invasion, planned to scorch the earth and retreat to their south coast. It was a very close thing.

At Pearl Harbor, the navy's battleship armada was crippled, freeing the navy from its fixation on battleships. Air power, both land and carrier, became the order of battle. The May 1942 Coral Sea Battle was fought by planes launched from fleets which never saw each other. Our navy called it a "draw," not necessarily an accurate description since the

USS BunkerHill

Navy lost two carriers, then half its entire carrier force. Japan lost one small carrier.

The 1942 Guadalcanal operation evoked six devastating sea battles. The worst defeat ever suffered by the navy was Savo Island, where, in ten minutes, we lost the four cruisers Canberra, Astoria, Quincy and Vincennes. Admiral Fletcher then withdrew the navy, stranding the marines with only supplies they brought ashore when they landed. In battles raging around Guadalcanal aircraft carriers Wasp and Hornet were sunk and Enterprise damaged. The cruisers Atlanta and Juneau were sunk along with several destroyers. The loss of the Juneau took the five Sullivan brothers to their grave. So many ships were sunk the waters around Guadalcanal were called 'Iron Bottom Sound.' Submarine commanders launched torpedoes, exposing their location, only to find fifty percent of their torpedoes were duds.

By November 1942, of the navy's six carrier fleet, four were sunk and two damaged. Whittled down to its last carrier, the crippled navy withdrew it from South Pacific waters studded with Japanese bases. Our navy had fought itself to exhaustion. For the next two years until the Philippine Sea Battle in 1944, there were no major carrier engagements. During this two year hiatus, Japan's dazzling air power, consisting of the best planes and pilots in the world, was crushed. In 1944, when the navy returned with new carriers and engaged Japan's carriers in the Philippine Sea battle, enemy air power had been so hemorrhaged that navy pilots called it the Marianas Turkey Shoot. It was during those two years the army and its air forces clawed their way up the Solomons' chain, across Bougainville, New Britain, New Ireland and the Admiralties, hopscotched the 1,500 mile length of New Guinea. Rabaul and Truk were isolated and left on the vine like tomatoes, rotten and dying. Japan didn't replace their pilots. They kept their best pilots out there and we killed them. From 1942 through 1944, the Army Air Forces smashed the cream of Japan's air armada, but bereft of news coverage, all this disappeared in a black hole of history.

In the 1943 Battle of Bismarck Sea, it was the Army Air Forces that sawed through a large invasion force of transports and destroyers headed for Australia, achieving what General Billy Mitchell predicted fifteen years before. Planes destroyed an enemy fleet at sea. James Murphy, a B-17 pilot who fought all three days of that battle, told me at the Nimitz Museum Program on Pacific Air Operations that fifteen transports and eight destroyers in the convoy were sunk.

The battle opened with B-17s bombing the convoy from high altitude. Some B-17s were shot down by Zero fighters. As the Americans parachuted down, Zeros machine-gunned them to ribbons. The rules were set. For the next three days American bombers and fighters worked the convoy over in a killing spree, skip-bombing, strafing, and sinking every ship. The B-17s came in high, medium B-25s and A-20s came in low. Some B-25s with eight forward firing .50 calibers came in at 500 feet with such concentrated firepower ships literally exploded.

After the ships were sunk, the fighters continued strafing, knifing through lifeboats and rafts. Planes roamed the sea, shooting survivors clinging to life rafts. The waters were a bloody pink froth, red and churning from sharks in a feeding frenzy. Some pilots vomited. From a 15,000 man convoy, only a few hundred Japanese finally washed ashore in New Guinea. Absent was Sir Walter Scott's premise: "The stern joy which warriors feel in foes worthy of their steel." Navy historian Samuel Elliott Morrison called Bismarck Sea the most devastating air attack on ships of the entire war.

The invasion of Port Moresby was aborted by Army air power, ending the threat to Australia then and there. An entire convoy, its soldiers, sailors and invasion equipment went to the bottom. Never again did Japan attempt to convoy troops where Army air forces could strike. Replacements were fed in by barges and subs at night. Using submarines as supply vessels removed them from the reason for their construction. Their supply role was resented by the crews who called themselves "moguras" or moles.

Japan's arrogant belief in their superiority blinded them that it was better to have lots of competent pilots than a few skilled ones. The shredding of their elite flyers with no reserves or replacements left them with young inexperienced pilots who were no match for American planes and pilots. When the Navy's revitalized carrier fleet returned in 1944, Japan's air forces had been broken, causing Admiral Carney to complain: "The damn 13th Air Force has just about ruined the war for my carriers."

REFERENCES

Bergerud, Eric, *Fire In The Sky*, Boulder, Colorado, Westview Press, 1999

Winslow, W.G., *The Fleet the Gods Forgot*, Annapolis Naval Institute Press, 1982

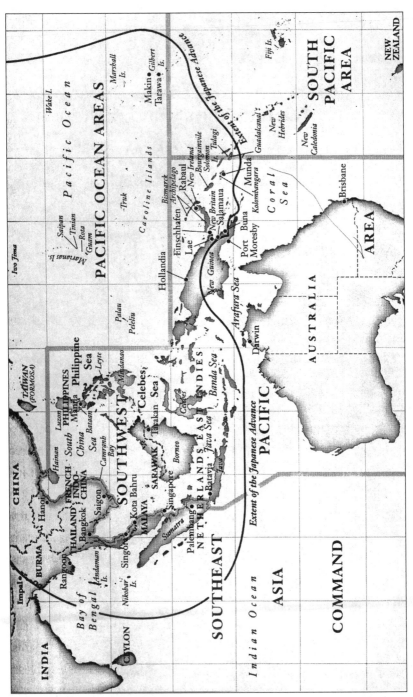

A map of the Pacific Theater.

CHAPTER SEVEN

The Three Missions that Darkened the Rising Sun

Victory in the Pacific was earned by a combination of army, navy and marines. Navy and marine contributions to victory were great and enduring, but their oft-repeated history eclipses the other services. Army Air Forces in the Pacific might well have been the silent service.

By the end of the war's first day, army air power had all but disappeared. The airfields in Hawaii were strafed into wreckage. Waves of Japanese "V" bomber formations appeared over Clark Field in the Philippines, where the B-17s and P-40s lined up wing tip to wing tip were smashed on the ground. The evidence is conflicting why eight hours after Pearl Harbor this disaster occurred.

Despite this inglorious inaugural, it was the Army Air Corps (later designated Army Air Forces) which flew three decisive missions of the war. They were the Doolittle raid on Tokyo, the shoot down of Admiral Yamamoto and finally, Hiroshima. Incredibly, two of those feats were performed by a single Army Air Force plane.

"Thirty Seconds Over Tokyo," as the Doolittle raid became known, came just four months after Pearl Harbor. On April 18, 1942, Jimmy Doolittle and sixteen Army B-25 bombers were coaxed into the air off a short and stormy deck on the aircraft carrier Hornet in the tempestuous North Pacific. That dashing raid on Tokyo shattered Japan's spirit of invincibility. Humiliated, Japan reported: "Out of nowhere, dark green airplanes appeared over Tokyo. Then, quickly as they appeared, they were gone." A thousand years of geographical virginity had been violated, an impact far more devastating than the actual damage. Japan's boast that the sacred homeland would never be attacked was silenced in an irreparable loss of face. This foray resulted in an abrupt change in strategy. Japan planned to establish a 7,000 mile *cordon sanitaire* protecting Japan's home islands.

One year to the day after the Tokyo raid, April 18, 1943, came arguably the single most significant mission of the war. Lt. Rex Barber, flying in a flight of P-38s from Guadalcanal, flashed through a screen of protecting Zero fighters and gunned down the bomber carrying Admiral Yamamoto. Japan's military icon, who planned the strike at Pearl Harbor, who swept the American, British and Dutch Navies from the seas and who turned the South Pacific into a Japanese lake, was eliminated in one lightning blow. The Nippon tsunami peaked at that moment. Japan never recovered and never won another battle. The rollback became relentless, never stopping until it engulfed the sacred home islands.

General Doolittle said: "Navy had the transport to invade Japan. The ground forces made it possible, and the B-29 made it unnecessary." In August 1945, a lone Army Air Force B-29 named "Enola Gay" ended the war at Hiroshima… and introduced the world to nuclear war.

REFERENCES

Glines, C.V., *The Doolittle Raid*, N.Y., Orion Books, 1988
Winton, John C., *War In The Pacific*, N.Y., Mayflower Books, 1978

CHAPTER EIGHT

Cactus Air Force

When I first saw Guadalcanal from a distance, it didn't look like a pestilential hell hole, but beneath a verdant canopy lay a steaming cesspool. Guadalcanal was a small island in a South Pacific archipelago called "The Solomons." This speck of jungle green jutting out of a clear blue ocean became the frothy focus of one of the most intense land, sea and air battles in history. On this tiny enclave, surrounded by a hitherto invincible enemy, Marines and flyers hung on and fought back, in a six-months Battle of Bastogne. It was more than a name. It was emotional and desperate fighting. The 13th Air Force earned its wings on Guadalcanal.

In July 1942, an Army B-17 on patrol filmed activity on this outpost. Japan was constructing an airfield from which its planes could intercept sea lanes to Australia, pinning the U.S. to Hawaii and the west coast. Those pictures shocked the Joint Chiefs out of their European myopia.

In August 1942, when the Guadalcanal campaign began, Japan was riding the high tide of conquest. Indonesia was conquered, the Philippines over-run, the British knocked out of Malaya, the Dutch out of Indonesia, and New Guinea invaded. Guadalcanal was the last stop to Australia. Japan was seemingly invincible. Their navy had not lost a single major ship. Their carriers were probably the finest naval weapon in the world. Their planes dominated the skies. Japan bestrode Asia like a Colossus. Had they extended their empire to Australia, Japan might have become a nation beyond defeat.

In an operation aptly named "Shoestring," the First Marine Division was rushed like an emergency fire department to the hot spot. They hit the beach on August 7. Enemy naval forces attacked the American fleet. In a few minutes we lost four cruisers, and a thousand sailors. This spooked Admiral Fletcher, who withdrew the navy, taking marines' supplies and artillery with him, stranding the marines. Marines said Fletcher added a fourth color to the flag.

When they saw our navy withdraw, Japan didn't take our Guadal-canal incursion seriously. Contemptuous of our puny effort, they never focused their overwhelming superiority. Thinking they could nickel and dime us into retreat, General Ichiki projected August 21 as the "enjoy-ment of fruits of victory day."

Fanned by "victory disease," they viewed Americans with contempt. Yamamoto haughtily ordered the pesky Americans "swatted away." Japan's navy officers, fearing the U.S. Fleet would not come out to meet them, directed their mail forwarded to Midway. Euphoria gripped Japan. Victory parades were conducted, with waving banners and flying kites. Officers threw one party after another, believing their codes unbreakable and their tactics indomitable. This episode was reported by one:

"Civilians clamored to go abroad with the army. After receiving creden-tials, Okada asked for a pair of army boots. Staff officers were puffed up like toy balloons. One of them, plump as a pig, said: "Boots? Don't worry about boots. You'll get beautiful ones out there—damned beautiful enemy boots. Americans are effeminate and cowardly, who don't conceive night to be a proper time for battle, but believe it is excellent for dancing."

Seabees completed the airstrip with captured Japanese equipment. It was named Henderson Field for a marine pilot killed at Midway. As soon as a short runway was serviceable, a motley assortment of army, navy and marine fighter planes begin filtering in through layers of enemy naval and air interception. When the army crews came in, marines gave them straw mats to sleep on and Japanese bowls to eat out of. They were told if they wanted underwear there were captured loin cloths that fit every size. The first Army Air Force units to enter combat in the South Pacific were under Navy's ComAirSoPac (Commander Aircraft South Pacific), commanded by Admiral John McCain.

Much is known about the Marines who seized that island and held on to it for three grim months until relieved by the Army. Little is known about that bunch of army, marine and navy pilots operating off this bombed and battered strip. They were the "Cactus Air Force," Cactus being the code name for Guadalcanal. Planes and crews dribbled into that meat-grinder, one or two at a time. Grumman Wildcats flown by navy and marine pilots, then some P-39 Air Cobras, P-40 Warhawks and P-38 Lightnings flown by the army. Cactus Air Force had no identifiable parent. It was treated accordingly by news releases of the navy.

As often happened in the Pacific, the first plane to land was the army's amphibious PBY5A Catalina. Then, on August 22, Capt. Dale Brannon, commanding the 67th Fighter Squadron, led five P-400s in. Nine more landed on August 27. P-400s were the European version of the Bell P-39, a plane with an in-line engine behind the pilot. A 37mm cannon in the

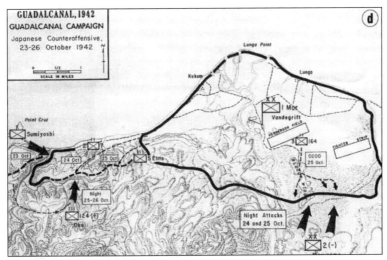

Guadalcanal Campaign Map

nose fired through the hub of the propeller. The P-400, originally made for the British, did not have oxygen equipment. Japs called it "needle-nose." Americans called it "flying rock" because it did not glide. P-400s had a star on their wings circled with a red ball. The red ball was removed because enemy planes sported a red ball, promptly dubbed the "flaming asshole." Without oxygen, they were no match for the high flying Zeros. The 67th pilots flew at low altitude, a pigeon shoot for Zeros pouncing down on them. Zeros zipped, darted, twisted and climbed straight up. The 67th Fighter Squadron said their lumbering P-400s acted like a herd of cows attacked by a wolf pack. At times they were so out-numbered that when hordes of Zeros headed in, the few planes were told to take off and hide. They kept going because it was easy to kill Japs who came in such big bunches. The 67th dwindled to three planes (the joke: "What's a P-400? A P-40 with a Zero on his tail!"). In November and December, the Army Air Corps' five other South Pacific squadrons, the 68th, 12th, 44th, 70th, and 339th arrived.

Japan's pilots were bold and experienced from years of combat in China, and hardened by rigorous training such as swimming under water and doing one hand push-ups. Pilots said "our planes go 150 mph down-hill and Zeros cruise above that speed." Perversely, the Zero fighter plane may owe its origin to Howard Hughes. In 1934, Hughes built the H-1. The fastest plane in the world, he set a speed record from California to Newark. The plane attracted interest everywhere, including Japan. Hughes offered it to the army, which rejected it. He stored it in a hanger in California. Mitsubishi later produced the Zero so closely resembling the H-1, Hughes believed it was copied from his design. The Zero was a winged culture shock. Gone were our illusions that Japanese were buck-toothed, near-sighted pilots flying flimsy kites. We met the finest fighter plane of its day. So swift and nimble it outmatched our planes and dominated the skies. Japan had kept this secret under wraps. No other nation was so security conscious. Their slogan was "Every foreigner is a spy."

George Chandler, a 13th Air Force Ace, admired the Zero. He says: *"The Zero was more maneuverable than our fighters. They had range, but not self-sealing gas tanks nor armor. Fighting a Zero was like swatting flies with a baseball bat, hard to hit, but if you did, it's all over."* The first time I saw one, I was struck by its smooth simplicity, much like the Spitfire.

Major Westbrook, leading Ace of the 13th, said: *"The Zero is the most beautiful plane you ever saw, graceful as a bird. Never try to dog-fight a Zero because that is not habit-forming."* Lighter than the Zero was the Oscar. One Cactus pilot said: *"Four of us caught a little Oscar. It was the most maneuverable plane I ever saw. We made passes at him for thirty minutes. We never touched him. Each time we lined up he'd turn into you and fly past. We gave up and came home, but he put a hole in my wing."* Their Betty bomber had great range and was fast as our fighters. As if that weren't enough, Japan held the advantage of operating superior forces from interior lines.

Nature was as mean an enemy as Japan. The writer Eric Larrabee described it: *"Guadalcanal was rain, mud, humid air in which nothing ever*

dried out and clothing rotted. There was disease, malaria, jaundice and dysentery, fungus and tropical ulcers that ate away the flesh."

Nights were spent in soaked clothes under sopping blankets while rain poured through shelter halves in

Main highway through the jungle

rivulets. Mosquitoes bit through clothes. Some men went out of their heads from incessant stings. When Henderson Field was dry, cloying black dust fouled engines. When it rained, the runway turned into a thick gooey mass. Pilots crashed regularly at the end of the sticky, crater-pocked air-strip. There were no bomb hoists, and

Building a jungle airstrip

ground crews had to lug 500-pound bombs through black ooze, then muscle them into place by hand. Refueling was exhaustingly tedious. Aviation gas in fifty-five-gallon drums had to be hand-pumped into fuel trucks and then into the wing tanks. There was no service equipment; coconut logs and oil drums were used to jack up planes.

Cactus flew during the day and repaired at night. Parts were so scarce that when planes crashed, crews descended like vultures stripping parts. Ground crews swapped wings and tails, wheels and engines. Mechanics worked dripping wet with rain in their face, passing scarce wrenches back and forth. It was their job and they did it. A handful of tired, grimy, hungry men kept a few beat-up planes flying. They worked all night so pilots would have planes ready the next day. Somehow they kept planes flying and bristling with the ugly killing tools of war.

Problems were compounded by a short strip and human sickness. The 3,000 foot strip was half what it should be, sometimes further short-ened by bomb craters. Malaria kept thirty percent of the pilots grounded. They subsisted on spam and dehydrated food. There was no such thing as a shower. Everybody was weak and exhausted. Because of pilot short-age, many flew who should have been grounded. Some flew five missions a day. Everybody got a little flaky. One lieutenant put on his dress uni-form and stood by the side of the road waiting for the bus.

Cactus flew off a wounded strip. Brakes would be set, flaps lowered, and throttle pushed full forward. Planes would creep forward, lurch and skid down the runway, spraying mud over the cockpit. Mud wrestled to flying speed, some made it, others crashed and burned. When planes returned after sundown, they came alone in the dark with mountains on all sides.

Marine Major Joe Foss, the Cactus Air Force pilot who won the Congressional Medal of Honor after shooting down twenty-six enemy planes, said: "Life on Guadalcanal was daily hell. The nerve-shattering life or death missions, combined with malaria, dysentery and poor food, was simply too much for some men. They broke under the strain."

Mission report of the 67th Fighter Squadron: "*P-400s are literally falling apart. Guns wouldn't fire, engines and electrical system are going out. These planes are in no condition to fly. Everything is only going due to extreme effort of men and total disregard of the planes' condition by pilots.*"

The first of Japan's many counterattacks came September 12, when Gen. Kawaguchi sent his best men out of the jungle, screaming and throwing firecrackers. Japanese language doesn't contain cuss words, but their English showed many had lived in America. "Japanese boys kill American boys. Japanese drink blood like wine. To hell with Babe Ruth." They came forward slapping their rifle butts and chanting "U.S. Marines be dead tomorrow." Marines' machine guns mowed them down. They pushed forward over dead bodies stacked across barbed wire. They ran out of soldiers before marines ran out of bullets. They fell back. So confident was Kawaguchi he would breakfast on American supplies, he left his food behind. When he retreated into the jungle, Japan realized these were not the same white men they walked over in Singapore, Hong Kong and Indonesia. These were United States Marines.

Japan got serious. Frustrated, Yamamoto ordered American air power destroyed. Racing down from Rabaul and Truk came carriers, battleships, cruisers, destroyers and transports. A task force built around two huge battleships, Kongo and Haruna went into position off the beach. Cactus pilot Dante Benedetti said: "*Both Kongo and Haruna were armed with enormous 18-inch guns. They plastered Cactus with 1,000 huge shells. Kongo's gunnery officers walked their shells right up the runway and into the tents. The results were apocalyptic. Huge coconut trees shattered and pieces flew like enormous blazing torches. Airplanes were shattered. Gas and ammo sent white-hot searing flames roaring into the sky. We trembled in our shallow slit trenches, shaking like a dog passing razor blades. It was horrible. This nightmare continued for an hour and a half. Then bombers and artillery pulverized Henderson the rest of the night. Flight Surgeon Henry Ringness, though horribly wounded, dragged his shattered body through the bloody mud to treat the injured. His spinal cord was severed and he soon died."*

Another pilot described that night: *"The shelling started on the runways, then the tents. In foxholes men cringed and prayed. When the shelling stopped, bombers came over in waves. When the shelling and bombing stopped, the field was a shambles. Trees were blown away, tents shredded. The dazed men were in shock."*

Douglas Pricer described the aftermath: *"On October 14, the sun rose on a moonscape of smoldering mud with pieces of everything, including people, protruding."* Henderson Field had all but ceased to exist. Benedetti's squadron was gone. Its commanding officer, executive officer and operations officer were all dead. Their aircraft had been destroyed. The squadron once had 35 aircraft. They now had three, and it was doubtful they could fly.

A colonel summed up: *"We don't know whether we'll be able to hold the field. We have gas for one last mission. Load your airplanes with bombs, go out and hit them. After the gas is gone, we'll have to let the ground troops take over. Your officers and men will attach yourselves to some infantry outfit. Good luck and goodbye."* Admiral Ghormley prepared to abandon Guadalcanal.

When the planes returned from that mission, they found a C-47 had flown in drums of gasoline for one more flight. "There were no bomb carts, and it took ten men to hoist a 500 lb. bomb by hand. Army trucks were hauling dirt to fill in the runway. Men were beating out fires with blankets, litter bearers were hauling wounded, crews were shoveling dirt on burning planes and ammo was exploding everywhere. Soon enough, the Japs came crashing through the jungle to occupy Henderson Field. Over the field, Zeros were circling, obviously waiting for a signal to land."

Yamamoto was planning a "surrender ceremony" as the famed Sendai division attacked. Typically Japanese, it was complex. Attacking from the rear, they outnumbered the marines, surged up Bloody Ridge and took the crest of the hill. As the enemy infiltrated marine lines, Captain T. A. Thompson led his last three P-400s, strafing the ridge just above the heads of Edson's Marines. The P-400s zoomed in with machine guns blazing, cutting the Japanese to ribbons. They would circle, strafe the massed soldiers, circle and strafe again. The enemy fell back. The attack was over, they retreated in shame. General Ichiki, who had brought his dress uniform to wear at the surrender ceremony, ripped his regimental flag and blew his brains out.

Day and night Henderson Field was bombed, shelled and attacked by infantry. Cactus faced annihilation. Survivors were stunned men who death had breathed on and passed by. For six months the issue was in doubt. The American perimeter was compressed into a hell hole two miles long. Gasoline was drained from tanks of wrecked planes. The pilots were preparing to fight with pistols and rifles. It was classic David and Goliath.

Those early days are described in a well-written book, *Vampire Squadron*, by William Starke:

"*Each night a lone bomber, named 'Washing-Machine Charlie', would buzz the field. Weary men went cursing to foxholes filled with mud. But a bombing doesn't last long. A shelling, however, is indescribable hell! And it can last for hours. When the shells scream overhead, you cringe, expecting a hit. When there is a let-up you tremble, knowing they are getting your range and the next one will hit. A shelling is sheer terror from which you never recover.*

"*Lt. Jack Bade got the Air Medal today. He spotted ten fighters attacking our bombers and he dove to their aid despite jammed guns and a bleeding head wound. He wove back and forth in a scissors maneuver, turning into any Zero which attempted to pass through until the enemy gave up the attack.*

"*A Jap fighter pilot cut one of our parachuting pilot's legs off with the Zero's prop. Another boy bailed out, breaking both legs. He said "After four hours in the water a great big beautiful airplane, a PBY, spotted me. He landed in a very heavy sea and picked me up. I know the fighter pilots would not exchange jobs as we figure flying PBYs is too risky.*"

"*Lt. Matson recorded a one of a kind experience. A Zero dove into him head on, smashing the cockpit. Matson bailed out, his mouth full of plexiglass. As he floated down three Zeros began strafing him. Matson trying to persuade he was one of their own, shook hands with himself above his head, gave them toothy smiles, protruding his teeth to look as Japanese as possible, and saluted. The Zero pilots bought it and departed. Before hitting the water, Matson gave himself a morphine injection. He passed out and was picked up by a PBY.*"

Doug Canning flew with Cactus. I asked him for any particular recollections. He said:

"*My flight, Canning, Goeke, Barr and Farquar, plus four more P-38 pilots, were on an escort mission with SBDs and TBFs to attack Jap destroyers. As the leader of the P-38s, I spotted the destroyers and flew to the rear, and led my flight from the rear to the destroyer parade. The ack-ack fire was very scary. Meantime, the undetected SBDs and TBFs made their attacks.*

We sank the destroyers.

"By this time night had fallen and we were over the Pacific, no lights to guide us home. So with a prayer, I set compass course to Guadalcanal. When I figured we were about ten minutes out, I got on the radio and asked the tower to turn on the searchlights. There were two, one at each end of the runway, pointed straight up. Since there were no radio navigation aids these were our only hope to locate our field. Two beautiful searchlights came on and we went into land. Truck lights illuminated the runway. I landed and taxied back to my revetment. I noticed a Marine trotting alongside the airplane. After getting out, he handed me a beer and said he wanted to do something for a pilot who had done so much for his fellow troops. What a perfect way to end a glorious mission."

During August, September and October, the "Tokyo Express" paraded up and down the "Slot," chewing up the Cactus Air Force on the runway, shooting up Henderson Field and landing soldiers. 20,000 enemy troops poured into Guadalcanal. The Tokyo Express soon grew wary of the prickly Cactus Air Force and made runs at night when Cactus was blind. Cactus now owned the day. In October, army units began relieving the decimated and hollow-eyed marines.

Like two scorpions in a battle, Cactus flyers killed the enemy wherever they met:

"Dick Amerine of the 67th Fighter Squadron came down in a jungle where he ran into Japanese troops. He found one asleep, killed him with a rock, and took his pistol and shoes. He killed two more soldiers with the butt of his pistol and shot a fourth. A one-time student of entomology, Amerine kept himself alive by eating ants and snails. It took him seven days to walk the thirty miles back."

Japan refused to believe they couldn't whip the Americans. They kept throwing in planes and pilots from Rabaul and Truk. But Cactus fought the best Japan had and won. After six months, Japan's hope of conquering the South Pacific died. Tokyo Radio pronounced "the island is dead." "I failed because I underestimated the enemy's fighting power. I deserve the sentence of a thousand deaths. Our army is used to fighting Chinese," said General Kawaguchi. This was their first encounter with the marines, young Americans who had volunteered to fight. General Suguyama went to the palace to obtain Hirohito's approval to begin Japan's first ever military retreat from "The Island of Death." The Imperial Navy's last run down the Slot was made exactly six months to the day after the

Americans landed.

In February 1943, Japan gave up Guadalcanal and sneaked its soldiers off in a midnight Dunkirk. The war's outcome was no longer in doubt. The route to outcome, however, was barred by suicidal fanatics. Japan's formidable navy and air forces continued hammering Guadalcanal from bases in Bougainville and Rabaul. The island then became our forward base in the South Pacific. The 13th Air Force was born there. In a historical irony, it was from the airfield Yamamoto tried so desperately to retake, that 13th Air Force P-38s took off and shot him out of the sky.

Australian "coast watchers" were the eyes and ears of Cactus. They were white missionaries and plantation employees who were loyal to the Allies. They hid in the jungle and sent radio messages concerning enemy movements. Stranded, alone, and constantly hunted, they lived on taro roots and luck. They gave Cactus time to scramble planes and be waiting. Christian missionaries converted many of the Solomon Islands natives. The Japanese treated them scornfully, defecating on their crude altars and forcing the women to perform obscene acts with their crucifixes. Consequently, the natives detested the Japanese and befriended the Americans, often rescuing American flyers. Their reward was canned meat. No Jap patrol was safe. They pounced on barges and killed the crews. They slipped into camps at night, killing Japanese and stealing weapons and food.

The Solomon Islands natives were friendly and tenacious. Jacob Vouza was a legend. He tried to arrest the Japanese for invading his homeland. The marines took to Vouza and vice versa. They gave him an American flag for his scouting missions. He was caught on patrol. Discovering his flag, the Japanese demanded information from him. His refusal infuriated them, so they tied him to a tree with ropes, bayoneted him seven times in the chest and left him for dead. But Vouza bit through his ropes and crawled three miles on his hands and knees. Although near death, he refused treatment until he reported all he had seen. After he recuperated, General Vandergrift awarded him a Silver Star and made him a Marine Sergeant Major.

On June 16, a coast watcher spotted hundreds of Zeros and Vals coming in to Guadalcanal. This was the climactic air battle for Guadalcanal, seeking to avenge Yamamoto's death. Every plane on Guadalcanal was airborne, while the incoming armada was miles away. With 300 planes in action, miles of sky were filled. Planes were falling out of the sky. Enemy losses were five to one. Only forty enemy planes returned. The greatest air battle in the South Pacific to that time turned into slaughter in the sky.

13th Air Force Fighter Squadrons with their new P-38s shot down seventy enemy planes against six of their own.

Cactus Air Force ranks among the greatest fighting units in history. It was not an organized unit, had no formal command structure, was made up of pilots and planes from the army, navy and marines, and dissolved when the battle was over. Isolated, outnumbered, backs to the wall, it held against the hitherto invincible Japanese juggernaut. These men arose each day, and, like the Light Brigade, rode into the valley of death. Once they were down to three planes. Their survival was doubtful, with Japan controlling the surrounding land, sea and air. Yet these men sharpened skills, honed tactics and developed an esprit that bloodied Japan's best pilots and mauled its planes. Those Army Air Squadrons formed the 13th Air Force, which settled its score by introducing Admiral Yamamoto to his ancestors.

Thomas G. Miller summarized the Cactus Air Force:

"It all turned around this battered airstrip. The marines safeguarded the field with their lives. The Japanese Army lost thousands of men trying to recapture it. The two navies lost dozens of ships and thousands of sailors. From this field, always outnumbered, flew the few dozen planes and few hundred men of the Cactus Air Force. In large part it was those men who beat back four powerful attempts to seize their airfield. It was against the rock of their courage and skill that a numerically larger Japanese Air Force broke, and in its breaking took to their deaths the empire's best pilots. The air arm of the Japanese Navy never recovered from the savage losses of those few weeks in late 1942."

Thus did Guadalcanal go from obscurity to legend. But for many of the soldiers and flyers who fought there, this is their grave. This is where they died. This is where they will always be.

Lt. Charles Van Bibber of the 339th Fighter Squadron wrote about those Guadalcanal pilots who remain there forever:

The Phantom Flight

"It's a clear cool dawn on Guadalcanal as the sky announces the day,
*   To the east there's a warmth in pink and blue,*
To the west, it's cool and gray.
*   From high above comes the fading sound, of a mighty engine's roar,*
Mechanics relax their ceaseless work, to scan the skies once more.
*   Too early for the dawn patrols, returned from their rendezvous,*

Too early for the bombers and TBFs, they're still out there in the blue.
The hum of the motors fades away, in the ever brightening sky,
*   And the work of war goes on again. Men sweat, and fight, and die.*
What ships are these, what pilots fly on this Phantom Patrol at dawn?
*   Too high to be seen by human eye, their invisible echelon?*
Those on earth may never know, but ask the man who flies.
*   Has he ever seen those mystery planes, in his travel thru the skies?*
The pilot lights a cigarette, for a moment his face is grim.
*   And a faraway look comes in his eye, and he tells you what they*
*   meant to him...*

Oh yes, I've seen those Phantom Flights, in the misty shades at dawn,
*   For the pilots who fly those mystery ships, are friends from near and*
*   far,*
They never come close enough to see, but we well know who they are.
*   They're Bobby Rice, and good old Heen, they've flown many a mile,*
And old Tex Rankin cheers our way, with his happy-go-lucky smile.
*   Sylvester, Stivers, Baker, Hoyle—they're part of this echelon.*
With a friendly smile they say, 'cheer up, don't act as tho' we were
*   gone...'*

Yes, some will say that they've all passed on, to that airfield in the sky.
*   But they still re-form each day at dawn, to joke and fight and fly.*
It's a clear, cool dawn on Guadalcanal, as the sky announces the day,
*   To the east there's warmth in pink and blue, and to the west it's cool*
*   and gray,*
From high above comes the sound of a mighty engine's roar,
*   And mechanics relax their ceaseless work, to scan the skies once*
*   more..."*

REFERENCES

Caidin, Martin, *Fork-Tailed Devil: The P-38*, N.Y. Ballantine Books, 1971
Hoyt, Edwin P., *Guadalcanal*, N.Y. Jove Books, 1982
Miller, Thomas G., *Cactus Air Force*, N.Y. Harper, 1969

Section II

THE JUNGLE AIR FORCE

When war broke out, the U.S. Army Air Corps was one of several army commands. Its Pacific outposts consisted of two bases, one in Hawaii and one in the Philippines. The treacherous attacks by Japan deprived the Air Corps its chance to rise and fight. At Pearl Harbor the planes were bunched tightly to protect against sabotage. By the time the last Japanese fighter flew away, little was left of Army Air Corps Hawaii. At Clark Field in the Philippines, B-17s and P-40s parked wing tip to wing tip were destroyed almost to the last plane.

At the beginning of 1942, the Pacific Army Air Corps was a rag-tag collection of P-39s, P-40s and worn out B-17s, which managed to fight their way through Japs and jungles to accrete in Australia. Hunkered down there, it was a sad and dispirited remnant. Its battered planes had no right to be in the sky, yet there they flew, patched until they fell apart. With no relief in sight "morale was lower than whale dung at the bottom of the ocean."

The long road to Tokyo began in jungles and islands south of the Equator, far from the sanctuary of the Rising Sun. The army surrendered in Bataan in a humiliating defeat. After losses in the Java Sea and Coral Sea and six disastrous battles off Guadalcanal, the navy was reduced to no battleships and one carrier, which scuttled back to Hawaii. It would be two years before the next carrier battle.

When the giant navy task forces returned in 1944, they contained bristling battleships, cruisers and destroyers, fast attack transports, swarms of landing craft and twenty-one new Essex class carriers with space for 3000 planes. It was the mightiest naval armada in history.

But during the two preceding years, not a day passed that the Air Corps, later called Army Air Force, were not in or under attack. Growing muscular, they vowed that in the future anything that flew, even birds, would be wearing the air force insignia. They clawed their way north out of Guadalcanal, across the Solomons, Admiralties, New Britain, Munda,

Bougainville, the length of New Guinea, isolated Rabaul, Truk and Yap, and left them rotting and dead. Those two years tore the heart out of Japan's air armadas, killed their best pilots and destroyed their first-line planes.

During all that time Europe was the war of record. Gut-wrenching hardships and incredible accomplishments of those men and their planes in the vast, isolated South Pacific are not recorded in majesterial writing by writers of renown. They lie buried in the history's dust bin.

CHAPTER NINE

An Air Force in Odyssey

The Homerian epic recounting the travels of Odysseus, the wandering Greek warrior, was named *The Odyssey*. Its title came to mean a lengthy voyage marked by changes of fortune. The constant travel of the 13th Air Force was an Odyssey, whose history is a panoply of maximums. It performed on the largest military stage in history. Its missions were the longest. Its conditions the harshest. Its weather the worst. Its enemy the most savage. The 13th was amphibious and itinerant. Its bases were strips of land taken as forward points on the road to Tokyo, and discarded in a love 'em and leave 'em routine as soon as the next strip became available.

Its Odyssey traversed two continents, twelve seas and islands beyond count. It never had a home. It pitched tents on forty-five different islands. Paperwork was haphazard. It lived on coral reefs and jungle mud, its time line blurred by movement. People it encountered were cannibals and head-hunters. There was no escape from sickness and disease, insects and snakes. Dehydrated food was the menu du jour. Sickness felled more men than combat. Improbably hatched on an unknown island, its men and planes rose every day for four years, fighting a primeval war in which its captured airmen were tortured, beheaded and sometimes buried alive. It fought side by side with its own band of brothers, the Army, Navy and Marines. Its allies were Australians, New Zealanders, British, Dutch, Chinese, Filipinos and, when friendly, natives. It traveled constantly, leaving enemy ruins in its wake and ripping the heart out of Japan's air force.

On the thirteenth day of the thirteenth month following Pearl Harbor, the rowdy, pugnacious Army Air Corps units rattling around with Navy, Marine and New Zealanders in the Cactus Air Force, came into their own. On January 13, 1943, the 13th Air Force was officially activated. Its orders were: "Defeat the enemy air force over Guadalcanal and defend Australia against an invasion." These gun fighters now had their own air force. It came to be known as the "Jungle Air Force."

There was something different about the 13th Air Force. It wasn't conceived by creating an air force on paper, staffing it, training it and sending it off to war. It hatched from the Cactus Air Force, that prickly bunch of pilots and crews that held Guadalcanal for months against impossible odds. Its killer skills traced back to that hardscrabble origin.

When the 13th was officially declared an air force in 1943, it obtained an identity to go with its élan and audacity. It undertook missions with tenacity and pride, killing its enemies quickly and ruthlessly. When it flew the mission that shot down Admiral Yamamoto, Japan's maximum war- rior, the 13th's Odyssey had just begun. It fought in the South, Southwest, Central Pacific, and China-Burma-India theaters, the only air force to fight in all four. It fought Japanese battleships and barges, bombers and fighters; trains, tanks and trucks—everything that moved.

It operated from "one damn island after another" in Guadalcanal, Admiralties, Bougainville, Green, Russell and Stirling Islands, Ondonga, Munda, Treasury, Sansapor, Wakde, Noemfoor, Biak, Morotai, Mindoro, Leyte, Cebu, Negros, Lingayen, Palawan, Mindanao, Luzon and Okinawa. It moved so often it could pick up stakes and move on an hour's notice, like a circus troupe. It flew the longest missions of the war against the smallest targets.

The 13th was unique in creation and operation. No other air force endured such primitive conditions. No other air force suffered its history to disappear. Its remarkable accomplishments were killed in the crossfire of inter-service rivalry, self-serving news releases of theater commanders, and allergy of war correspondents to jungle foxholes. The Air Force Historical Research Agency admittedly failed to properly document its history. When confronted with the omissions, the bureaucracy declined to act. Its feckless non-response buried the history of a feisty killing- machine that scythed a numerically stronger enemy including its Goliath, Admiral Yamamoto.

Beginning in March 1943, and starting from Guadalcanal, the 13th clawed its way up the Solomons across Santa Isabel, New Georgia, Rendova, Kolombangara, Vella Lavella, Choiseul, Treasury and Shortland.

It spearheaded army and marine conquests in the Carolines and New Georgia. From Los Negros they knocked out Woleai so effectively the 5th Bomb Group received a Presidential Citation. Japan's air power in the Solomons went kaput, brought on, according to an intercepted enemy message, by "the vigor of 13th Air Force strikes." Enemy aircraft in the 13th's area dwindled to none by November1943. The enemy evacuated the South Pacific, ending the war there and leaving behind 100,000 troops. In ten months the 13th fulfilled its first mission, to neutralize enemy air power in the South Pacific.

The 13th fought itself out of a job. Needing work, it became Paladin, a gun-slinger for critical assignments. Its next assignment was neutralizing Rabaul, the impregnable enemy base. Rabaul had been hit repeatedly by the 5th Air Force and the navy, but the 13th knocked it out. The 13th first hit Rabaul in November 1943. Japan defended fiercely, siphoning planes from as far as Manchuria. As fast as the new units arrived, they were shot out of the skies by angry, swarming 13th fighters and bombers, supported by Navy and Marine fighters. By February 1944, when the curtain came down on Rabaul, the 13th had destroyed 266 enemy planes and wrecked the harbor. Rabaul's 100,000 man garrison was intact, but with airfields wrecked, planes smashed and harbor filled with dead ships, the mightiest base died. Japan refused to withdraw until there was nothing left to withdraw.

With Rabaul neutered by air power alone, the 13th assisted the navy drive through the central Pacific. In March 1944, the 13th flew the first air force raid against the huge Japanese base at Truk. Flying 13-hours to a target 1,000 miles away, unescorted B-24 bombers of the 307th Long Rangers took the enemy by surprise. They scored 200 direct hits, churning the runways and destroying 49 planes on the ground. Enemy fighters quickly arose, and in a fierce dog-fight 31 Japanese fighters were shot down by B-24 gunners. The 13th received its first Presidential Citation. The 13th, along with the 7th Air Force and navy flyers, pulverized this stronghold, knocking it out of the war. Maximum range missions were flown against bases at Yap and Palau—strange of name, but bristling like angry porcupines. Yap was a barnacle in the Pacific which Japan fortified after receiving it as a "protectorate" in World War I. As the first to strike Yap, the 13th suffered heavily. But, in running gun battles which followed, the 13th shot down so many enemy planes, Yap no longer threatened the navy plowing across the central Pacific.

In June 1944, the 13th became part of the Far East Air Force (FEAF), although retaining its individual identity. It participated in the Marianas Campaign for Guam, Tinian and Saipan, bringing Japan in range of the great B-29s.

With Japan's eastern perimeter destroyed, the 13th vectored west to cover the Eighth Army bogged down in New Guinea since 1942. New Guinea was an enormous, primeval sub-continent whose terrain was unchartered and whose inhabitants were cannibals. From its long narrow tail on the east, it expanded to a bird's head on the west. Its jagged mountains poked high above the clouds at 13,000 feet, looking down on steep gorges and rushing rivers. Covering it all was a solid, fetid jungle, nurtured by monsoons and inhabited by stone age people. Across this 1,500 mile unmapped wilderness, the 13th hop-scotched, setting up shop at outposts with strange names like Noemfoor and Sansapor. Then across Geelwink Bay to Biak, wrested from the enemy only after a prolonged fight. Biak brought Ceram and Ambon in the Banda Sea under attack. Crossing the Flores Sea they isolated Timor. Then another flat-footed leap across the Molucca Sea to Morotai in the Halmaheras. From Morotai in giant stretches, the 13th prowled the Celebes Sea and the Makassar Straits. Enemy bases at Manado and Kendari, which funneled the resources of Indonesia to Japan were cut off by the 13th from the air and by submarines from below. Balikpapan was bombed and the Philippines were under attack. MacArthur was now ready to return to the Philippines.

In October 1944, MacArthur landed at Leyte, fulfilling his vow to return to the Philippines. The 13th was there. The Philippine Archipelago stretches 1,000 miles from north to south, containing hundreds of lush and verdant islands, rich in resources, benign in climate and friendly in people. Spain scalped these islands for centuries until the Spanish-American War in 1898 ended that occupation. America provided development without colonization. When occupied by Japan, they became a nearby convenience store, defended to the death. So fierce and skillful was General Tomoyuki Yamashita's defense, three U.S. infantry divisions were wasted in the mountains of Luzon. War in the Philippines ended only when the Emperor ordered Yamashita to surrender. He was not defeated.

13th bombers and fighters flew the entire Philippine campaign from southern Mindanao to northern Luzon. Where the enemy set foot, the 13th came to evict him. Its first bases were Cebu, Negros and Mindoro. The 13th was the first to hit Manila's Nichols and Neilson airdromes, Corregidor and Cavite. In two weeks from March 27 to April 9, the 13th knocked out 600 enemy motor transports. Its medium bombers flew longer missions than heavy bombers in Europe. MacArthur's Eighth Army rooted out the enemy with the 13th in lock-step, establishing bases at Palawan in the west, Mindanao in the south and Luzon in the north. Bill Harris, the 13th's great Ace, told me about taking his P-38 Squadron to Lingayen as the first U.S. planes there.

Next came the Australian campaign for Borneo's oil at Tarakan, Brunei and Balikpapan. To reach such juicy targets required the longest bomber missions of the war. The 13th was first over Balikpapan, the main source of Japan's fuel. Six smashing 2,000-mile raids were the longest B-24 missions up to that time. Opposition was furious, but the 13th destroyed Balikpapan. They isolated Ceram, Lutong and Bandjermasin, drying up oil for the guns of Japan. They crossed over the Sulu Sea and the Makassar Straits, as the Aussie's "Air Assault Force." The oil of Indonesia was the only strategic target in the Pacific. Oil was so valuable one Japanese official declared that one drop of oil is as precious as a drop of human blood.

From Palawan the 13th flew the longest fighter missions of the war, its P-38s spanned the South China Sea to Malaya and Indo-China. Its bombers flew 3,000 miles to Java, an 18-hour 40-minute flight, the longest ever flown by loaded B-24s. Its fighters flew missions of 2,100 miles to Singapore and 2,500 miles to Java. The 13th was the first air force to fight Japanese battleships, tangling with the giant battleships, Yamato and Konga at Brunei. Determined bomb runs against those battle wagons bristling with the largest guns ever mounted on ships produced heavy casualties. 18-inch guns fired 3,000 pound shells so large they were visible in their 30-mile trajectories. Stunned, one pilot reported those shells looked like Volkswagens flying across the sky. The flak was so thick, he said, that even the autopilots were bailing out. Although the battleships survived, a large cruiser did not.

As the war approached Japan, so did the 13th. From giant Clark Field in Luzon, the 13th Squadrons staged through Okinawa, flying against Formosa, Korea and Kyushu. Its flyers were so skillful and its depredations so deadly, the 13th was designated by General Spaatz to be the Tactical Air Force for the invasion of Japan. In August 1945, President Truman ordered a survey of air attacks on Japan from the Military Analysis Division of the War Department. It reported the 13th Air Force was "the war's most efficient killing machine."

Lacking ability or resources to research thousands of microfilm rolls at the Maxwell Air Force Base record center, I've cobbled together a list of squadrons and planes aided by Mauro Messina, diligent publisher of the 13th Veterans Bulletin. Although not precise, it's close enough for government work.

The 13th flew a variety of planes: B-17 Flying Fortress, B-24 Liberator, B-25 Mitchell, B-26 Marauder, P-38 Lightning, P-39 Aircobra, P-40 Warhawk, P-61 Black Widow, C-46 Commando, C-47 Skytrain, L-5 Sentinel and PBY5A. It sported these units:

13th Bomber Command consisted of the 5th, 307th and 42nd Bomb Groups flying B-17s and B-24s, B-25s and B-26s. Medium bombers were Martin B-26 Marauder and North American B-25 Mitchell. The cigar-

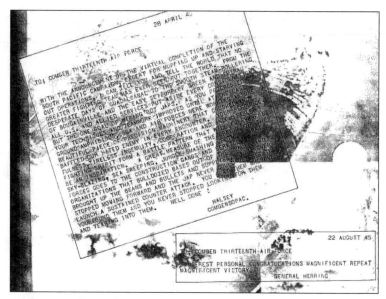

Communique from Admiral Halsey announcing the end of the South Pacific campaign

shaped B-26 was a hot plane, but not successful in the Pacific where distance defeated its range. Its small wings earned it the name "Flying Prostitute" because it had no visible means of support. The rugged North American B-25 Mitchell was our best bomber.

5th Bomb Group comprised four Bomber Squadrons: 23rd, 31st, 72nd and 394th, flying B-17s and B-24s.

307th Bomb Group called the "Long Rangers" comprised four Bomber Squadrons: 370th, 371st, 372nd and 424th, flying B-24s, called "The Flying Boxcar." Although ugly, its Davis wing provided range and tricycle landing gear allowed short take offs. Not as sturdy as the B-17, it was welcome in the Pacific. B-17 crews joked the worst place during an attack was in a formation of B-24s because the enemy always attacked B-24s first. An ideal long-range reconnaissance aircraft, it was not a flotation device, however, and when ditched sank like a rock.

42nd Bomb Group comprised five medium Bomber Squadrons: 69th, 70th, 75th, 100th and 390th, flying B-25s.

868th Bomber Squadron was a unique outfit flying B-24s with night searching radar. Prowling the night, they were the "Snoopers."

13th Fighter Command, contained the 18th Fighter Group, composed of the 12th, 44th and 70th Fighter Squadrons. The 347th Fighter Group contained the 67th (P39s), 68th (P39s and P-40s), 70th (P-39s), and 339th (P-38s), plus the 44th (P-40s) and 12th (P-39s) Squadrons. Ultimately, all fighter squadrons flew P-38s.

Night Fighter Squadrons consisted of the 6th, 419th and 550th. They flew P-61s.

4th Photo Group consisted of the 17th and the 38th Photo Reconnaissance Squadrons and the 18th Photo Mapping Squadron, flying stripped down P-38s called the F-5.

403rd Troop Carrier Group consisted of three Squadrons: 13th, 63rd and 4th. They flew C-47s and C-46s.

25th LS flew L-5 Piper Cubs.

2nd Emergency Rescue Squadron flew Catalina Patrol Bombers, designated 0-A 10 by the Army and PBY-5A by the Navy. Amphibious, it operated on water and land. This was my Squadron. We also operated B-17s with airborne lifeboats slung on the bottom called Flying Dutchmen. We also had a C-47, B-25 and P-38.

The 13th is bereft of "official history," which was not written until many years later from communiques of theater commanders. News correspondents did not find their way to our front-line squadrons for real time reporting, and the jungle is a poor place to keep records. The Yamamoto Mission, a decisive tactical and strategic victory, was hushed at the time and down-played later. *Fire In The Sky*, "the history of air war in the Pacific," treats the shoot down of Admiral Yamamoto with two sentences: "P-38s of the 339th squadron based on Guadalcanal launched an astounding long-range raid that succeeded in downing two Bettys carrying Yamamoto and his staff. That legendary admiral and many of his top officers perished in the Bougainville jungle." More galling than denigration is deception. The 450-page *World War II Encyclopedia* published by Greenwood Press in 1999 reports this mission thusly: "Yamamoto, the Japanese Admiral who planned the attack on Pearl Harbor, was shot down by U.S. Navy planes while he was on an inspection trip. The Navy pilots knew of his flight plans and were on a deliberate mission to take him down."

Although never possessing more than 300 operational planes, the 13th:

- Flew 97,038 combat missions
- Sank or damaged 1,350,000 tons of shipping
- Effected 1000 rescues
- Destroyed 1,439 enemy aircraft
- Flew the longest bomber missions of the war in B-24s—3,000 miles
- Flew the longest fighter missions of the war in P-38s—2,000 miles
- Flew the longest combat missions of the war in PBY5As—twenty hours
- Had the largest theater of operations
- Flew in twelve different campaigns
- Flew the first plane to land on Balikpapan and on Brunei in Borneo
- Fighter Aces Murray Shubin shot down five Zeros on one mission and Westy Westbrook downed six Zeros in three days
- Supplied the Moros in Mindanao by landing on lakes in the highlands

Mark Peattie, a Japanese history scholar at the Hoover Institution, identifies the point when our planes outclassed Japan. *"The Zero fighter, dainty as a dragonfly, dangerous as a rapier, and possessed of great firepower, was ultimately driven from the skies by American planes with more powerful engines improved further by turbo-superchargers. Our planes now had increased power, range and performance."* The Lockheed P-38 Lightning became the backbone of Army fighters. In the blurring, terrifying speed of war, its brute power could out climb and out dive Zeros. To Japan, it was an object of fear and terror, and they called it "Fork-Tailed Devil." A twin engine fighter with twin tails, the pilot flew in a cupola between the engines, giving it distinctive shape. It was the war's only successful twin engine fighter, with 400 mph speed and performance to 30,000 feet. Propellers turned in opposite directions, eliminating torque of single engine planes. Four 50-caliber machine guns and a 20-mm cannon gave tremendous fire power. With all its guns in the nose the pilot pointed the plane to shoot.

These are miscellaneous entries from the 13th Air Force log showing the sweep of this bunch of nomads:

"October—over Bougainville, B-24 crews parachuting were strafed by Zeros. Bill Harris got three Zeros in one mission.

"Christmas Day—sixteen 44th P-38s engaged sixty Zeros. 'Westy' Westbrook shot down two, giving him six victories in three days.

"18 January 1944—a force of Zeros so large, eight P-38s were lost, our first and only licking.

"February 1944—Japanese pulled their remaining 57 planes out of Rabaul. Thus ended the aerial fight for Rabaul.

"March 1944—went after Truk, the largest remaining Jap base. In a 1600 mile round trip, Zeros met the incoming Liberators in a running fight. Phosphorous bombs were dropped on our formations which suffered heavy damage. The 307th received a Distinguished Unit Citation.

"13 May—heavies supported the June invasion of Saipan by hitting Yap, a 1,023 mile trip.

"August—Long Rangers (307th) and Bomber Barons (5th) moved to Wakde Island, a hunk of coral stripped bare by shell fire. The Long Rangers were visited by a USO show featuring Bob Hope, Jerry Colona and Frances Langford. Bob said "I love this beautiful island, with its magnificent palm trees, two of them with tops."

"September—Crusaders moved to Noemfoor. Mediums and fighters supported landing at Morotai.

"23 October—twenty-six B-24s of the 307th attacked a force of three battleships, four cruisers and five destroyers. Long Rangers scored a dozen near misses on the Yamato. Three B-24s were shot down and fourteen damaged. The 13th had now scored hits on three Japanese battleships, one of which (the Hiei) they helped sink. It was a record shared by no other air force.

"November—the 347th hit Makassar, but three P-38s shot down by heavy flak. Lt. Col. "Westy" Westbrook, the 13th's leading Ace was lost.

"November—Long Rangers pounded the Philippines until the Nips were driven off their airdromes and had to take off on roads.

"January 1945—P-38s of the 18th Fighter Group landed on Lingayen. First fighter group on Luzon since 1942. Bomber Barons and Long Rangers raided Cavite Naval Base and Manila.

"April 1945—403rd Troop Carrier Group flying supplies to guerrillas on Mindanao, landed on small strips in enemy territory. Over Saigon, 70th Fighter Squadron White Knights shot down a Sally bomber.

"April 1945—Mission to Formosa by 18th Fighter Group destroyed six Jap fighters, blew up a locomotive and ten cars.

"28 April—12th Lightnings flew a sweep to Borneo. The next day flew an Indochina sweep.

"May—868th Snoopers flew record-breaking missions, 2,660 miles in seventeen hours and forty minutes to Soerabaja.

"3 June—B-24s hit Batavia, Java, a round trip of 3,000 miles in eighteen hours and forty minutes, another record breaker.

"July—the 67th, which flew the first fighter strikes at Guadalcanal, flew the last one to Singapore.

The least significant part of this Odyssey is my personal participation, long on scope and short on distinction. The winds of war wafted me across just about every major air force battleground in the Pacific—Tarawa and Guadalcanal; Nadzab, Finschaven and Biak in New Guinea, followed by Morotai in the Halmaheras. In lock-step with MacArthur's liberation campaign, we massaged every airbase in the Philippines at one time or another… Leyte, Mindoro, Cebu, Panay, Mindanao, Palawan and Luzon. From Philippine bases we covered air strikes on the Dutch East Indies at Celebes, Borneo and Java. We became Borneo experts, covering the Aussie invasions of the oil centers at Balikpapan, Tarakan and Brunei. Here our squadron's activities were sufficiently intense to receive a Presidential Unit Citation. We finished the war at the great Clark Field base on Luzon, from where we flew missions to Okinawa, Formosa and the China Coast until VJ-Day mercifully intervened.

Author David Witts with "Butch"

CHAPTER TEN

Power in the Pacific— From On High

Nobody prepared for a war in the South Pacific. The battlefields were in areas unknown. It involved a type of fighting no one had ever seen before—amphibious warfare. Battles did not swirl around great cities like Stalingrad or Berlin: There were no industrial areas or population centers. The strategy and structure of war in the Pacific involved air bases. Control of the air meant control of the seas. Fighting was for tiny strips of land from which planes could operate. But first they had to be built—hacked out of jungles, or chipped out of coral. Sometimes they were wrested from the Japanese like poison thorns in places like Guadalcanal, New Guinea and Morotai.

The terrain was strange and hostile. Suffocating jungles were fury by day and terror by night. Flat coral beaches and hot sands over which men crawled were exposed to an entrenched and bore-sighted enemy. Honeycombed caves were deep and undented by shelling. When the bombardment lifted, those caves came alive with human-like snakes crawling out and spitting fire.

American military technique relies on speed, mobility and firepower. George Washington and his rag-tag Revolutionary Army was no match for Britain's massed Red Coats, except for speed and surprise. General Patton swept to the Rhine in race track maneuvers that cut off enemy troops by tens of thousands. Not so in the Pacific. There were no roads. Swamps swallowed wheels. Progress was measured in yards per day against a suicidal enemy who had to be scraped out of caves and snipered out of trees. Firepower and speed lost advantage against an enemy that could not be seen. Targets were site specific, small and isolated. Land battles were fought over airstrips. Air power was the ultimate force in the Pacific, from the first bomb dropped on Pearl Harbor to the last one at Nagasaki. But there are no monuments or memorials. Air battles can't be evoked. Nothing remains but the endless sky.

Although held back by Washington's European tilt, once army air power muscled up and got out from under navy control, it was decisive. The maxim that generals prepare for the last war was validated. In the interim between World Wars, army generals and navy admirals resisted an independent air force. The War Department insisted that "victory comes only from the battlefield with the defeat of the enemy army. The air force has no mission except support of the army." Only General Billy Mitchell championed air power. He contended the plane was not a new weapon, but a new way of waging war. The airplane made it possible to overfly armies and navies directly to the heart of the enemy country where victory lay. Mitchell learned air power in World War I. He felt that air power could destroy naval fleets and sought a test. Secretary of the Navy Josephus Daniels refused, snorting: "Mitchell will discover if he ever tries laying bombs on a navy vessel, he will be blown to bits before he is near enough to drop salt on the navy's tail."

Somehow Mitchell obtained the "unsinkable battleship Ostfriesland" from the German fleet to test his theory. In July 1921, eight old biplanes rumbling along at ninety mph, dropped bombs on the German dreadnought, sinking the giant ship in thirty minutes. "Gun Club" admirals refused to believe what they saw, insisting: "The battleship is the backbone of the nation's defenses." Mitchell persisted. A few months later he obtained the battleship Alabama for a test and sank it. For proving his point, Mitchell was court-martialed. Japan, however, observed Mitchell's lesson and built an air force. Our naval strategy was vested in floating pachyderms, sunk in war's first hour by Japanese planes flying from aircraft carriers 250 miles away.

Charles Lindbergh, America's Lone Eagle who achieved fame as the first to fly solo across the Atlantic, was treated to an exhibition of Germany's Luftwaffe by Goering himself. Lindbergh was so impressed, he extolled Germany's air power. For his clairvoyance, he was scorned.

The Battle of Britain which stymied Hitler's invasion of England was fought by air power. In 1940, some old British biplanes sank the modern Italian navy at Taranto, which feat emboldened Yamamoto to copy it at Pearl Harbor. Our navy received a forced conversion to air power once its battle wagons burrowed in Pearl Harbor mud. The British capital ships, Prince of Wales and Repulse, confidently sortied from Singapore without air cover, only to be handily destroyed by Japanese planes in what Churchill called his worst day of the war. Yamamoto, with efficient and chilling pace, had defeated the British, Dutch and American navies without losing a capital ship. The battleship was dethroned as Queen of the Fleet. That was the epiphany of the battleship navy deferring thereafter to aircraft carriers, a strategy forced rather than planned.

The Army Air Corps' enlightened brass conceived the high flying bomber as an aerial pill box, heavily armed and fast as fighters, obviating need for fighter planes. It didn't work out that way in the Pacific. Lacking industrial or urban targets, Pacific targets were planes, ships and airfields. So ineffective was high-level bombing and so painful were the losses, that General Curtis LeMay switched to low level fire-bombing over Japan. Pathfinder planes would drop incendiaries marking the target with a giant "X." Then army B-29s roaring in at low-level laid down an inescapable blanket of fire. Fifty-six square miles of Tokyo were razed. Eighty thousand civilians died, scorched, broiled and baked. The flames melted metal, boiled rivers and humans burst into fireballs.

New Guinea cannibals

Despite all the latter-day caterwauling about the A-Bomb, more people were killed in Tokyo fire bomb raids than at Hiroshima and Nagasaki combined. Army air power brusquely ended the Pacific War as suddenly as it had begun. At that moment, warfare became less muscular and more technical.

Targets in Europe meant flak and fighters on the way in and on the way out. Approach to Pacific targets was always over the ocean, so we didn't enter the tunnel of fire until near the target, but going down meant capture and certain death unless rescued. Over Europe, crews could bail out and survive, even though it might be in a German stalag where the pilots were told: "For you, der war is over." In the Pacific, a plane going down had two choices: ocean or jungle. Jungle was the worst. Crashing in dense trees was a death sentence. When ditching, if the nose went down on impact, it was "Katie Bar the Door." Fighter pilots had one-man life rafts attached to their parachutes. Bombers carried inflatable rafts and yellow flotation vests (called "Mae Wests," for reasons I don't recall). The lucky ones got picked up by PBYs and sometimes by subs. The unlucky ones died of shock, were eaten by sharks, fried in the sun or were captured.

Natives of the South Pacific were not swept up in the war. The musi-

A South Pacific head hunter

cal comedy South Pacific was a wonderfully orchestrated story on Bali Hai, except that it wasn't the way it was. Friendly natives were encountered in the Solomons, which benefitted from missionary schools . The people I saw in New Guinea were stone-age cannibals, and in Borneo the Dyaks adorned their belts with skulls.

In the Dutch East Indies, now called Indonesia, Sumatra, Java and the Celebes were inhabited by lighter-skinned people who had progressed under Dutch Colonization. Dutch colonialism had so embittered them against whites, natives initially welcomed Japanese as liberators. It didn't take long for Japanese brutality to remove scales from eyes. Their "Indonesian Patrol" prowled for downed flyers who they turned over to the Japanese for rewards. Reliably friendly were the Filipinos who fought alongside our forces and constantly risked their own lives in guerrilla activities. Our squadron was involved in some of those activities in Mindanao, discussed later.

REFERENCES

Wheeler, Keith, *The Road To Tokyo*, Richmond, Virginia, Time-Life Books, 1979

World War II Encyclopedia, Vols. *10, 17, 18, 19, 20*, USA, Orvis Publishing, 1972

Jablonski, Edward, *Pictorial History of World War II*, N.Y., Doubleday, 1977

Gailey, Harry, *War In The Pacific*, Novato, California, Presidio Press, 1995

CHAPTER ELEVEN

Sayonara - Yamamoto

"There have been few, if any, missions in the history of our air force in which such outstanding victory has been achieved in the face of seeming insuperable difficulty." Lt. Gen. M. F. Harmon, April 24, 1943

In April 1943, the time of the Yamamoto mission, I had not yet joined the 13th Air Force on Guadalcanal. However, I've talked with George Chandler, Bill Harris and Rex Barber, all 13th Air Force Aces, and Doug Canning and Besby Homes who were on the "Killer Flight." My contribution to preserving this historic event consists of gathering first-hand narratives, reporting George Chandler's extraordinary endeavors to correct historical errors which dogged the mission, and obtaining General Doolittle's personal comments. C.V. Glines is a distinguished historian with whom I visit at meetings of the University of Texas at Dallas History of Aviation Board. His book *Attack on Yamamoto* cannot be bettered. Quotes from him are included.

The epic mission of the Pacific War, the blow from which Japan never recovered, was shooting down their idolized military leader, the driving force of Japan's war machine, Admiral Isoruku Yamamoto. Arguably the war's most significant mission is little known. It marked the high-water mark of the Japanese tsunami, after which they never won another battle. It was apparently authorized by President Roosevelt as the first assassination of an enemy leader authorized by the U.S. Government. It involved the most secret secret of the war, i.e., we had broken their code and were reading their mail in real time.

This mission was planned by one 13th Air Force pilot, and heroically concluded by another. It was hushed at the time and unheralded thereafter. It was a 100% mission of the Army Air Force, but flown under navy command, insuring it would be downplayed. Admiral Halsey downgraded recommendations for Congressional Medals of Honor to Major John Mitchell who planned the mission and Lt. Barber and Capt. Lanphier who flew the "Killer Flight."

In the book, *Yamamoto*, written by Edwin P. Hoyt, neither the 13th Air Force nor the remarkable "Killer Flight" led by Mitchell, Barber and Lanphier was mentioned. The climax was skirted in a single sentence:

"A flight of P-38s was laid on from Henderson Field. They flew to Ballae, intercepted the planes just as they were preparing to land and shot down Yamamoto in spite of the covering Japanese fighters."

Secrecy shrouded the mission, and controversy swirled around which pilot actually sent Yamamoto's plane into the jungle. Half a century later, I interviewed Rex Barber, the victory pilot, George Chandler, whose efforts to correct the record have been Herculean, Bill Harris, the greatest living Ace of the 13th Air Force, along with Doug Canning and Besby Holmes who also flew that mission. George Chandler interviewed Major John Mitchell who planned and commanded the mission. He provided the tape, along with General Doolittle's letter to Capt. Lanphier. Eyewitness reports of three Japanese airmen who survived the mission were obtained from the Nimitz Museum and from Doug Canning who spoke with them through an interpreter.

The mission was flown by the 13th Air Force while under navy command. The Pacific was divided into the army zone commanded by MacArthur, and navy zone commanded by Nimitz. This mission fell in the navy zone, but big problem: navy had no carriers or planes with range to reach Bougainville. Pummeled in sea battles off Guadalcanal, the navy was down to one carrier, which it was not about to send into that wasp nest buzzing with enemy planes and ships. The navy grudgingly deferred to the army and its long-range P-38 Lightnings. Despite the mission's spectacular success, Major John Mitchell who led the mission, and Lt. Rex Barber who destroyed the target, saw their recommended Congressional Medal of Honor awards replaced with the Navy Cross by a petulant Admiral Halsey.

Admiral Isoroku Yamamoto was Japan's military icon, its maximum warrior and Commander of the Japanese Fleet, then the world's most powerful navy. He was the "Sword" of his emperor who planned the attack on Pearl Harbor and Midway. He permitted no criticism of his operations and was known for intensity of speech and an indomitable will. To his men Yamamoto was a god. He boasted he would ride down Pennsylvania Avenue on a white horse and dictate peace terms in the White House. Having studied at Harvard and traveled extensively in the U.S., he understood America's potential. Although he opposed war with the young nation across the Pacific, once the decision was made, he plunged into its planning. He said, "I fear we have awakened a sleeping giant and filled him with a terrible resolve." That prediction played out over Bougainville.

Yamamoto, married and with four children, did not drink, but allowed himself other indulgences. He enjoyed several geisha mistresses, who, when visiting him, were ceremoniously ushered aboard his flagship. His lifelong love, Kawai Chiyoko, published his love letters in 1945. An addicted gambler he bet on every game of chance, especially shoji, Japanese chess. His first gamble was Pearl Harbor, his second, Midway, his third was Bougainville, where his luck ran out.

Japan's strategy involved capturing Port Moresby in New Guinea preparatory to invading Australia. Code breakers alerted us to a huge invasion convoy heading to Port Moresby. In March 1943, the Army Air Force intercepted that convoy of twelve troop transports and ten warships in the Bismarck Sea. What followed was one of the most savage battles ever fought—The Battle of Bismarck Sea. Army planes sank the entire convoy in a vengeful slaughter described by the New York Times of March 15, 1943 as "low flying army planes turned lifeboats into bloody sieves. It was the same ferocity Japs loosed on Allies. Only a few bobbing survivors washed ashore."

This staggering loss displeased the Emperor. To erase the shame of Bismarck Sea, Yamamoto launched Operation I-Go. He struck at Guadalcanal in April with a massive raid of 486 planes. Standing beside the Rabaul runway in dress whites, he waved his cap as the mission took off. He announced his decision to visit the forward bases in Bougainville on April 18 and encourage them to greater sacrifice. The rivalry between Japan's army and navy was worse than ours, yet the Area Commander, Army General Imamura, pleaded with him to stay out of the combat zone. Admiral Joshima pleaded with his superior not to expose himself to aerial ambush. As Japan's foremost warrior, he insisted on a precise, swaggering plan to visit his front line. Confident their code was unbreakable, they were equally sure no American fighter could fly the 1,000 mile round trip from Guadalcanal to Bougainville. The radio message from Rabaul to Bougainville signaling his itinerary became his death warrant.

April 13, 1943, Station Hypo in Pearl Harbor intercepted a message from Yamamoto's headquarters at Rabaul, informing Bougainville that:

"On 18 April CC combined fleet will visit RY2. Depart RR at 0600 in medium bomber escorted by six fighters. Arrive RY2 at 0800. Proceed by minesweeper to Kahili, arriving 0840. He will make a tour of inspection and visit sick and wounded."

Commander Layton rushed the intercept to Admiral Nimitz. Yamamoto's flight to Bougainville would bring him within range of army fighters on Guadalcanal. Nimitz recognized that: "aside from the Emperor no man in Japan is more important. If he were shot down, it would demoralize the nation." It is said that with Roosevelt's personal approval, Secretary of Navy Frank Knox sent a Presidential Priority message: "If forces in your command have capability, intercept and shoot down Yamamoto and his staff. Initiate planning to destroy the target at all costs." (He didn't wait for a legal opinion from the State Department.)

April 16, Admiral Halsey radioed Admiral Mitscher at Guadalcanal: "It appears the Peacock will arrive on time. Fan his tail."

There was argument among the commanders as to how the mission should be flown. Finally, Admiral Mitscher said that since Mitchell had to fly the mission, it was up to him to decide how to do it.

Mitchell was the epitome of American flying commanders. He left Mississippi in 1939 to enlist in the Army Air Corps. He received basic training at Love Field in Dallas in an open cockpit Stearman. Then on to Randolph Field, the West Point of the air. Then to Hamilton Field in California, which he called the country club of the Air Corps. On Guadalcanal, he became the first 13th Air Force Ace. He was a supreme fighter pilot who trained his pilots to kill, but also to stay alive. He decided to put an end to Washing Machine Charlie, the midnight reveler who flew over Guadalcanal with his puttering engine, activating the air alert which sent soldiers scrambling to foxholes. Mitchell took off early, orbited high so his exhaust could not be seen and did a falcon number on Charlie. The marines were so grateful they baked him a cake.

Major John Mitchell, Commanding Officer of the 339th Fighter Squadron flying P-38 Lightnings, selected his pilots and charted their courses, plotting time, air speed, distance and winds to arrive at a spot 425 miles away within a ten-minute time frame! He estimated the speed of the Mitsubishi bombers, called "Bettys." The flight had to be on the deck to avoid detection, eliminating any landfall reference. Relying on nothing but compass and estimated ground speed, it was the longest long-shot. Timing was everything. There would be only fuel for the round trip plus ten minutes of combat power once belly tanks were dropped. Should Yamamoto be ten minutes off schedule, or if his flight was not spotted within ten minutes, Mitchell would have to scrub the mission. Significantly, this was one year to the date following Doolittle's raid on Tokyo.

George Chandler, himself a fighter Ace, encouraged my writing about the 13th Air Force. At a squadron reunion, he talked with Major John Mitchell, taping the conversation. He authorized my including Mitchell's words:

"I was called to a briefing in the Marine dugout at Henderson, where we got our orders. Admiral Mitscher was there with 30 or 40 people milling around and talking. The navy wanted to get him in the boat when he transferred to an island. I couldn't tell one boat from another and besides even if we got the boat, he could get in a life jacket and escape. I didn't want to take my P-38's down on the deck where they are at their greatest disadvantage and have 75 Zeros pound down on them. At the briefing there was a hassle on how to do it. Finally Mitscher said 'if Mitchell's going to fly the mission, then its up to him to plan it.'

"I fault the Navy for giving us a plan with true headings. That didn't do us any good since we had to fly a magnetic compass heading. They asked if there was anything they could do and I said, 'Yea get me a good compass.' The only time we knew whether our compass was accurate was when we lined up on the runway because we know the true runway heading. I drew the flight plan on a piece of tablet paper which I taped to my knee.

"I fault the Navy for not telling us there would be two bombers when they knew it, but let us think there'd be only one. Otherwise I would have put two flights up, one for each bomber.

"I relied on Yamamoto's punctuality. His take-off was scheduled at 0600. I figured his speed would be 180 mph. Based on this estimate, our known speed, and a guess of winds on the way, I plotted a zig-zag course of five different legs to the intercept point. This would keep us away from islands known to have radar. We would fly on the deck at fifty feet to keep from being spotted, although this placed our P-38s at their least operational efficiency and blinded the mission from reference points during the entire flight. At the end the 'Killer Flight' of four planes would climb up and attack the target.

"I would lead the remaining planes to Kahili to head off any Zeros so the Killer Flight would be free of interference once Yamamoto's flight was sighted. We would be in position at that altitude to handle the fifty-odd Zeros we expected as an honor escort for the Admiral. We figure he'll land at 0945. We'll jump him ten minutes before when he should be into his letdown. I told the flight, we're going to be on the deck. Your depth perception isn't worth a damn if you stare at the water, and you'll be in it before you know it. And radio silence. No transmissions for any purpose until we have the target in sight.

"At 0820, I hand-signaled the first course change. The P-38s swung to 290 degrees. We flew the second leg in twenty-seven minutes, then turned 305 degrees. Thirty-eight minutes and 125 miles later, I veered to the fourth leg of 20 degrees for a twenty-one minute run due east. All we knew about the wind was there would be a 5-knot wind off the port bow. However we changed direction 4 times and the drift changed each time. We later learned Yamamoto had ordered their uniforms to be fatigues, but two guys came out in dress whites. If he had sent them back to change, we would never have made the intercept.

"We took off at 0700, circled once to get all 18 planes in the pattern. Two aborted before we got in the pattern. I gave hand signals to the others to get them into slots. We flew without radio or check point. Nothing but a compass and a watch, down on the waves which all look alike. We arrived at the intercept point at 0945, one minute off my schedule. We still couldn't see land. Then Doug Canning said 'Bogies, 10 o'clock high.' I said, 'Skin off your belly tanks, they're your meat, go get 'em.' We thought there would be about 75 Zeroes coming in to escort their top dog. I thought with that many Zeroes we would have a turkey shoot.

"At first I was not sure since the navy briefed us there would be one bomber, but I saw two Betty bombers in close formation at 4,500 feet. Then I saw six Zeros in flights of three, one on each side of the bombers. I knew we had Yamamoto.

"I called the squadron to drop their external tanks and attack. Lt. Holmes could not shake his belly tanks loose. He turned away from the "Killer Flight," taking Lt. Hine, his wingman, with him. This left only two P-38s to shoot down two bombers and fight off six fighters. It was unlikely that two P-38s at low altitude would survive six high altitude attacking angry Zeros. Lanphier and Barber were on their own. The Killer Flight was down to two planes against insuperable odds. Those who decry this 'assassination' should change places with Lanphier and Barber.

"Lanphier and Barber went to 100% power and came in at right angles to the bombers which were sitting up there, fat, dumb and happy. They never saw the P-38s coming up from below. Then the Zeros spotted them. Three Zeroes peeled off and dove, but Lanphier turned up into them and they scattered. Rex stayed with the bombers, which was the mission. Barber had to get the Betty before the Zeros got him. He rolled hard right and fired into the lead bomber. The second bomber didn't even know they were under attack until they saw tracers. The Betty started smoking. The fight was over in a brief time, which most dogfights are. Lieutenant Hine went down with his wingman and knocked the Zeros off Barber's tail. Holmes damaged the sec-

ond bomber. Rex finished it off. Then I said 'Everybody get the hell out of here'. Pearl Harbor was avenged!

"There's no way to foresee everything. He was there, and we were there. Maybe it was luck. Maybe it was Fate that pre-ordained our mission would be successful. When we got back there was lots of jubilation and slapping and shouting, 'We got Yamamoto, got Yamamoto.' But nobody was supposed to know anything."

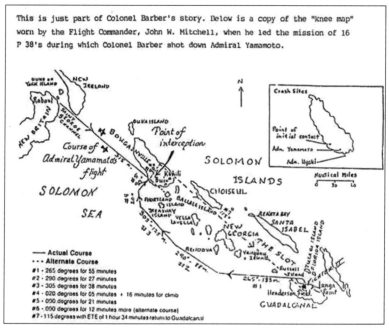

Yamamoto interception map

In less than five minutes, Admiral Isoroku Yamamoto, Japan's chief military commander, six of his staff officers, and thirteen crewmen of the two bombers were dead. This is the dispatch Mitscher sent Admiral Halsey after the mission:

"Pop goes the weasel. P-38s led by Major J. William Mitchell USAAF visited Kahili area. About 0930, shot down two bombers escorted by six Zeros flying close formation."

Halsey replied:

"Congratulations to you and Major Mitchell and his hunters. Sounds as though one of the ducks in their bag was a peacock."

After the mission none of the pilots recalls a debriefing. Major Mitchell, Captain Lanphier and Lieutenant Rex Barber were recommended for the Congressional Medal of Honor. Admiral Halsey downgraded the recommendations. An intelligence report on the mission written by Captain Joe McGuigan was furnished me by Doug Canning. Doug Canning says: *"Every effort was made to hush up the mission. We were told that if we said anything about the Yamamoto flight we would be court-martialed."*

MacArthur ordered: *"Revelations of the Yamamoto incident by returnees from the Pacific Theater are serious. Order all those under your command not to reveal information."*

Yamamoto was found dead in the cabin seat with his seat belt on. Yamamoto's watch stopped at 7:45 a.m. What impressed the rescue party was pure white toilet paper in his pocket: "You use good paper when you get to be C in C." The dead bodies were cremated on Bougainville and taken to Japan.

Yamamoto's death was kept secret even from his headquarters at Rabaul. His ashes were flown to Truk and placed aboard his flagship, the Musahi. An envelope found in Yamamoto's safe, contained a poem written by Yamamoto:

"Since the war began, tens of thousands of officers and men of matchless loyalty and courage have done battle at the risk of their lives, and have died to become guardian gods of our land. Ah, how can I ever enter the imperial presence again? With what words can I possibly report to the parents and brothers of my dead comrades? Wait but a while, young men—one last battle, fought gallantly to the death, and I will be joining you!"

On May 7, the battleship Musahi sailed from Truk carrying the ashes of Yamamoto, arriving in Tokyo Bay on May 21. The news was released months later. When Tokyo Radio announced that Admiral Yamamoto met a gallant death, the announcer broke down in tears. The Emperor decreed Yamamoto be accorded a formal state funeral, a tribute given to only eleven others in the nation's entire history. The news of Yamamoto's death had been conveyed officially to the family and unofficially to his favorite geisha, Chiyoko Kawai, on May 18.

Yamamoto's state funeral was held June 5, 1943. The roads were lined with three million Japanese. Half of Yamamoto's ashes were placed in a grave next to the grave of Admiral Togo whom Yamamoto greatly admired. The other half was taken to his home town Nagaoka in the grounds of a Zen temple. In 1943, a full-length statute of Yamamoto was erected at the Kasumigaura Flying School. During the occupation, MacArthur ordered all military statutes destroyed. Yamamoto's statute was dumped into a nearby lake.

Rex Barber Speaks.

Rex Barber, who made the kill, is a true American hero. He was quiet, unassuming and unpretentious on the ground, but in the air he metamorphosed into an aggressive fighter. He flew 110 combat missions before being shot down over China. He was awarded the Navy Cross, two Silver Stars, the Purple Heart and several Air Medals. He lives in Oregon. I asked Rex to tell me the first thing that came to his mind about the mission. He told me: "The night before the mission, belly tanks were flown in from Nadzab in a B-24. The mechanics worked all night in a rainstorm to rig a 310 gallon tank to the belly and a 165 gallon extra fuel tank to the side."

Barber described the mission :

"I was doing three hundred miles an hour, and overshot the Bettys. I banked sharply to the right to fall in behind them, rolled level and saw only one Betty a thousand feet above the jungle. I was slightly left, a little above, and less than a hundred yards behind when I opened fire, aiming at the right engine. Pieces of cowling flew off, and it began smoking. I drew my fire into the fuselage, left wing root and engine. Reversing direction, I came back through the fuselage and tail. The Betty suddenly banked steeply to the left, and because I was so close behind, I nearly hit its upturned right wing. We were now less than five hundred feet above the jungle, and I last saw the Betty going down with its right engine smoking heavily."

When Barber looked back he saw a column of smoke arising from the jungle and saw Zeros shooting at him. Two or three Zeros were riddling Barber's plane. Barber broke free of the Zeros at tree top level and headed toward the sea. Ahead of him over the ocean suddenly appeared the second Betty Bomber under attack by two P-38s. He moved in close. Barber described the scene:

"After Holmes and Hine made their pass at the bomber, I saw its right engine smoking. Holmes' bullets hit the water behind the Betty, then walked through the right engine. White vapor started trailing behind that engine. Hine also fired, but his rounds seemed to hit ahead in the water. I pulled in behind the Betty, opened fire, and continued firing until I was about twenty

feet behind the bomber which was so close to the ocean I could see the prop
blasts from the engines making wakes in the water. It suddenly exploded and,
because I was so close, I could not avoid flying through the debris. I flew
through black smoke and debris and a large chunk hit my right wing, cutting
into the inter-cooler. When this debris smashed the leading edge, it disabled
the turbo supercharger and severely limited power from that engine. Another
large piece hit my gondola. I landed at Fighter Two almost out of gas. My
crew chief showed me four bullet holes through my left prop and three in the
right prop. There were 104 bullet holes in the wings, tail, and fuselage."

Talking with Rex Barber provides an insight not found in official reports of the Yamamoto mission. Rex was born in 1917. He came to Guadalcanal in December 1942 as a P-40 pilot, but flew P-38s once they arrived. He said the Yamamoto mission got reported "all out of context." After Guadalcanal, he was recycled to China where he flew twenty-eight missions under Chennault. Although shot down, he evaded capture by hiding for two months.

He was dismayed at America's post war foreign policy. Like everybody who fought in World War II, he was very proud of our military. To see its proud legacy squandered left lingering bitterness. Barber said: "When North Korea violated their treaty and moved south, we lost 50,000 lives and ended up where we started. When Russia blockaded Berlin, the State Department wouldn't let us break the blockade. At the Bay of Pigs, one of his units was pulled off the line the night before the landing troops got slaughtered, and the world got Castro. America should stand up for what is right. Not go out and fight every battle in the world, but announce what we will protect and defend and not be dunced around by wimpy civilians like we were in Viet Nam. Don't be a bully, but when we get stepped on, we should step back hard."

One of the survivors of that remarkable mission is Doug Canning. This is what he told me:

"After Halsey cancelled the Congressional Medal of Honor Awards and
replaced them with Navy Crosses, the rest of us got a classified Air Medal
signed by Secretary of Defense Forrestal. Also we were told by General
Harmon as a reward we were to return to the States and be promoted one
grade the minute we stepped on US soil. Plus the warning that if we ever said
anything about the mission we would be court martialed.

"Initially, all pilots were members of the 339th Fighter Squadron, with
the first four to be led by John Mitchell as Mission Commander, with my
leading the second four, Tom Lanphier to lead the third four. His flight was

designated the "Killer Flight." The intent was for Tom Lanphier's flight to attack Yamamoto's plane and the rest of us to commence a high-speed climb turning towards Kahili where it was anticipated many Japanese fighters would be taking off to escort the Admiral. I believe the field we called Kahili was called Buin by the Japanese.

"At Fighter II we had two squadrons of P-38 pilots, but only one squadron of P-38s. These squadrons were the 12th and the 339th Fighter Squadrons. The 12th flew missions one day and the 339th the next. After the initial posting of pilots for the flight, Major Louis R. Kittel of the 12th Squadron logically stated that since the two squadrons flew alternate days, half the slots should be assigned the 12th Squadron. Mitchell agreed, and a new posting was made: First four—Major John Mitchell leading with Lt. Jack Jacobson as his wingman. I was designated his element leader with Lt. Delton Goerke as his wingman. Second Four—the "Killer Flight"—Capt. Tom Lanphier leading, with Lt. Rex Barber as his wingman. Lt. Jim McLanahan to be Tom's element leader, with Lt. Joe Moore as his wingman. I do not remember the flight positions of the 12th pilots, but they were Major Lou Kittel, Lts. Lawrence Graebner, Roger Ames, Everett Anglin, William Smith, Albert Long, Eldon Straton and Gordon Whittaker. The designated spares were Lt. Besby Holmes and his wingman, Lt. Ray Hines who was lost on the mission from causes unknown to this day.

"The final briefing was the morning of 18 April 1943, with take-off scheduled for 0700. We would fly at low altitude and out of sight of all islands. We were to maintain radio silence until the enemy was sighted. I still remember a marine colonel saying: "We were not to come back until the Admiral was dead.

"While taxiing, Jim McLanahan's tire was punctured by a piece of Marsten mat, so he had to abort. Joe Moore, after take-off, could not get his belly tanks to feed and he too had to abort. The two spares filled in on Lanphier's flight, and we were on our way. Flying at fifty feet with only ocean to watch, it was extremely hot with no cooling system, and the sun glazing the canopy, the cockpit was an oven. To pass the time, I counted sharks and eventually counted forty-eight on the way up. Then as we made our turn into Bougainville, the distant mountains came into view and I observed two Betty Bombers escorted by two vees of Zeros above and behind the bombers, with one threesome on its left and the other on its right. I immediately called out 'bogies ten o'clock high'. Mitchell directed Tom to proceed to the target and for all of us to drop our belly tanks and get ready. The twelve of us made our turn and started climbing towards Kahili. I saw a Zero ready to make a rear attack on us. I made a quick descending turn and *wound up on his tail. As I was about to shoot, my canopy fogged up and I could see nothing. I broke off my attack, climbed vigorously and endeavored to clean off the canopy with my handkerchief. When I could see out I was at 20,000 feet over Torokina Bay and by myself. There were no enemy planes or friendly P-38s in sight. I heard no messages over the radio nor had I seen any action below.*

"I decided to fly back to Guadalcanal. There were no enemy planes until I flew over Kahili, where I could see coral dust boiling up as Zeros were wildly taking off. Being badly outnumbered, I proceeded on, and finally caught up with Besby Holmes, who was low on fuel and whose engines were running so rough he could not read his tachometers. Now, my radio was working and he told me his problems. Knowing I could synchronize my propellers to his by sighting through my props, I told him what his tachometer should be reading.

"Finally, we approached the Russell Islands where a new runway was being built, Besby did not have enough fuel to reach Guadalcanal. He would try to land. I went ahead and buzzed the runway. The Seabees in their steamrollers thought I was just putting on a show so they waved back and did not budge off the runway. So I dove on the runway as though I was going to land. I pulled up into a tight "widow maker," a great show maneuver, put my gear down and proceeded as though I were going to land. The Seabees scrambled off the runway with all their equipment. In the meantime, Besby came in and barely was able to stop on this unfinished runway. I proceeded back to Fighter II, where I was the last one back from the mission."

The Sub-Plot

There is a simmering dispute over who actually fired the shells that pierced Yamamoto's body, fostered by secrecy and conflicting versions. Captain Tom Lanphier, the other P-38 pilot on the Killer Flight with Barber, boasted he got Yamamoto. Since reports of the mission were hushed up, there were no official documents to dispute his claim. Although Rex Barber was angered at Lanphier, he never took his case public. Lanphier, on the other hand, sought a political career using this exploit as its centerpiece. He peppered the media with his claims. With no contradiction, they were accepted.

George Chandler, himself a P-38 Ace of the 339th Fighter Squadron on Guadalcanal, resents Admiral Halsey's downgrading the Congressional Medal of Honor to Mitchell and Barber. Chandler's tenacious efforts with the Office of Air Force History, Air Force Board For Correction of Military Records, United States Courts, Victory

Confirmation Board of American Fighter Aces Association, Chief of Staff USAF and Secretary of the Air Force encountered bureaucratic torpor and intransigence. George Chandler described their efforts in *Report of the Second Yamamoto Mission Association*:

- When the P-38 pilots returned to Guadalcanal on 18 April 1943, there was immediate contention over who shot down Yamamoto. The P-38s did not have functioning gun cameras, because the film they received absorbed moisture and would not run through the cameras. So it was one pilot's version against another pilot.
- Immediately after the war, Lanphier publicly claimed that he alone shot down Yamamoto.
- An Air Force study awarded half credit to Barber and half to Lanphier.
- In 1985, Lanphier insisted the Office of Air Force History give him complete credit. Dr. Richard Kohn declined his appeal.
- SYMA (Second Yamamoto Mission Association) appealed to the Air Force Board for Corrections of Military Records. The board made a split recommendation, awarding half to each pilot.
- SYMA appealed this decision. SYMA discovered new and convincing evidence. A letter written in 1984 by Lanphier was discovered in the General Doolittle files in the History of Aviation Collection at the University of Texas at Dallas. Lanphier wrote: "The bomber I shot the wing off of was intact when I first shot at it far inland from where Barber had to be at the time chasing a bomber over the sea." (Note: When Yamamoto's plane entered the jungle, it did so in the attitude of a forced landing).
- SYMA brought this new evidence to the Victory Confirmation Board of the American Fighter Aces Association. The Board concluded that Lanphier did not attack the Yamamoto plane and gave Rex Barber one hundred percent credit. The American Fighter Aces Association sent this information to the Office of Air Force History, and to the Chief of Staff, suggesting the air force re-examine their position.
- 18 August 1997, General Eberhart said the Office of Air Force History was not willing to change its position.
- John Mitchell was sure Rex Barber alone downed Yamamoto. At the 1985 reunion of the 339th Fighter Squadron, Mitchell pointed to Barber and said: "There's the man who shot down

Yamamoto. I don't care what you read in pulp magazines, you're looking at the man that got him, period."

• In 1995, the SYMA questioned the navy about the award of the Medal of Honor for John Mitchell, which had been denied by Adm. Halsey. It was approved by the navy, but then disapproved by the State Department. John Mitchell died a few weeks after receiving word of the rejection.

Lanphier's self-aggrandizing story is itself evidentiary. This is his version as reported in *Attack on Yamamoto*, by C. V. Glines:

"*I pointed my nose down and squared away in a dive toward him. His frantic efforts to elude me assured me he carried what we had come long way to destroy. I set up a classical high side gunnery pass. I chose that method of attack rather than go directly at the tail, which contained a couple of deadly heavy caliber stingers. By this time the Japanese gunners on the bomber were all firing at me. I fired a short burst of fifties to get the proper direction and check the range. There was no need to be in a hurry. There was still sufficient time to shoot the bomber down in my own way. My next burst of fifties kicked up the water just short of the bomber.*

"*Next time, I said aloud, pulling my gunsight ahead of the Betty. Now! I touched the trigger. The fifties chattered and vibrated. Bullets tore into the Betty, showing that my range and deflection were perfect. I pressed the button to fire my 20mm cannon and listened to the dull POM-POM-POM of the shells. The only numbers up for liquidation that day were all Japanese. The bomber's right wing came off and it plunged into the jungle and exploded.*

"*Two onrushing Zeros swooped across the top of my canopy. Like a rattlesnake that threatens even after death, the bomber I had set afire was still lethal. There was another Betty that had to be polished off if I expected to get back to Guadalcanal. Flying in extremely close, I lined my gunsight on the bomber's right engine and touched the triggers. The bullets tore into the engine and wing root and I could see little tongues of flame leap out. But the Betty wouldn't go down!*

"*Suddenly my Lightning faltered. The right engine conked out and the airspeed started dropping. If I didn't get this Japanese pilot he would roll over, split-S out, come up under me, and knock me out of the sky. I continued firing. I saw a burst of flame from the Zero as he went out of control. I was still alive and had saved Barber's neck for the second time that day. I had also added another Zero to my list of kills, making my total for the day one bomber and three Zeros.*

"*I continued toward Guadalcanal, knowing that I hadn't a snowball's chance of making it. I flew with my eyes glued to those fuel gauges. One tank ran dry. I switched to another. Back and forth, I switched tanks until there wasn't a drop left. I dropped my landing gear and set the '38 down heavily and rammed the brakes hard. The airplane came to a skidding halt near the far end."*

The report of the mission by Japanese pilots said that both right and left wings were with the wreckage. This means that Lanphier did not attack the Yamamoto aircraft. Japanese airman Yanigaya attended a symposium at the Nimitz Museum. Speaking through an interpreter, this is his account:

"Our pilots were not briefed to expect interception from American fighters. It was to be a routine escort flight and the Zeros were to fly about 1,500 feet above and behind the two Bettys. Zero pilots were delayed in seeing the Americans attack because they were accustomed to looking skyward. They did not think the P-38s would be coming from below.

"Under attack, the lead bomber nosed down spurting smoke and flames. A tall column of black smoke began to rise lazily out of the jungle. Taking advantage of his superior speed, the enemy pilot closed in rapidly. I watched the P-38's nose seem to burst into twinkling flame, and suddenly the bomber shook from the impact of the enemy's machine gun bullets and cannon shells. The P-38 pilot was an excellent gunner, for his first fusilade of bullets crashed into the right side of the airplane, then into the left. We knew we were now completely helpless and waited for our end to come. The P-38 hung grimly to our tail, pouring in his deadly fire."

This report came from the second bomber, because no one from the first bomber survived. Admiral Ugaki's diary reported:

"As I boarded Plane No. 2, I sat in the commanding officer's seat, removed my sword and handed it to Staff Officer Muroi. The weather made a fine day for flying. Six fighters escorted us—three on each side and above our planes. The chief pilot handed me a note reading 'Scheduled arrival time 0745 hours.' My watch then read 0730. At this moment the No. 1 plane made a sudden dive. It was emitting black smoke and flames. That was my last parting with Admiral Yamamoto. All I could see was black smoke rising from the jungle. There was nothing more we could do."

One of the surviving Japanese who was interviewed made comments I found interesting:

"I went back to Japan in 1944. By then two thirds of our squadron were

gone. I flew Betty bomber, called 'one shot lighters' because they went up like a torch. When we received orders for the Yamamoto mission, for security reasons, they were given at night after the lights were turned off."

Doug Canning said *"I saw none of the action by the "Killer Flight" after we turned toward Kahili, and these comments are based on my knowledge of the persons involved:*

"In 1988, I was in a symposium at the Admiral Nimitz Museum in Fredericksburg, Texas. Seven of the surviving U.S. Yamamoto mission pilots were there, as well as Kenji Yanagiya, the sole surviving Zero pilot. I talked with Yanagiya through an interpreter, Henry Sakaida. Yanagiya had been in the "V" on the left of Admiral Yamamoto's Betty Bomber. He verified all the statements of Rex Barber as to Rex's shooting down Yamamoto's plane. He verified that he saw Rex shooting from the rear and the left. Japanese records show that bullets in his back and head killed Yamamoto. The angle at which they entered was exactly as described by Rex and Yanagiya. I asked him why he had not called on the radio to warn Yamamoto's pilot we were there, but they removed their radios to make the plane lighter so it could climb and turn better. Instead, he dove to catch up to Yamamoto's plane firing his guns ahead of the bomber in hope the pilot would see his tracers and be warned of the danger to the Admiral. I asked what was the Zero pilot's punishment for letting the Admiral be killed. He said that each of the six escorting pilots were to fly missions until they were killed. The only reason he survived was because in a fight with a US Navy F6F, he lost his right hand and could no longer fly. Ever since I heard Yanagiya's verification of Rex shooting down Yamamoto's plane, I believe Rex alone should be credited with the victory. As to the second bomber, when Rex began his attack, the second bomber dove toward the ocean where Besby Holmes attacked it. As it headed down, Rex came along and finished it off.

"Flying back to Guadalcanal I heard Lanphier get on the radio and say, 'That s.o.b. won't dictate peace terms in the White House.' This really upset me because we were to keep complete silence that we had gone after Admiral Yamamoto."

Besby Holmes, another member of the mission, told me:

"I was running short of fuel. I called Mitch and told him I didn't think I could make it. Mitch said we'll try and find you. Doug Canning found me and drew up alongside. I felt better because if I had to ditch he could pinpoint me. An island appeared. It was the Russells where the Marines were constructing an airfield. I told Doug I was going to land there no matter

what condition the field is in. Doug dragged the airstrip scattering everything and everybody in it. I made a very short landing with four gallons of fuel left."

Bill Harris, the great living Ace of the 13th Air Force, wrote me after reviewing a draft of this chapter: *"I like your perspective of the Yamamoto shoot-down and will make a few comments:*

"At the time of this mission, I was in the station hospital at Henderson Field with a bad case of ear infection due to bathing in the Lunga River. I sure learned the error of my ways. The doctor would tap on my head to get my attention. The afternoon of the mission, I borrowed one of the doctors' jeeps and drove over to Fighter 2 just in time to see Tom Lanphier land and get in a jeep. He drove up the strip waiving his arms and yelling 'I got Yamamoto, I got the son of a bitch' and just kept yelling the full length of the strip. I sat in on sessions with George Chandler, John Mitchell, Rex Barber and other members of the mission hashing things out. When all is said, the final word was that mission was a great success. What really happened has been written by John Mitchell and the Second Yamamoto Mission investigation. It is interesting to note that everybody in the Killer Flight left the flight for various reasons. Nobody was left but Rex all by himself, and he got the job done. If Rex hadn't gotten the job done, I wonder if there would have been some repercussions.

"I remember a meeting either in Australia or New Zealand shortly after the mission. Rex and John Mitchell were down there, and were playing golf with some brass. A newspaper reporter came over and asked them point blank about the Yamamoto mission. It was not supposed to have been known. They were blamed for the press finding out about the flight, and instead of getting a Congressional Medal they were sworn to silence and got a Navy Cross."

Bill Harris sent me a copy of a letter from General Doolittle to Lanphier:

27 December 1984

Dear Tom:

Thanks for your note and the copies of the two letters. The human mind is a very complicated thing. When one thinks over and over of a certain event, in which he participated, or even watched—particularly if the action was fast—inclines to change it an infinitesimal amount each time—always in his own favor. After long periods of time he may change it 180% and never realize he has done so. This is one reason why, in recalling an event after a long period, people who all saw it—for example an accident—may later remember it very differently. Maybe I mentioned this to you before. My memory is getting very flabby. Do want to send every good wish for the New Year to you and Phyllis.

Jimmy

The last chapter of this historic mission may have just been written. Rex Barber died in his sleep on July 26, 2001. His wife Margaret said: "It was a surprise to me. Although he was eighty-four, I expected him to live another ten years. He thought he was invincible, and frankly every pilot I ever knew thought he was invincible. Credit was not important to Rex. He was just doing his job. He seldom talked unless others brought it up. It bothered him as a matter of military honor and personal honor. He said he knew what happened."

Members of the Barber family are proud of his accomplishments as a husband, father and civilian. Rex retired from service in 1961 and returned to Oregon. He was a mayor and an insurance man who would take in stray kids, never miss a Little League game and devoted his last thirty years to his community and family. He was so much more than the Yamamoto mission. Rex Barber, Jr. said: "The reason those World War II veterans did what they did was so they could come home and be parents like Dad was."

REFERENCES

Glines, C.V., *Attack on Yamamoto*, Atglen, Pa., Schiffer History, 1993
Brown, Richard F., *Lightning Strikes Four Times*, Phoenix, Arizona, Bradley Printers, 1996

CHAPTER TWELVE

Snafu Snatchers

Attrition on Pacific missions was severe. With no ocean landmarks and no radio navigation aids, navigation was "dead reckoning" by compass, watch and air speed. It often meant just that. Missions were long. Weather was tumultuous. Planes damaged or out of fuel always went down in enemy territory beyond our front line. The Japanese beheaded our flyers. Experienced aircrews were priceless assets. Getting them back in combat saved two years training per replacement. Each rescue was one man closer to getting the damn war over and going home. Efforts to rescue these crews were taken at whatever risk. Those missions were non-negotiable. A crew in a dinghy is a dot in a vast ocean. Finding them required great skill in precision searches. That's what my squadron did. Officially designated "Second Emergency Rescue Squadron,"

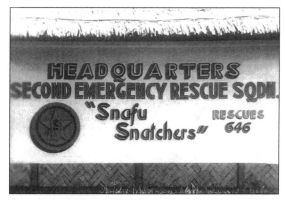

Snafu Headquarters

our twelve-plane outfit was called SNAFU SNATCHERS, because we landed on water and snatched "snafus" (situation normal all fouled up) from the enemy. We were a crack squadron, the first of its kind in the Pacific, flying PBY5As (the amphibious PBY Catalina Patrol bomber used by the army), but we also had a P-38, B-17, C-47, L-5 and B-25 for special missions.

From October 1944 to September 1945, our squadron's planes, code named "Daylight" and "Playmate," rescued around 1,000 flyers. The word "rescue" fails to describe the exciting conditions under which "snafus" were snatched while being fired upon by an angry enemy. Many rescuers were killed in action.

The success of these missions is a tribute to the sturdy steed which galloped to the rescue. The heart and soul of Pacific rescues was the indomitable Catalina bomber/flying boat. It came in two varieties: the pure flying boat (PBY) used by the navy, and the amphibious (PBY5A) used by the army. In the amphibious version, the wheels retracted into the hull for water operations and dropped down for terra firma. Operating on land and sea with a 2,500 mile range and twenty hours flying time made it unrivaled in the air. Slow but sure, it was a great sea bird soaring on long, lonely patrols, or becoming the "B" for bomber in its name. It flew some of the most dangerous missions of the war, swooping in and snatching downed airmen from the boiling sea or angry enemies.

A PBY in the air

If it's possible to be at once, both beautiful and ugly, the PBY fits that description. Its high parasol wing and graceful upswept fuselage resemble a bird in flight. Instantly recognized by its signature profile, it was loved by its crews and respected by every GI in the Pacific. Its broad mid-section housed bunks for carrying wounded. There were compartments for pilot, engineer, navigator, gunner and radio operator. It mounted a .50 caliber machine gun in each blister and a .30 caliber in the nose. Slow but sturdy, it was a plane of superlatives. It flew missions no other aircraft could perform. Often under fire, it snatched flyers bobbing in the water in missions a P-38 pilot said he was glad he didn't have to fly because they were too dangerous.

Military airplanes are mission specific, i.e., fighters, bombers, transport and training. They are not designed for cross-utilization. Not so the PBY. It did it all. It was said it couldn't bomb, but it did. Supposedly it couldn't strafe, but it did. The docile Cat could turn deadly hunter. Putting on a black nightgown, Black Cats prowled the night. It had nine lives, because it could find its way home on one engine, or chewed by bullets, or rivets popped from the buffeting ocean. It carried mail and supplies, transported wounded, fought enemy ships and subs, interfaced with the friendlies, and flew lonely patrols. They were sometimes called "Dumbo" from the friendly elephant in the Disney cartoon.

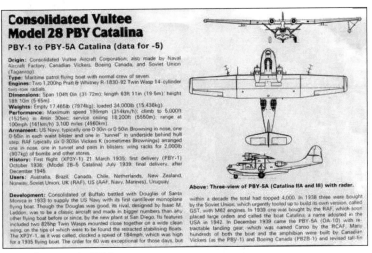

Consolidated Vultee Model 28 PBY Catalina

PBY-1 to PBY-5A Catalina (data for -5)

Origin: Consolidated Vultee Aircraft Corporation; also made by Naval Aircraft Factory, Canadian Vickers, Boeing Canada, and Soviet Union (Taganrog).
Type: Maritime patrol flying boat with normal crew of seven.
Engine: Two 1,200hp Pratt & Whitney R-1830-92 Twin Wasp 14-cylinder two-row radials.
Dimensions: Span 104ft 0in (31·72m); length 63ft 11in (19·5m); height 18ft 10in (5·65m).
Weights: Empty 17,465lb (7974kg), loaded 34,000lb (15,436kg).
Performance: Maximum speed 196mph (314km/h); climb to 5,000ft (1525m) in 4min 30sec; service ceiling 18,200ft (5550m); range at 100mph (161km/h) 3,100 miles (4960km).
Armament: US Navy, typically one 0·30in or 0·50in Browning in nose, one 0·50in in each waist blister and one in "tunnel" in underside behind hull step. RAF typically six 0·303in Vickers K (sometimes Brownings) arranged one in nose, one in tunnel and pairs in blisters; wing racks for 2,000lb (907kg) of bombs and other stores.
History: First flight (XP3Y-1) 21 March 1935; first delivery (PBY-1) October 1936; (Model 2B-5 Catalina) July 1939; final delivery, after December 1945.
Users: Australia, Brazil, Canada, Chile, Netherlands, New Zealand, Norway, Soviet Union, UK (RAF), US (AAF, Navy, Marines), Uruguay.

Development: Consolidated of Buffalo battled with Douglas of Santa Monica in 1933 to supply the US Navy with its first cantilever monoplane flying boat. Though the Douglas was good, its rival, designed by Isaac M. Laddon, was to be a classic aircraft and made in bigger numbers than any other flying boat before or since, by the new plant at San Diego. Its features included two 825hp Twin Wasps mounted close together on a wide clean wing, on the tips of which were to be found the retracted stabilising floats. The XP3Y-1, as it was called, clocked a speed of 184mph, which was high for a 1935 flying boat. The order for 60 was exceptional for those days, but within a decade the total had topped 4,000. In 1938 three were bought by the Soviet Union, which urgently tooled up to build its own version, called GST, with M62 engines. In 1939 one was bought by the RAF, which soon placed large orders and called the boat Catalina, a name adopted in the USA in 1942. In December 1939 came the PBY-5A (OA-10) with retractable landing gear, which was named Canso by the RCAF. Many hundreds of both the boat and the amphibian were built by Canadian Vickers (as the PBY-1) and Boeing Canada (PB2B-1) and revised tail-fin.

Above: Three-view of PBY-5A (Catalina IIA and III) with radar.

Data sheet on the PBY

The PBY name comes from its mission, Patrol Bomber. "Y" identifies its manufacturer as Consolidated Aircraft. Its name was "Catalina." When the war started, the PBY was seven years old and obsolete. However, the Catalina fought from the first day of the war. Many still fly today in such places as the Arctic and the Amazon. Two engines to carry a weight of 32,000 pounds made her cruising speed 90 knots, or 100 miles per hour. Crews described her performance as: "climb, glide, fly, land at 90 knots."

Awkward in design, redeeming qualities were range and rugged construction. She could take punishment. Her umbrella wing perched high above the fuselage and stubby nose. A large tail rose high above her body. The long fuselage, shaped like a boat hull, had floats on each wing tip that extended down for water operations. Slow speed and large size made her an easy target, and many were shot down, sometimes in gun battles as reported in *Black Cat Squadron*:

"The PBY opened the attack strafing the dock and some barges. They circled for a second pass, hitting the dock and a freighter with 500-pounders. The gasoline on the dock exploded and spread fire to four freighters and a warehouse. Not letting up, Schenck dropped six more 100-pounders into the inferno. Then he came back a fourth time and sank six barges with heavy machine gun fire."

By 1944 our planes and daring submarine commanders converted the Jap transport fleet to an endangered species. Supplying their bases over

B17 Flying Dutchman with lifeboat.

thousands of miles required a maritime taxi service. It was an endless string of "luggers" that looked like tug boats. They were identified as Sugar Dogs, Sugar Charlies and Sugar Bakers, depending on their length. How you determined length of a lugger during a mission was beyond me. We often picked "dog fights." Having no armor, our best tactic was surprise. The Dogs were armed with cannon and machine guns. Attacking them with our thin-skinned, hermaphrodite plane was a combo of macho and dumbo. The game was to sneak up on these dogs—pounce, punch and scoot. Surprise made the difference. Clausewitz called surprise "the prince of the battle-field." We were the "court jester."

Unless hits on planes were catastrophic, there was time to bail out. Aerodynamics of a falling plane feed on gravity and drag. Overcoming those forces requires strength and courage. Ditchings ordinarily resulted in deaths and injuries. Trying to make a monstrous metal box screaming along at 100 mph glide gently into rolling swells and stay out of Davy Jones' locker long enough to scramble out and launch life rafts, required skill and luck. Stories of pilots keeping those planes flying while their crews bailed out or ditched, are legion. They are also true. If they ditched, we intended to save them.

When the war mercifully ended, my squadron was on Clark Field in Luzon. I opted for a troop ship to return home. As a consequence, I was able to lug two footlockers home. They were stuffed with maps, photos, flying paraphernalia, souvenirs, battle flags, and the original squadron combat log. Memory fails to inform why I had it. Nobody ever showed up to claim it, so it remained in my footlocker for fifty odd years. All that memorabilia is now in the Hoover Institution. The log is eighty-one pages in original typing. Like everything else that old, it is incapable of repro-

SNAFU Snatchers in the flesh. Back row, left to right, are Pete Albano, Herman Schultz, Roy Caldwell, and Larry Roberts; Kneeling, left to right, are Buzz Grosvernor, Keith Parks and David Witts.

duction, so I had it retyped. Its stark realism of missions under stress, and under fire, commend it as history, real and raw. Here are some of the reports:

22 June 1945. Mission: Cover B-24 strike on Balikpapan, Borneo.
Lt. Arthur G. Carothers, pilot of Playmate 41, was returning from a mission to Borneo when he intercepted a distress message that a B-24 would crash land on the sea at approximately 00 35' N, 124° 35' E. Lt. Carothers set course and sighted six men of the B-24 crew on the beach. Lt. Carothers landed in a very rough sea, took the six men on board and attempted to take off at 1610. After a long and hazardous run, the ship bounded from a swell, held for a moment,

then crashed head on into an oncoming wave. The force of the impact ripped the pilot and navigator compartments wide open and catapulted the pilot, co-pilot and radio operator into the sea, still strapped in their seats. Eleven men escaped, but three were killed in the crash.

A downed crew on the beach

Fortunately, Lt. Bryan W. Guess, pilot of Playmate 42, was in the area and arrived just as Lt. Carothers was taxiing his ship inshore to pick up the six original survivors. While Lt. Guess circled Playmate 41, they watched the six survivors paddle out to the PBY, saw Playmate 41 make her last run, watched her as she finally struggled free from the grasp of the sea, falter in the air and fall back to destruction, carrying with her one member of the crew and two survivors from the B-24.

This B-24 with a crew of eight was returning from a mission over the Celebes when two engines cut out, forcing them to bail out or ditch. Four men elected to bail out. The pilot and co-pilot ditched the ship and escaped. The two remaining crew members were not seen after the four men bailed out. It is possible that they escaped from the ship and reached shore, but the sea is infested with Japs. If they did reach land, they may have been killed or taken prisoner, which are about the same.

Lt. Guess saw eleven men escape the stricken ship. Avoiding the experience of Lt. Carothers, he landed in a sheltered bay two miles distance and taxied to the eleven survivors, clinging to their life raft in the boiling sea. After all survivors were taken aboard, Lt. Guess taxied back to the sheltered waters of the bay and took off. Three members of the Playmate crew were severely injured in the crash and were given emergency medical treatment by the Flight Surgeon, Capt. Bailey, who escaped from the crash uninjured.

22 October 1944.

Lt. James F. Scott, pilot of Daylight 13, departed Middleburg to cover strikes on Ceram and to keep a sharp lookout for any survivors who may have gone down. At 1445, he received a call that an A-20 had gone down in Ambonia Bay. Lt. Scott proceeded to that area, finally sighting an oil slick and mirror flashes. Lt. Scott landed at 1600, taxied to the survivor and took him aboard. The survivor, Capt. E. L. Davidson, pilot of the A-20, ditched his plane following damage by enemy fire. His gunner went down with the ship. Fighter cover which flew overhead to protect the PBY departed at 1400 due to lack of fuel. At 1605, as takeoff was underway, several machine guns and splashes in the water around the rescue ship, drew their attention to a Jap fighter who was attacking them. With full throttle, Lt. Scott piloted his plane into a convenient cloud bank and escaped. One hour later, he broke out of the clouds beyond the reach of the Jap fighter, set course for his base and arrived at 1930 with an estimated ten minutes supply of fuel. Total time in the air was 12 hours and 15 minutes.

8 June 1945. Mission: special search for lost P-38 pilot. Lt. Earl Hutchings, pilot of Playmate 46, received a message from a Spitfire pilot stating he had sighted two dinghies. Lt. Hutchings sighted the two survivors, surrounded by native canoes. As he circled the rafts, the natives paddled ashore and disappeared into the jungle. Playmate landed and took aboard the survivors. The two pilots, Lt. D. L. Finch and Lt. J. W. Woliung, of the 41st Fighter Squadron, were returned to Zamboanga and transferred to the station hospital for treatment of severe sunburn and lacerations.

The survivors stated that while ferrying P-51s from Biak to Clark Field, they encountered a tropical front and became lost. Both pilots successfully ditched their planes side by side and escaped unhurt. They removed all their survival equipment, waded ashore and proceeded to a village. Their reception was cool, and, fearing the Japs had intimidated the local inhabitants, they withdrew from the village and selected an abandoned hut on the beach. They inflated their rafts and secured them at water's edge in readiness for a hurried flight. About midnight, Lt. Woliung heard footsteps approaching and yelled for them to halt. A flash of lightning at this moment disclosed their shack to be partially surrounded by Japs. The two pilots crawled through the opposite side of the hut, raced to the beach and untied their rafts. The Japs opened fire on the hut. The pilots paddled toward the sea, but the Japs heard them and directed their fire toward the sound. They were not hit and continued paddling all night. At daylight, they discovered numerous canoes putting out from the beach. Soon they were surrounded by natives who attempted to persuade them to return to the village. The pilots, warned of natives in these regions, declined and continued paddling.

About noon, they observed several boat loads of Jap soldiers putting out from shore. Their hopes of escape were fast dwindling when suddenly two Spitfires appeared. The Spitfires strafed the canoes, driving all of them ashore. In the meantime, Playmate 46 hurried to the position. They arrived just in time, as the Japs had again put out from shore and were rapidly approaching the life rafts. Lt. Hutchings landed near the survivors and took them aboard.

13 July 1944.
Lt. Stover, pilot of B-25 #469, stated that, with a skeleton crew and three passengers, he departed Hollandia 13 July for Morotai. Encountering heavy weather, he became lost and overshot his destination. He found himself over a group of islands and ditched his plane off shore near a native village. The ditching was successful. With the help of friendly natives, they were taken to the nearby village.

The natives informed them Japanese patrols frequented the island daily and for them to remain in one place was dangerous. They were taken into the jungle and concealed. The natives supplied them food and water. After nightfall, the survivors were transported by native canoe to an adjacent island. During the second night they were concealed in the chief's house, the chief standing guard while they slept. But a native informer notified the Japs of their presence, which necessitated their constant moving. They hid by day and traveled from one island to another by night, with the Japs ever in hot pursuit. They received a message written in a mixture of Malayan and English, stating the Japs knew of their whereabouts and were closing in for the kill. They immediately left the village and hid in the jungle. A rescue plane and a crash boat were dispatched. Since the Japs were closing, the survivors were preparing to make a dash for the open sea when the PBY arrived.

Sometimes we orbited, sometimes we went in. This report of 13th Fighter Command describes one such mission:

"With 20 Jap planes, Lt. Colonel Westbrook was the leading Ace of the 13th. While strafing a gunboat in the Celebes, Westbrook was shot down. Lt. Charles Strader, flying Westbrook's wing, made a second pass on the gunboat, and his plane was also hit. He was forced to ditch. For 24 hours he played hide and seek with a harbor full of Nips. A boat searching for him actually brushed against his life raft. But he had it deflated and covered by blue sailcloth. He went undetected. His rescue the next day by a Catalina Flying Boat of the 2nd Emergency Rescue Squadron was truly an outstand-

ing piece of work. The cat, which picked him up in the enemy's front yard, was in the air 20 hours flying more than 1,900 miles."
(This mission is described in detail by Lt. Strader in a later chapter)

An example of the rugged versatility of the plane is our squadron report on rescuing a downed B-25 crew off the coast of the oil center at Tarakan, Borneo.

8 April 1945. Mission: Rescue B-25 crew down in the bay near Tarakan. 1st Lt. Robert T. Davis, pilot of Playmate 37 departed Puerto Princessa at 0427, setting course for Tarakan. At 0800, about thirty miles from Tarakan, he was joined by his father escort of two P-38s. At 0817, a P-38 sighted a dinghy and led the Catalina to the survivors. At 0856 while crossing the southern tip of Tarakan at 1000 feet, all hell broke loose as the Japs opened up on the rescue ship. The first salvo struck Playmate 37, rocking it severely and throwing it temporarily out of control. A large hole was blown in the starboard wing, and a 40mm shell exploded in the blister. Lt. Davis carried out violent evasive action, diving to the deck and leveling off at 100 feet. Lt. Craig, the Navigator, conducted damage survey and informed Lt. Davis that the ship was still air and sea worthy, and that Sgt. August V. Roznovsky had been wounded in the face and Sgt. Fred B. Bernard sustained flak wounds of the chest and legs. Both men were wounded at their gun stations in the blister. Lt. Craig with the help of Sgt. Roznovsky dressed his wounds. By this time, Lt. Davis had landed and taxied up to the survivors who were assisted aboard by Lt. Craig and Sgt. Roznovsky. Lt. Davis cut the port motor as he drifted up to the dinghy bringing it under his port wing. While the last two survivors were being hauled aboard, he roared down the bay for a take-off.

The rescue required three minutes, during which time additional hits were scored by the Japs. Sgt. Roznovsky collapsed from loss of blood and was carried into the crew quarters where Lt. Craig dressed his wounds and administered morphine. The radio operator, Spl. Edward C. Baumgartner, remained at his station throughout the encounter, transmitting urgent signals "in the blind" to Palawan despite the fact Japs jammed all C/F frequencies.

Lt. Davis exhibited great skill and courage in landing his damaged craft under heavy enemy fire. While taking the survivors aboard, a 40mm shell passed through the blister, just missing Lt. Craig. Another 40mm shell damaged the tail assembly and the vertical stabilizer. In spite of the extensive damage, take-off was successful and the Catalina headed for Zamboanga, arriving at 1133. The wounded men and survivors were transferred to waiting ambulances and taken to the hospital where transfusions of whole blood were given to Sgt. Roznovsky.

All rescued were members of the 70th Bomb Squadron, 42nd Bomb Group. Lt. Berg, pilot of the B-25, stated that while at an altitude of 600 feet in a strafing run over Tarakan, 7 April 1045, his ship was damaged when a 40mm shell exploded in the right engine nacelle, setting it on fire. The fire enveloped the right wing in a sheet of flame. Damage to the hydraulic system prevented him from jettisoning his bombs or lowering his flaps. However, he descended in a long glide, landing safely on the water with the nose high. The turret was ripped from its moorings and crashed against the armor plate of the co-pilot's seat. All men in the forward compartment escaped through the top hatch, and those in the rear escaped through the left waist window. The tail gunner sustained scalp wounds and the radio operator sprained his ankle. The life raft was inflated and launched. The crew climbed aboard and paddled away from the ship which went down almost immediately. The remaining B-25s of the formation circled the survivors until 1320, spotted enemy gun positions and dropped their 250 pound demolition bombs on those guns.

The survivors, vigorously paddling their clumsy raft, set course for the western shore of the bay about five miles distance, where the jungle appeared to offer safety. Out in the bay, they encountered a twenty knot wind and a strong tide, which pushed them towards the Jap gun positions on Tarakan Island. By nightfall, they were but two miles away and drifting closer to disaster. Through the night, they rowed incessantly, and at daybreak, to their great dismay, were only a few hundred yards from the Jap positions. They could see Jap soldiers on shore and were sure they would be taken prisoners. However, as the surf rose, they concluded they were being left out there as bait for the rescue ship which they knew would be coming soon. Their hopes were raised when two B-25s appeared on the horizon at 0700 and covered them until the rescue ship arrived at 0853, accompanied by two P-38s.

The escape of the six survivors from the disabled and bomb loaded B-25 is an example of the value of training in ditching proce-

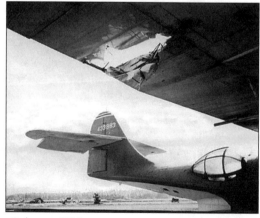

A shot-up PBY

dures for all aircraft crews. The rescued crew were most grateful to Lt. Davis and his gallant crew for their timely rescue from capture by the "Second Sons of Nippon." Damage sustained by the Catalina was: one large hole in the starboard wing; one broken wing strut and several ribs, broken elevator control capable; smashed blister; broken elevator trim tab; hole in starboard wing tank; jammed vertical stabilizer; and 110 other bullet and flak holes.

4 March 1945. Mission: To cover B-25 strike on Zamboanga.
1st Lt. Frank Rauschkolb, pilot of Playmate 42, departed Morotai at 0515, arriving at Melanipa Island, his orbit point at 0930. Immediately upon arrival at his destination, he received a radio message that three B-25s had been shot down off the target. The air was filled with distress calls and directions to the survivors. Lt. Rauschkolb headed for the target and sighted a crew down in the water about one mile off shore. As he was circling to land near the raft, Lt. Rauschkolb observed several Jap barges firing at him. He called for the B-25s to strafe the barges and keep them off until he could effect the rescue of the surviving crew. He landed and taxied to the raft through a hail of machine gun and mortar fire and took five crew aboard, the sixth having gone down with the ship. Except for minor bruises, none were injured. The B-25s kept the Jap barges off until the rescue was completed. The Catalina then taxied toward the second crew down on a reef, 500 yards off shore. As Lt. Rauschkolb approached the crew, shore batteries opened up on the rescue plane, but he continued on and took the six survivors aboard. During the taxiing, one engine cut out for fifteen minutes due to overheating. As soon as the survivors were aboard, Lt. Rauschkolb taxied through the coral reef to the open sea, out of gun range of the Japs. The sea proved to be too rough to take off, so Lt. Rauschkolb elected to taxi the fifteen miles to the other crew, which was down just off Melanipa Island near the southern tip of the Zamboanga Peninsula.

The rescue ship was guided to the third surviving crew by two B-25s. Water was leaking into the ship through flare tubes in the tunnel hatch, flooding the rear compartment. The crew members and survivors bailed vigorously to keep the water down. At 1130, the third crew was sighted and taken aboard. The ship proved to be overloaded, so Lt. Rauschkolb jettisoned 400 gallons of gas and began his take off run with twenty-five men aboard and a badly leaking hull. The ship was airborne at 1140 and headed for home. The two circling B-25s dipped their wings and likewise headed for him. The rescue plane arrived at Morotai at 1615, where the survivors were transferred to the 155th Station Hospital.

The survival of the seventeen out of eighteen crew members is a tribute to the training of the B-25 crews in ditching procedures. The crew member who was lost had left the ship and appeared to be unhurt. However, he suddenly disappeared beneath the waves. Presumably he was killed by enemy fire from shore as he floating in the water.

My squadron played a key role in a significant mission marked by both tragedy and rescue. It was a fighter sweep of P-38s against shipping in the Celebes port of Makassar. In November 1944, while most American units were occupied with the Philippines, Japan was developing great air and shipping strength in the Celebes area of the Dutch East Indies, threatening to flank MacArthur's return. The 347th Fighter Group headquarters staff along with the 67th, 68th and 339th Fighter Squadrons were ordered to de-fang this menace.

On November 22, 1944, a group of ten P-38s took off, led by Lt. Colonel "Westy" Westbrook, the leading Ace of the 13th, with twenty confirmed kills. Westbrook, like Bill Harris who succeeded him as the Ace of Aces, was an inspirational leader and a pilot's pilot. There were three planes in Westy's element, including Lt. Simon Snider and Lt. Charles Strader, both of the 339th Fighter Squadron—both survived the mission. Snider joined Westy in a high speed dive on a large ship. He described the events: "*We both were firing all our guns. I could see our fire was ripping the decks, but the target turned out to be a disguised flak trap (large flak boat). The most intense fire I ever saw was hitting us. Even so, Westy stayed on target and our combined fire silenced all the deck guns as we passed over the boat. Westy's right engine was burning, he feathered his prop and leveled out to pancake in. Suddenly his plane nosed down and smashed into the water. Other P-38s buzzed the crash site, but Westy never appeared.*"

The third pilot, Lt. Charles Strader, followed on and said "*there were guns all over the ship and they all focused on me. It was a blanket of fire. I lost both engines. I didn't bail out, because I knew I'd be shot in my chute. My speed was enough to carry me. I stretched the glide, but knew I'd hit hard. I jettisoned the canopy and hit so hard my head snapped so I thought my neck was broken. The plane began sinking. I tried to release my seat belt, but my shoulder harness snagged, pinning me to the seat. I grabbed my hunting knife from its leg holster and cut the straps. I was now deep under water when I popped out of the cockpit, but a strap on the life raft caught on the horizontal stabilizer, preventing me from getting to the surface. We had been trained to never inflate the Mae West when deep in the water because it might crush your chest. I was down so deep I couldn't see the surface, so, having nothing to lose, I yanked both carbon dioxide bottles and the vest inflated. My oxygen mask was still attached to my helmet, so I was breathing even though under water. I popped to the surface and passed out. When I came to, I was floating with my helmet and oxygen mask still on. I inflated my small life raft, took my shoes off and looked around. I was in the middle of a large Jap convoy and ships were burning in every direction. A four-stacker destroyer was headed directly at me.*

The original newspaper caption read, "Rescue plane is taxiing toward raft, with Nip-held island seen in background. Flight surgeon and enlisted medical personnel are ready to give first-aid."

I pulled the blue and yellow sail cloth over me with the blue side up and let air out of the raft until it was partially submerged. I sneaked a look, and could see the destroyer was going to hit me dead center. Suddenly I was pushed aside, and looking straight up I could see the Japs hanging over the rail looking for me, but they were looking out instead of down. Somehow I was not sucked into the prop as the ship raced ahead.

"I lay in the raft until late afternoon. Suddenly I realized I was surrounded by natives in boats. Two of them dived in the water and swam to my raft. I tried to hide under the cover, but one lifted the edge to look in. What he saw was my .45 pointed between his eyes. He dropped the cover and swam away. The boats disappeared. I fell asleep and was awakened by something bumping my raft. I could see large fins circling. After what seemed a very long time, they left and I fell asleep. When dawn broke I had drifted to a small island. I waded ashore, but heard voices. They were not English. I felt safer at sea and paddled into deep water, where currents carried me away from the island. There were still fires visible from burning ships. The afternoon of the second day I heard the most beautiful sound, a pair of P-38s out

looking for me. I focused my reflection mirror at the closest P-38. He dove down the mirror's flash like a beam toward me and waggled his wings. I knew a PBY was on its way. Before it arrived, the native boats returned. Fortunately, the PBY beat them, but the pilot couldn't cut his engines due to a dead battery. He cut one engine, lowered his landing gear in the water and circled me until he got close enough to drag me in. As soon as I was on board, they gave me a shot and I passed out. The next thing I remember was being released from the hospital."

CHAPTER THIRTEEN

The General and the Jungle

New Guinea is the second largest island in the world, 1500 miles across, blanketed with jungle and ribbed by impassable mountains reaching to 13,000 feet. It stretched across the waters north of Australia like a huge buzzard. New Guinea was the gateway to Australia on the south, to Indonesia on the west and the Philippines on the north. It anchored Japan's Southwest Pacific perimeter.

My crew joined the 13th Air Force at the replacement depot at Nadzab, or "Repple Depple" as the combat cotillions called it. The 13th bases I endured in New Guinea sprouted every condition—heat, stench, jungle rot, diarrhea, snakes, scorpions and snipers. The record for the biggest snake was held by New Guinea—thirteen and a half feet long! Occasional therapeutic relief came from "jungle juice," not a natural product of the jungle. We often received mail from classmates then in England and France. The one aspect of their living we did not envy was the only malady unknown in the jungle, venereal disease. Situationally we were spared ignominious "short arm inspection," a demeaning procedure whereby one's genitalia was inspected for defects.

I toured Milne Bay, Nadzab and Biak, idyllic New Guinea recreational areas where the vegetation was always freshly watered with 300 inches of annual rainfall. Huge areas on the map were simply blank spaces stamped "unexplored." The only "maps" we had were Australian and Dutch. They were neither precise nor accurate. It is not encouraging to have maps with the notation printed on them: "Please correct and report all inaccuracies discovered." Like an Italian traffic signal, they were a suggestion. Dense jungles blotted out the sun. Everything was wet. It was a white man's graveyard, gloomy, mysterious and portending death from nature's vengeance, or Japanese snipers. Malignant organisms prospered there. Rats marched across tents like a drill team. There was no fresh water. To bathe required going out in the rain and lathering up with a bar of lye soap. Fickle rain usually stopped after the celebrant achieved full lather. I learned the "New Guinea salute" which required two hands. One hand brushed flies, the other delivered food to mouth. Trucks vanished in mud. Torrential rainfall came daily for nine months, then the monsoons began.

That was then. Now I am bemused at the language in New Guinea travel brochures: "The remote highlands are a land of lush, fertile valleys draped between craggy limestone peaks and watered by countless streams and rivers. Watch the natives showcase their splendid ceremonial costumes, their faces painted with vivid yellow and red ochre." The pictures I have of the cannibals are less romantic. They have bones in their noses, enormous head gears of bird feathers and grotesque body guards. The description given by Mitchener as "god-forsaken back-wash of the world" resonates with my memory of wasps as long as your finger, spiders as big as your fist, hideous crabs scuttling across your feet and clouds of mosquitoes on your face.

After spear-heading MacArthur's drive up the southwest Pacific archipelagoes and dealing 135,000 Japanese out of the war, in 1943 units of the 13th Air Force began pulling out of their Guadalcanal and Munda bases, moving west to New Guinea. When the first crews from the 13th landed in Milne Bay, they happily spent a month on FAFSOA (Fifth Air Force Sitting On Ass Policy) otherwise called "ground alert." My squadron flew the New Guinea Campaign from Nadzab on the east to Sansapor on the west.

"American Caesar" was the name given General MacArthur by William Manchester in his remarkable biography. It was in New Guinea that I first served under MacArthur. Although I never set eyes on him, I hold him in esteem because I, along with thousands of other guys, owe our lives to his concern for his men. The New Guinea campaign was brilliant strategy, overcoming great odds, isolating the most enemy soldiers and sustaining the smallest losses in that bloody war. MacArthur's forces killed Japanese at the astounding ratio of twenty-two to one.

MacArthur and Patton were the greatest allied commanders of the war. Both studied Confederate Cavalry tactics at West Point, the essence of which was "hit 'em where they ain't." Patton used those tactics, employing mobility for end runs. MacArthur was forced into it because he lacked resources for frontal assault. His standing orders were "bounce off the Nips, go around the Nips, but keep moving. The paucity of resources at my command made me adopt this method as the only hope of accomplishing my task." MacArthur isolated a 200,000-man army trapped in New Guinea, a 100,000-man army in the Dutch East Indies, another 100,000 in the Solomons, Halmaheras and Admiralties. In Rabaul alone the 100,000 enemy troops isolated there were more Japanese than defended Iwo Jima.

Patton and MacArthur were prima donnas, anti-communist and consequently they were derided by the press. Irrelevant events were played up to denigrate their accomplishments. Patton slapped a soldier he suspected of faking an injury, an incident which dogged him. Although MacArthur was ordered to Australia by Roosevelt, he was derisively labeled "Dugout Doug." Solicitous of his soldiers' lives, the compelling statistic is that MacArthur's forces sustained fewer casualties in four years of war from Australia to Tokyo than Eisenhower sustained in the single Battle of the Bulge.

A Japanese general paid tribute to MacArthur: "This was the strategy we hated. The Americans, with minimum losses, seized a weak area, built an airfield and cut the lines to our strong points which were starved out. We respected this strategy because it gained the most while losing the least. Americans attack all day, fight all night and shoot all the time."

In July 1942, Japan landed 13,000 men on New Guinea's north coast at Buna, ready to cross the Owen Stanley Mountains and take Port Moresby facing Australia. A small, gutsy Australian ground force and U.S. Army flyers challenged the invaders in rain and mud along the Kokoda Trail. In what Samuel Eliot Morrison called "the nastiest fighting in the world," these allies stalled and then eviscerated the aggressor. The Japanese Army, its soldiers diseased and starving, were reduced to cannibalism, cutting "steaks" from the bodies of Aussie soldiers. Those who made it back to Buna were barefoot and wearing rice bags, their uniforms long since dissolved into rotten rags. The Imperial Japanese Army finally tasted defeat.

In that brutal New Guinea backwater U.S. Army troops began fighting desperate but little known battles. New Guinea showed America the sort of foe they were up against and the kind of country they would have to fight him in. MacArthur's first encounter occurred with his 42nd Division at Buna in January 1943. For six months, the two armies locked in stalemate. Two American divisions were chewed up. With no roads and no navy, army supplies were parachuted by the Army Air Force "Biscuit Bombers." Thwarted, MacArthur wrote that no commander in American history has been so poorly supported. He sent General Eichelberger in with instructions: "Bob, take Buna or don't come back alive." No prisoners were taken by either side. Japan called us "butchers." "The Japs resisted from behind rotting bodies forming fortifications. The living fired over bodies of the dead. Corpses were stacked on barricades like sandbags." At Buna, the Allies suffered 9,000 casualties, a bloodier battle than Guadalcanal. MacArthur vowed: No More Bunas. Never again did MacArthur splash his army in frontal assaults against massed fire power, as the marines did in every battle, tactics which MacArthur denounced as "tragic and unnecessary massacres of American lives." Marine casualties were forty percent at Tarawa, fifty-six percent at Pelelieu, seventy-six percent at Iwo Jima and eighty-one percent at Okinawa.

I detested New Guinea, as did every man who served there. It's understandable why much of New Guinea is unexplored and uninhabitable except for creepy, crawly things and stone age people. A soldier wrote: "*Did you ever try eating rice and sardines three times a day for three months? It makes me burn every time I read about people back home complaining about rationing and the hours they work. Twenty-four hours a day we're on the go and no days off. The Japanese attacked regularly at night, screaming in Banzai charges. It's no fun at 2:30 in the morning standing in a slit trench, especially if it's raining and it always is. Life in the jungle was atrocious. There were the scorpions whose sting sent you mad, lack of food, malaria, typhoid, snakes and topical disease. Fighting in the jungle was terrifying and merciless, neither side taking prisoners.*" It's a wonder family raised teenagers remained sane, fighting savages in that setting. Some didn't.

Even the enemy hated it. Ogawa Masatsugu told of his experiences in New Guinea, *The Island of Death*. "*Soldiers who struggled along before us littered the sides of the trail. Their bodies were swollen and rotted. What little they wore was taken from them. Boots were taken instantly, so the dead lay barefooted. The worms crawling over them gave them a silver sheen. The dead bodies became road markers. They beckoned to just follow us corpses and you'll get there. That was true until we came to the gorge with no bridge.*" The British said Japanese are "natural jungle fighters," when they bicycled down Malaya and spooked Singapore into surrender. They weren't "natural." Japan's wars had all been north of the equator. They had never seen a jungle, much less fought in one. What they had was a fanaticism and a disregard for their own life. I never knew of a Japanese rescue of their air crews. It's tough to win a war against people who want to die.

There are no front lines in the jungle. You never saw the enemy. Japanese strategy was simple—no survivors. Each soldier fights until he dies. Each Japanese must kill ten Americans. Relentlessly they fought over a tiny scrap of land, sometimes the size of a football field. Japanese snipers hung for days in trees for one shot. Sometimes, it was easier to carve a new strip out of the jungle than to wrest one from the hands of suicidal Japanese occupants. Every landing on a jungle strip was a thrill.

MacArthur had the advantage of Magic message intercepts. He learned Japanese plans and exploited their weakness. He selected the time and place of battle, jabbing and jumping, out-flanking and by-passing. Instead of attacking the big base at Wewak, he leaped behind and caught Hollandia looking the other direction. His tactics quickened the war, by seizing every advantage from breaking their code. He took one stronghold after another: Milne Bay, Wau, Salamau, Lae, Nadzab, Madang, Aitape, Hollandia, Biak—positions which Japan dug in to hold for years. Japan never suspected their codes were broken; instead they gave credit to our long range air patrols for spying.

The additional range wrung from planes thanks to Charles Lindbergh's tactics, enabled MacArthur to ambush Hollandia, taking it in one of the most successful, but least known battles of the war. This drive cut New Guinea in half and allowed MacArthur to advance to Biak and Sansapor in western New Guinea, which the 13th began using as advance bases. Now we were 300 miles from Halmahera, the Japanese base, protecting the Celebes Sea, and only 600 miles from the Philippines—the door to the Philippines was now open.

In July, our Long Rangers and Bomber Barons moved to Wakde Island, a hunk of coral off New Guinea. It had been stripped bare by shell fire. They were visited by a USO show featuring Bob Hope. When Bob stepped out on the stage, he said "I love this beautiful island, with its magnificent palm trees... two of them with tops."

In August, the 42nd Bomber Group, called the Crusaders, moved to hot, dusty Hollandia. In September, the Crusaders moved again to the Sansapor rain forest.

After Hollandia, this coastal ballet leaped to Biak, a terrible place honey-combed with caves, where Japan made the murderous discovery that instead of defending the beaches, they would hole up in caves, where rooting them out was bloody and personal. Then on to Noemfoor, at the western tip of New Guinea. The enemy air force was smashed and their troops cut off. Unable to retreat, they withered away. Thirteenth mediums and fighters supported MacArthur's September landing at Morotai by attacking bases in the Palaus on Ceram, Beroe, Kai and Halmahera.

That parade of invasions caused one officer to complain: "If my company makes one more invasion, the medics will need forty-two straight jackets because there are only forty-two of us left." The brutal New Guinea campaign ended in early 1944, by which time Pacific War had raged for two years. The Normandy invasion was still six months away.

MacArthur, without heavy guns, used the air force as his artillery and cavalry. A patch of jungle or coral reef would be seized, covered with Marston mats, steel links hooked together like giant erector sets, and a new air base was born. From there the war hop-scotched another 300 miles to the next enclave. He moved his planes forward in great leaps. When he encountered an entrenched enemy that outnumbered his resources, he told his air forces "you incapacitate them." (MacArthur's use of air power is replicated today across the formidable Afghan terrain where the army supports the air force, rather than vice versa.)

The New Guinea campaign ended with MacArthur's return to the Philippines. The enemy was bypassed, their supply lines cut off. Of 200,000 Japanese troops sent to New Guinea, only 10,000 survived, a mortality rate of ninety-five percent.

In September, MacArthur invaded Morotai in the Halmaheras and set up a bomber and a fighter strip. Within thirty days, Army Air Forces so pounded the enemy that no aircraft remained on Halmahera. From here missions radiated, attacking Celebes bases along the Makassar Straits and south to the rich islands of Ceram and Timor, surrounded by seas with romantic names like Sulu, Celebes and Java.

In the ongoing rhubarb between the army and navy, the navy wanted to approach Japan through Formosa. MacArthur emphasized our moral obligation to the Philippines. He told Roosevelt to his face: "the country would never forgive you if you left 70,000 Americans under a Japanese flag." Roosevelt later said that no one in his life ever talked to him the way MacArthur did. Roosevelt authorized the return to the Philippines over navy objections. October 20, 1944, when MacArthur waded ashore on Leyte, he was the last four-star general to command at the front. General Yamashita said he thought the picture of MacArthur's landing on Leyte had been mocked up, and had he known the General was actually at the front he would have launched a suicide raid on MacArthur to avenge the death of Admiral Yamamoto. The Japanese navy didn't tell the army about its catastrophic defeat in the Philippine Sea, and General Suzuki, commander of Leyte, planned to seize MacArthur and demand surrender of the entire U.S. Army.

June 15, 1944, 13th Air Force was transferred to the newly created Far East Air Forces under Lt. General Kenney along with Kenney's own 5th Air Force. This paper transfer did nothing to bring recognition to the 13th, since all air force communiques originated from General Kenney, now Commander of FEAF. From his lofty perch at 5th Air Force

Headquarters, Kenney could barely see the 13th, always at the front.

A first-hand example of this tactical use of air power was given me by Bill Harris, the 13th Air Force Ace. Bill took his squadron north to Lingayen in the Philippines while most of Luzon was still under Japanese control. During this operation, the remarkable painting "Moonlight Over Lingayen" was made. Bill presented me with a print. He said:

"You asked about the strip at Lingayen Gulf. It was located just north and slightly east of the town and right on the beach. Gen. MacArthur's men landed there and held a perimeter about three miles in from the beach. The Sea Bees came in and put down palm fronds on the sand and then laid steel matting. We arrived four days later and started dropping bombs and strafing in the traffic pattern. Really made long missions, some of them all of twenty minutes and then load up and go again.

"From the air you might remember a sugar factory right on the beach which was very visible, that had a building probably 150 feet high. The strip was about 100 feet east of it lined up north and south. One of the 5th P-51 pilots landed there a few days after we were in business, but when he took off he turned too soon and hit the building dead center, which didn't damage the building, but sure finished the P-51 and pilot off."

REFERENCE

Mayer, S.L., *MacArthur*, Ballantine, N.Y. 1971

CHAPTER FOURTEEN

Rabaul—The Ultimate Bypass

The Japanese defeat at Rabaul was a decisive event, but like shooting Yamamoto, it was obscured. Rabaul was Japan's Singapore, "an impregnable fortress," garrisoning 150,000 troops of Japan's army, fleet and air arms. Its enormous Simpson Harbor bristled with artillery. It was a sword over Australia. It shielded the Solomons and New Guinea to the south, reached north to the central Pacific, and blocked the road to Tokyo through the Philippines. The very name Rabaul still gives cold chills to the airmen who fought there.

Rabaul Harbor, 1942

Situated in MacArthur's Army zone, Rabaul was so formidable it required joint army and navy action. Halsey flew to Australia to confer with MacArthur and, although they had never met, Halsey reported that "after five minutes with MacArthur, it seemed like lifelong friends. I was impressed with his extensive knowledge."

During 1942 and 1943, Rabaul was attacked by navy, marine and army pilots who characterized Rabaul as "full of cruisers, big attack ships and hundreds of barges. The ack-ack was so thick you could walk on it and Zeros were all over the sky." The number of Japanese aircraft was overwhelming. Rabaul was struck time and again by the navy and the 5th Air Force. On November 2, General Kenney threw the 5th Air Force's best punch, losing seventeen planes. Kenney said, "it was the toughest fight the 5th Air Force had in the whole war." It remained for the 13th Air Force to finally knock those cavorting Zeros out of the sky.

The role of the 13th comes directly from Mauro J. Messina of the 13th Air Force Veterans Association. He says:

"The 13th successfully completed its first assignment by November 1943. Then from newly seized bases, like a Special Forces Team of today, the 13th was sent out of theater against the Japanese giant that MacArthur's larger 5th Air Force, based safely behind the lines, had been unable to destroy. The 13th's base on Guadalcanal was deep inside enemy territory, and 24-hours a day for months was subjected to unrelenting Jap attacks from the air, land and sea.

"To the 13th's angry airmen, Rabaul represented an opportunity to vent their fury. Rabaul now faced attacks of unexpected ferocity. Our cost was high against fleets of planes and walls of flak, but the brave, bold, angry airmen had learned how to survive and destroy. Their renown was great amongst the enemy, but unknown to their countrymen.

"By March 1944, the 13th and supporting aircraft destroyed Rabaul's immense air fleet of 800 planes, except for a final fifty-seven which escaped to Truk. The 13th so reduced enemy resistance, that Nimitz and MacArthur reached the China coast six months later. Such a great accomplishment achieved in three theaters during the worst of the war by a single air force should have brought honors and glory. Instead, libraries today have no information that a 13th Air Force ever existed."

The ferocity of Rabaul was reported from a 13th Air Force B-24 called "Blessed Event." Shells from Japanese fighters knocked out the controls and smashed the instruments. The pilot, co-pilot, bombardier and nose gunner were wounded, but "Blessed Event" pushed on despite further hits which killed the navigator and wounded the top turret gunner, who nevertheless continued to fire, shooting down three Japanese planes. "Blessed Event" headed home with one rudder missing and gasoline pouring from 120 bullet holes. Guided by its wounded pilot, the B-24 collided with a fighter while landing. It lost one of its wheels, but ground to a stop on its belly with one crewman dead, one dying and eight wounded.

George Chandler, the 13th Air Force Fighter Ace who has done so much to preserve our history, passed along his vignette on Rabaul: *"I was leading the P-38s escorting B-24s. We could see Rabaul for twenty minutes while we were inbound. The bombers were lined up. We could see dust from Zeros taking off, but we figured with the bombers at 15,000 feet and us at 20,000, they would drop their bombs, turn off the target, drop their nose, pick up speed, and we would all be out of there without a fight. It was not to be. The B-24s didn't get lined up right, so they turned and lined up for another run. Again, they didn't drop bombs. By this time the Zeros are level with us. Another 270 degree turn to line up for the bomb run, but the Zeros were diving on us. We fought our way through, and watched all the bombs miss the entire island and land in the ocean. It was fortunate we didn't have air-to-air communications with the bombers."*

A 13th Air Force pilot shot down over Rabaul who lived to tell about it was Lt. Ken McCloud. He had splashed two Zeros before his plane was riddled with bullets, forcing him to bail out. He spent nine days on the sea battling storms and sharks in his one man raft. He stayed alive catching rain water and luring birds to his raft, which he skinned and ate raw. He caught an albatross which he soaked in sea water and sun-dried it. Using his raft cover as a sail, he steered away from Rabaul and was picked up by a PBY nine days later.

Another adventure was that of Lt. Hart, found in his raft after seven days. He had consumed only half of his rations and water. His squadron buddies suggested he go back to sea until he used all his rations!

From the diary of Japanese pilot T. Iwamoto: *"Prior to 1943, we had hope and fought fiercely. Empty sleeping places are a stark reminder that even our skills were not enough. We are expendable. There is no hope of survival. They bombed fish from the air for food. After each bombing, thousands of dead fish floated in. Some men died eating poisonous varieties. It was either put it in the tunnels and have it rot, or put it out in the open and have it destroyed."*

On March 3, 1944, Rabaul was decimated in what the Japanese called "a hellish bombing." Only 120 of the 1400 buildings in Rabaul were left standing. Defending Rabaul cost Japan their best pilots, so weakening their navy air force, Japan never mounted another first-rate carrier attack.

The 8th Consolation Unit in Rabaul housed some 500 "working girls." An Australian coast watcher was told by natives of a brothel for field grade officers only. The exact location of the building was relayed to the Air Force. The strike came at night under a full moon when business was going full blast. No confirmation of the raid was received, but it certainly was a squadron morale booster.

By isolating rather than invading Rabaul, the sparing of American lives was boundless. Samuel Elliott Morrison reported: "Tarawa, Iwo Jima and Okinawa would have paled in comparison with the blood which would have flowed if the Allies attempted a landing on Rabaul." However, 125 American flyers were shot down over Rabaul, identified by the War Graves Commission as having been executed.

Even after the "hellish bombing" of March 1944, Rabaul still took a lot more killing. 13th Squadrons flew training missions over Rabaul as they sharpened their bombing and strafing skills. After the surrender, when the allies entered Rabaul they found 100,000 emaciated, starving troops. The 13th settled the score for Guadalcanal, bringing Bhagavad Gita to Rabaul: "I am become death, shatterer of worlds."

Today, Rabaul is trafficked by scuba divers. To those earlier visitors, the tourist brochures are knee-slapping funny: "The very air has the sensuous feel of a rich soft fabric. You sense that you are approaching Eden. It is like a romantic mirage."

REFERENCES

Gaskill, Wm., *Fighter Pilot In The South Pacific*, Manhattan, Kans., Sunflower Press, 1997

Sakaida, Henry, *The Siege Of Rabaul*, St. Paul, Minn., Phalanx, 1996

Harris, Brooklyn, Bill, *A Pilot's Story*, Klamath Falls, Ore., Graphic Press, 1995

CHAPTER FIFTEEN

A Tale of Two Targets— Balikpapan and Ploesti

Two decisive missions of World War II were flown against great oil centers—Ploesti in Europe and Balikpapan in the Pacific. Ploesti was the principal source of oil for Germany, as was Balikpapan for Japan. The rationale for both targets was identical—destroy the hearts that pumped life into the host war machines. Both bombing attacks were flown by the same type aircraft—long range B-24s. Both were at maximum range. Both flew over land and water. Both were first strikes. Both installations brutally punished the attacking planes. The differences, too, were dramatic. Ploesti was never put out of business. The strike on Ploesti, one of the war's most publicized missions, was also one of the most catastrophic.

Ploesti played out in a series of disastrous blunders. The lead navigation plane crashed. Another plane took the lead. It got lost and flew over German headquarters at Bucharest, alerting both the Luftwaffe and miles of flak guns. One flight missed the target on the first run, then flew back over it, only to meet another flight head on over the target. One flight missed the target entirely. Some planes jettisoned their bombs and crash landed. Of 178 planes on the mission, only thirty-three were flyable the next day. Sixty planes and their ten man crews were lost. Those losses were among the highest of any mission during the war. News correspondents extensively reported their stories and *Time Magazine* ran a feature story. Six Congressional Medals of Honor were awarded the flawed Ploesti mission. None was awarded the successful mission to Balikpapan. Several books have been written about the Ploesti mission; none about Balikpapan.

Balikpapan is a cameo of the Pacific war, fought in Europe's shadow. The Balikpapan mission succeeded according to plan. Flying all night in the dark over 1,000 miles, each navigator reached his destination on time. Every plane bombed on schedule. Balikpapan, on Borneo, the world's third largest island, fueled Japan's war effort. It took three years of fighting for our planes to get within range. It then required the longest bombing missions ever flown to reach it. Balikpapan was smashed by Army Air Forces and put out of the war.

Discovery of oil in Indonesia, comprising 6,000 islands, led to the formation of Royal Dutch Shell. Indonesian oil became Japan's instant objective once Roosevelt embargoed oil from America. Balikpapan was the major oil refining facility in the South Pacific. Its oil was of such high quality it was pumped directly into boilers as fuel. Balikpapan oil had to be denied Japan. The 13th Air Force was first to slash Balikpapan with unescorted B-24s in the longest bombing missions flown. In follow-up raids, the 13th was joined by the 5th Air Force, and later by long-range P-38 fighter protection. The Army Air Forces not only knocked out Balikpapan, they then destroyed Borneo's two other oil facilities at Brunei Bay and Tarakan for good measure.

When the 13th Air Force finally got long range bombers in 1944, Balikpapan came in range. The 13th had flown long range bomber missions of 1800 miles without fighter escort against Truk and Palau, but Balikpapan was a 2,500 mile round trip. Flying this distance against Japan's heaviest defended installations without fighter escort prompted Colonel Thomas Musgrave, Commanding Officer of the Bomber Barons to confess, "Frankly we were scared to death." This mission meant carrying 20,000 pounds above the maximum capacity of B-24s. A fly-by-line plan was designed so as gas was consumed, crew members and heavy objects were shifted to adjust weight and conserve gas.

September 29, 1944, shortly after midnight, the 13th's Bomber Barons and Long Rangers began taking off every sixty seconds, climbing through darkness. Each plane was timed by stopwatch and was flashed a starting signal by green light from an aldus lamp. The first forty-eight Liberators rolled down the runway with perfect timing and were airborne in forty-eight minutes. For sixteen hours the entire 13th waited and sweated. After eight hours, a radio message reported the planes hit the target and were fighting their way back through heavy fighter interception. Balikpapan was left in flames, but planes and crews suffered terribly.

Captains Elliott Arnold and Donald Haugh described the mission :

"We had to make a round trip of 2,500 miles, much further than the Ploesti raid on refineries in Romania. Seventy-two airplanes flew against the most heavily guarded target in the South Pacific. We crossed New Guinea, Ceram, Moluccas, Celebes and the Makassar Straits. Planes would be in the air sixteen hours without fighter protection. The minute we took off, we were behind enemy lines.

"Balikpapan, the largest refinery in Indonesia, was heavily defended by *deadly anti-aircraft. The B-24 was designed to carry 48,000 pounds. This mission required a 70,000 pound load, eleven tons over weight. Crash trucks lined the strip because if a plane cracked up it was to be shoved off the strip immediately. Planes in trouble after take off had to stay in the air until the last plane got away before they could return. If Japs strafed the strip during take off, they were to be ignored and take off was to proceed. If a mechanical developed so serious a plane could not stay aloft until all planes cleared the strip, orders were to fly over water, bail out and let the ship crash."*

"Take off was at midnight to arrive over target at 0800 . The route was over mountains and ocean. Planes flew individually all night and rendezvoused over the Celebes at daybreak, a thousand miles from takeoff and 220 miles from target. Each navigator had to navigate a thousand miles at night by celestial navigation and reach a given point within a twenty minute window.

"The first twenty-four planes were airborne in exactly twenty-four minutes. At dawn they crossed the Celebes on schedule. The navigators had flown a thousand miles in the dark, yet reached their pinpoint within minutes of each other. Suddenly two Jap twin-engine planes began paralleling just out of our gun range. They were radioing our course, speed and altitude to the Jap anti-aircraft at Balikpapan.

"The checkpoint thirty miles from the target was clouded over. Jap fighters came up in droves. They flew into and through the formation, every gun shooting. They were ordered to stop the raid at all costs. The bombers plodded on. Cannon and anti-aircraft flak were everywhere, yet Jap fighters kept attacking through it. The air was filled with phosphorous bombs. Only when the bombardier could see were the bombs to be released. Musgrave had to swing the formation in at another angle to see the target, giving the fighters and flak more time. The bombing was precise. Almost half the Balikpapan refinery was destroyed. Our losses were heavy.

"As the planes turned home, Jap fighters attacked for one solid hour. Two more bombers were shot down and many others damaged so badly they had to ditch. The planes were over the target more than an hour. Time over target normally is in minutes. The lead ship was hit and nose-dived into Balikpapan. Lt. Oliver Adair took over the lead ship's position. Then Adair's ship was hit. His waist gunner, Sgt. Charles Held had his machine gun shot out of his hands. He grabbed the loose gun and started firing, holding the hot barrel in his hand. One crewman pleaded 'Oh my God, let me get out of here'. On the way home they chopped out the turrets to lighten the load. They worked three hours with axes on the ball turret, but it wouldn't cut. A crew member pulled his pistol and shot off the rivets. When the ship *landed on Morotai the brakes locked and the ship plowed through trees. One stump flew into the plane and hit Sgt. Held in the leg. The nose wheel buckled and flew back into the plane, crushing Sgt. Held's other leg. When the other planes came in the first five planes were still in perfect formation, even though riddled with holes, parts of the tails and turrets gone. Capt. William Stewart, Operations Officer, burst into tears when he recognized his own ships."*

The mission was repeated a few days later, again without fighter escort. Opposition over Balikpapan was even more intense and our losses were so heavy, they were equivalent to losing an air force a month. On the third and fourth strikes, 13th Air Force P-38s escorted the bombers. The fighters shot down nineteen Japanese planes. One Zero rammed a B-24.

This poem was written by a B-24 gunner:

> *Oh, Hedy Lamarr is a beautiful gal.*
> *And Madeline Carroll is, too;*
> *But you'll find if you query, a different theory.*
> *Amongst any bomber crew.*
> *For the loveliest thing of which one could sing.*
> *This side of the Heavenly Gates*
> *Is no blonde or brunette of the Hollywood set,*
> *But an escort of P-38s.*

Letters from Balikpapan. Theron W. Borup was a gunner on a 13th Air Force B-24 shot down over Balikpapan. His family made available some personal correspondence, providing a first-hand insight into the spirituality of those times. February 14, 1943—from a letter Theron's wife handed him as he went overseas:

"My Dearest: If I had the emotional strength to talk to you and tell what is in my heart, I should like to tell you how much sunshine you have brought into my life. I should like to tell you how much your love has meant to me and how much your ideals have brought the best in me to the surface… Always remember this—that wherever you are I will be with you every minute until you return to me. Gladys"

November 1944, Theron wrote his family:

"At the age of eight when I was baptized, I was much impressed about being good… I tried to so live that I would not lose this gift. Once it saved my life. The longest bombing flight ever made would be our attempt to knock

out the huge Japanese oil refinery located in Balikpapan. We had to be on the flight line at 11:30 p.m. At 11:00 p.m. our breakfast was served but so many fellows had heard about it they ate the food before we got there. At the side of the plane under a coconut tree I offered a prayer. I had the feeling that I would be shot down but would not lose my life."

"The combat was furious. Our plane burst into flames and the pilot told us to jump. Japanese planes shot at us as we were floating down. Soon I was in the water struggling to inflate my life jacket. I was exhausted. Six of us got together, the others were shot while parachuting. The crew elected me to be the captain to keep the matches so no one could smoke as it dries out the throat. I kept the canteen of water. For three days we floated in enemy territory. One night a storm came up and waves were very high and our five little rafts were nearly torn apart. The officer asked me "Do you pray, will we be saved"? I replied that I pray regularly, and assured him we would be saved. The fourth morning the wind calmed. Three days had gone by without food or water. We saw a submarine, but they passed by. The next morning it passed us by again, we knew this would be the last day. Then came the prompting of the Holy Spirit. I prayed in the name of Jesus Christ. In a few minutes they were along side of us. How glad I was that somewhere in my growing years, my parents and church teachers inspired me to so live that I might have the gifts and protection of the Holy Ghost, and to know God and His Son Jesus Christ live."

March 1945, a fellow squadron member wrote Theron from a hospital:

"Hello thar Theron old boy: I just received your letter of Feb. 27, 1945, and was sorto glad to hear from you. They were sending some B-25s back to the states and needed crews, so we volunteered and got on a crew. We flew back by way of New Caledonia, Fiji, Canton, Xmas, and Hawaii. Back home, they never heard of the 13th. The guys think I'm giving a snow job when I tell them about our little experience. We were getting bombed every night at Morotai. The first Sgt. got hit. A Zeke came in low strafing. Do you remember Red Broker? He was killed in a crack up down on Homefoor. Cunningham and Elliott was knocked off. Yep, boy those bastard Japs gave us plenty trouble in old Morotai. We had 6 raids Xmas eve. Capt Elder got the Silver Star for that mission, we were put in for the DFC, but that was canceled when they found out we were picked up. I got the purple heart. Anyone who flew the first two missions on Balikpapan got the DFC. Your account of the Fifth Air Force is plenty accurate, hell Borup, you seen them drop their bombs in the water."

January 12, 1945, Theron received a letter from a friend:

"I pray God will heal and bind up your wounds. Our hearts seem to be

weighted down with sorrow but so many others are also. We were fighting so our children could live in peace."

March 1945, a letter to Theron from other parents who also lost a son over Balikpapan: *"We have been trying to find details of that flight. The War Department has not given us much information. We received a letter written last November stating they were sending home his personal belongings, but they have not arrived. Don't you think it would be possible for him to keep afloat, even tho wounded, and perhaps be picked up by a ship? His mother died about 6 years ago, and we are thankful she is spared this great sorrow. His younger brother is now in the navy. He has been to Africa, Italy and Sicily. His older brother is in England. He has a married sister, whose husband is now in the Philippines. I notice your return address is care of Baxter Gen'l Hospital. We sincerely hope you are not injured seriously and will be out again in a very short time."*

March 12, 1945, brought Theron a letter from the parents of a son lost at Balikpapan: *"I guess we must concede that Roy has gone to his much earned reward. I am indeed glad to know he was not captured by the Japs. He will have no more awful missions to make. He is safe and happy, I know. We live in deeds, not years, in thoughts, not breaths, in feelings, not in fingers on a dial. We should count time by heart throbs."*

The 13th medium bomb groups later joined the heavies in pulverizing Balikpapan preparatory to the Aussie invasion which recaptured the oil field. For this the 42nd Bomb Group received a Presidential Unit Citation for action in June 1945:

"Operating in support of the Australian invasion, made the longest range missions flown by medium bombers 1700 miles over open sea... Taking off from a damaged runway and encountering tropical weather fronts, the planes fought through intense anti-aircraft fire. From minimum altitude, the group dropped 460,000 pounds of napalm and demolition and expended 415,000 rounds of ammunition in strafing. They destroyed gun positions, roads, vehicles, 73 military buildings and huge stores of gasoline the enemy had placed to be ignited and released on Australians when they hit the beaches. They also protected the underwater naval demolition teams as they smashed the off-shore barricades."

CHAPTER SIXTEEN

Home Sweet Home— Mud, Mosquitoes and Malaria on Morotai

After bopping across the length of New Guinea, we nested for a spell on Morotai, a wretched island in the Halmaheras group, midway between New Guinea and the Philippines. Euphemistically called "The Spice Islands" by the Dutch traders who brought their tropical spices to Europe. The 13th Air Force gave it a more realistic description, as the place where, if the Lord ever gave the earth an enema, Morotai would be the point of insertion.

Lying in torrid latitudes near the Equator, Morotai was a stepping stone to the Philippines on the north and to the profitable Indonesian targets of Celebes, Borneo, Java and Sumatra to the west. It was an outpost to be captured, occupied and abandoned once its utility atrophied. It was popularized as 'the most bombed island in the Pacific'. Japan had thirty airfields within flying range. Tokyo Rose derided it as: "the graveyard of the 13th Air Force." Nestled up against the large island of Halmahera, Morotai was a tourist jaunt for 40,000 Japanese troops on Halmahera. They particularly favored night time tours. Japanese could not pronounce words with double "L," so we used passwords such as "lollapalooza" and "lollipop." Since only an airstrip was needed, MacArthur took this small island, dwarfed by a larger island, lurking with enemies. They were still there after the war ended.

On a lonely island that USO shows seemed unable to locate, any companionship was welcome. An antidote for jungle fever was to have a pet. Mine was Chico, a lively chattering monkey. Chico liked me, I liked Chico. We were flying buddies since Chico liked to fly. Amazing how personable those little apes were. Chico and my co-pilot developed instant dislike. It ripened into a feud. Buzz would curse Chico and throw things at him. Chico responded with a chatter of monkey expletives. He'd roll back his lips and spout invectives. Although translation was lacking, intent was clear. Chico played tricks. He would snatch Buzz's socks and deposit them in the top of a coconut tree. Sometimes he'd lay in wait for Buzz to leave his toothpaste tube unprotected, and then dart in, bite holes in the tube and scamper off, making sounds I know were scornful simian laughter.

Author David Witts with "Chico"

Words fail to describe jungle war. It's a claustrophobic tangle, without front lines where death awaits every step.   Mind and body degrade. Gloomy and full of death, it crawls with giant ants, scorpions, leeches and snakes. Shoes rot, sores erupt and insects swarm. Nature is at its strongest, men at their weakest. The jungle inflicted more casualties than combat. Daily doses of the yellow Atabrine tablet so colored the face that length of time overseas could be gauged by skin color. The longer there, the more lemon colored. It was rumored that Atabrine pills made you impotent. That never worried me, because being potent hadn't done me much good. Everything reeked with the inexpungeable jungle odor. Disaffection for such places is that nobody ever goes back. Servicemen visit European battlefields in droves, but whoever revisited New Guinea or Morotai?

Home Sweet Home

With no place to go and no way to get there, the army air forces were divorced from R&R, except for flight crews who were functionally mobile. Air bases were isolated without roads to any place. Camp movies and Tokyo Rose provided interludes. Tokyo Rose was popular because she broadcast music appealing to lonesome listeners. She played Glenn Miller and Tommy Dorsey, rudely interrupted with an occasional dramatic outburst, "We know where you are and tomorrow you die!" I never saw a USO show or a Red Cross girl until we moved up to Clark Field and got into Manila. Movies were the magic carpet that for an hour or so whisked you out of the jungle. Scratchy, they were a link to home. The "theater" consisted of logs or ammo boxes perched in the mud. Fancy names such as "Jungle Bowl" or "Coral Cabana" suggested the primitive accoutrements. The 'screen' was a back-drop of undetermined nature. Air conditioning was never a problem, although rain was. Ponchos would deflect the rain, with trade-off being hot and sticky. Scenes that produced most laughter were Hollywood actors making like soldiers. Alan Ladd confessing to Veronica Lake "I'm a GI

Jungle Bowl

myself," or John Garfield jerking a .50 caliber from his crashed plane and hip-shooting the jungle, brought real hoots and hollers.

Mail call was a pleasant interlude, but a sometimes-thing. Eager faces greeted and prehensile fingers grabbed the only jewel in the jungle—that letter from home. It was the moment that relieved reality. An occasional

dark cloud hung over the soldier whose name was not called or, worse, when he received a "Dear John" letter. Letters were read and re-read, fondled and slept with. Writing letters home was done on a small sheet of paper called v-mail. The pages were photographed and the film flown to the states where it was developed and delivered. An APO number (Army Post Office) was the local address, since locations were not identified. Officers were supposed to censor out-going mail, a job nobody liked. Since captured airmen were tortured for information, flyers were restricted to need to know, but I can't think of any crucial information I ever had.

Jungles mid-wifed inventions. Air crews were wonderfully creative. One outfit got cold beer by filling a drop tank, hauling it to 30,000 feet in a P-38, freezing it, and diving back to happy warriors. Showers were Rube Goldberg contraptions, mostly pipe with holes punched for refreshing salt water. The South Pacific lacked harbors and docks. One officer recalled:

"We unloaded 20,000 gallons a day from a barge, swam it ashore, loaded it into trucks and then handed it into planes. There were no lights, and for pre-dawn take-offs ground crews set out bottles of oil with strips of paper for wicks. Invariably the prop-wash extinguished the bottle flares and the next plane had to wait until the lamps were relit before taking off. Operations clerks placed a jeep at the end of the runway so the headlights would guide the pilots."

The book *Morotai—a Memoir of War*, written by fighter pilot John Boeman, describes lodging for new air crews:

"Each crew is responsible for their own tent. I noticed some tents that had wood floors. We asked how to get one of those and were told acquiring what you need is up to you. Get cots, too. It rains here every afternoon. By mid-afternoon, through scavenging, we had lumber. We propped up the center pole and put up our cots, just as the rain began to fall in torrents."

My establishing residence in Morotai was less adventuresome since we inherited a tent from a predecessor in title. Cots in the mud cried out for upgrade. Boxes laid down as wood floors were luxury items. Everything left on the ground mildewed. Shoes, when taken off, were hung off the cot. The wardrobe closet was a barracks bag suspended from a tent pole, otherwise it became a rat habitat. Anything needed was always at the bottom of the bag.

Sack-time was sought by bodies in torpor. Sacks were variously a poncho on the ground, an air mattress or a cot. "Super Sacks" were wood frames with inner tube rubber strips nailed across the top. On top of the rubber strips was laid an air mattress. That combination equaled Five-Star lodging.

No one ever saw an indoor toilet. Sanitation was a slit trench. Metal plates over the trenches provided tranquility during rainstorms. A helmet held between the knees filled with salt water was the wash basin.

The chow line consisted of fifty-gallon fuel drums sliced vertically and mounted over open fires:

"Each man held open his mess kit on which cooks slapped down slabs of spam, dehydrated potatoes and canned corn. At the end of the line was a lister bag of chlorinated water. After finishing our meal, we scraped leavings into a garbage can, washed our mess kits in boiling soapy water, and carried them by their long handles back to our tents."

Dining tables were steel planking or boards laid across poles. Meal service was usually in the rain, so food items became indistinguishable in the mess kit. The commentary between food purveyors and consumers was an ongoing source of vitriol. During a tropical downpour at Morotai, I remember one guy, contemplating what had been plopped in his mess kit, testily inquiring of the mess sergeant

Wash basin

"you s-o-b, what is this swill?" Never looking up, the chef growled back "it's bat shit, you s-o-b." The curious diner grumbled: "Oh, I thought for a minute it was something I couldn't eat."

Food was so bad it didn't matter whether it was hot or cold. "Hydraulic" eggs came out green. Butter was "axle grease," canned and guaranteed not to melt at 100-degree temperature. It didn't. Cooks reduced dehydrated potatoes to rocks. Spam, not today's acceptable progeny, was animal fat and animal skin. "C" rations and "Jungle" rations in tin cans, were sometimes preferred to the luck of the chow line. Australian "bully beef" was to be avoided at all times. It was a substance not readily identifiable but appeared to be intestines, skin and suet galvanized and distinguished by an odor encountered in stockyards. Chocolate that found its way to the tropics had some ingredient that kept it from melting in the heat. Of course, it wouldn't melt in your mouth either.

Grocery delivery is explained by this analysis: *"We got a load of frozen sheep meat from Australia. The navy picked up the meat and they took the chops. At New Caledonia they took the hind legs. At Esperitu Santu they took the forelegs. Guadalcanal got the rest of the carcass, except for the liver. At Munda we got the sheep liver. By the time it reached us, it was green."*

Bread was full of weevils. Our flight surgeon told us not to worry about weevils, because cooking killed germs and provided protein. His advice: "Just pretend you are eating raisin bread."

Without refrigeration, there was never any fresh food. On rest leave in Australia, when I laid hands on an orange, my first fresh food in months, I wolfed it down, skin and all.

Our supply officer was a sleepy Alabaman named Harves. A great guy, he had trouble keeping records. Government red tape never takes a holiday. Once I saw smoke pouring from Harves' tent and asked what is that all about? I was told, "Oh, that's just Harves adjusting his records."

A rain-repellent foxhole

Foxholes were a life support system. Sometimes you inherited one, sometimes you dug one. Soil conditions were always horrible—mud in New Guinea, coral at Morotai. Aviation cadets didn't study foxhole construction. As a flying officer, I considered myself above digging foxholes, grumbling "these are wings on my collar, not shovels." Occupational reticence vanished at the first air raid. We learned to dig deep and cover the top with logs, garnished with sandbags. A sheet of tin provided a rain repellent roof. Three shots signaled incoming bandits. Flying suits were zipped up while running. The tent record was thirty seconds from warning to foxhole. A bomb string walking in your direction turns one's thoughts from wings to shovels.

Mosquitoes were so huge they sparked fables. A fuel truck pumped fifty gallons of gas into a big mosquito before realizing it was not a P-38. Once two mosquitoes were lifting the net off a burly sergeant. They argued whether to eat him there or haul him away. It was decided to eat him there, because if they took him back, the big 'uns would get him.

The rats of Morotai were so big they could stand on their hind legs and play volleyball. The Varmint Distinction Award went to Sergeant Godsmark of the 44th Fighter Squadron who reported:

"…crabs in the jungle lived in holes under your bunk. They were constantly digging new holes and would drag anything into the holes. I remember seeing socks disappear before my eyes. One fellow's wristwatch disappeared down one. He tried to dig his way through coral to the watch, but gave up. Seeking revenge, he poured 100-octane gas down the hole and tossed in a match. Flames shot out of about 20 holes in the vicinity, followed by a few jet propelled crabs, but they weren't wearing watches. The crabs had the last laugh, as the odor of decayed crabs poisoned the air in his tent."

Bill Harris, the 13th Air Force Ace, is a genuine hero and a source of recollections. He passed on to me his crab report:

"During the time we were flying off of Munda was the annual migration of land crabs back into the hills. There were millions of them and they covered the strip and the living area. They were continually moving from the beach to the hills. When the airplanes landed, it mashed them on the strip and sprayed the mess up in the wheel wells and all over. The strip got so slick brakes were almost useless. The smell was terrible. The crabs would come right through the tents, the cots would have to be put up on rocks and nothing could be left on the ground. The weather was so hot we couldn't close the tents so the crabs just walked on through. After about two weeks the migration stopped. Crabs on Munda and stuff like that, are they of any interest? I can tell you where the most mosquitoes were, the scorpions, centipedes, the crabs, snakes, the bats that would dive bomb us, but really now who cares, would people believe it anyhow?"

Bill also wrote: *"I sure agree with your chapter on the mud in the tents. The first time we got out of the jungle, mosquitoes and mud, and had a wood floor, was when we moved up to Palawan. After we moved again, I left everything there for the 5th to move into, including my nice bamboo house with a wood floor, I had built for one hundred pesos. That sure was a bad day. Until I read your chapter on the Palawan Massacre I had never heard of it."*

REFERENCES

Congdon, Don, *Combat, The War With Japan,* N.Y. Dell, 1962
Boeman, John, *Morotai,* Manhattan, Kansas, Sunflower Press, 1989

CHAPTER SEVENTEEN

Stress, Strain and Junior Birdmen

The Army Air Corps was too freshly hatched to have traditions. The only "tradition" I recall is one indulged by air crews who took off from California for combat. Those who made the big hop from San Francisco traditionally spent their last night at the "Top of the Mark." The Mark Hopkins Hotel boasted a sky room caged by picture windows, heavily trafficked by departing airmen. It was "Big Band" music time, with drums rattling and the brass section standing and swinging their horns to and fro to tunes like *Chattanooga Choo Choo, Moonlight Serenade, Stardust, Don't Sit Under the Apple Tree With Anyone Else But Me*, and *You'd Be So Nice To Come Home To*.

During the course of the evening, crews whose take-off was set for the morrow, made their exit by way of the grand piano on the bandstand. A crew would cluster around the piano, and, with hands across shoulders, sang the *Whiffenpoof Song*: "Gentlemen fliers off on a spree, doomed from here to eternity…" It wasn't meant to be melodramatic, but it was. The room fell quiet. As the last notes played, men were silent. There was not a dry eye among the ladies.

Along the food chain, navy got first bite since they hauled the stuff. Next came the marines, instinctive hunter-gatherers, who stole what they wanted. Then the foot army, whose scrounging skills were on constant alert. Finally, the air crews. At the end of a 10,000 mile supply line, we had priority only on Australian Bully Beef. Marine and navy air squadrons were rotated and relieved. Army squadrons were supple-

David Witts on leave in Sydney, Australia

mented. Tours were often extended and ground crews were stuck in place until war's end. Occasionally, we sneaked "Fat Cat" missions to Australia for amenities. Pacific air crews got rest leave after 25 missions. My pictures of 'rest leave in Sydney' in the Hoover Archives provide documentary insight.

The Air Force Surgeon General reported: *"In the 13th Air Force thirty percent of casualties resulted from fatigue and stress. Crews with over ten months of combat undergo changes to such an extent that ever restoring them is questionable."*

Lee Tipton of the 13th Air Service command said: *"Recreation didn't exist, there was a lot of depression. The twenty-six months I was there, I had three days off duty."* Flight surgeons deployed at the squadron level were kept busy. Sometimes they flew missions, watching for men that cracked under fire or tending wounded. On returning from a mission, these angels of mercy doled out two ounces of whiskey per crew member, a potion often hoarded until it attained critical mass.

Aftermath of a typhoon

Equatorial weather is the planet's worse, plaguing planes and pilots. Its menu du jour offered typhoons, thunderstorms, avalanching rain and bone-cracking turbulence. Weather reports did not emanate from behind Japanese lines, which is the only place we flew. High mountains were sprinkled everywhere, often fog-shrouded. Pervasive humidity corroded metal, condensed in instruments and short-circuited wiring. Volcanic and coral dust were agents of abrasion. Twelve-hour missions meant the twenty-five-hour inspection cycle came up every two missions, entailing a 100 man-hour commitment. Without airdromes and hangars, these inspections were conducted in downpours or 130° heat. We never took the measure of the jungle.

Facilities of fixed bases were denied the 13th, always hot behind the ever-advancing front-line. A grounded plane was a wasted plane. Ingenuity made do with scavenged supplies and jerry-rigged parts. Men

who had kept tractors and Model-T Fords running were creative mechanics. They were the sinew of the planes and knew their engines like a mother knows a child. They worked like dogs with no chance of rotation, their planes always ready for their crews. Major Dale Brannon, the first squadron C.O. of an Army Fighter Squadron on Guadalcanal, described these men: "With barely enough food, little sleep, bombed and damaged equipment, these men worked up to and beyond the limit of physical endurance. In the midst of death, destruction, tropic heat, hunger and weariness, these men were devoted to duty beyond description. The side that has men like these just cannot lose."

Air war was a young man's war. We were fascinated by airplanes. I remember as a boy that on hearing a plane, I'd run out of the house to gaze at it flying over. Americans are natural pilots, weaned on wheels and nurtured by speed. Judging speed and closure, distance and depth came quite naturally. The real engines of the Pacific air war were not mechanical, but human. Young people grew up with guns, they loved to shoot and hunt. Use of guns was instinctive. Men who headed air units were young. There were no veterans. It was almost a children's crusade. Nineteen-year-olds were leading bomber missions and thirty-year-olds were generals. We grew up fast because we weren't given time to grow up. I recall a sign over an officer's club: "No colonels admitted without their parents."

Young people were proficient flyers where much depended on reaction. Reaction is good, doubt is bad. There's a casual arrogance to youth rendering them impervious to foreboding. They think "nothing's going to happen to me." I never worried about getting killed, even though I longed for the Congressional Medal of Honor. Subliminally, we were aware of Shakespeare's line "we owe God a death," but hoped God would extend our line of credit. Occasionally there'd be a flight cruising through those soft blue skies where it seemed you could see forever, where clouds were little gauzy ribbons, and where a flirtation with death seemed remote. Whatever the alchemy of fate and luck, Pacific air crews were constantly in combat and never free of the red and ragged business of war.

Promotions came rapidly and from inside the group. It was said "there are old pilots and bold pilots, but there are no old, bold pilots." Supply officers in Sydney complained about behavior of crews on rest leave. They told General Kenney "make your brats grow up and behave." Kenney retorted "I don't want them to get fat, old and respectable, because if they do they would no longer shoot Nip planes and Nip boats!"

Jim Edmundson, a squadron commander for the 31st Bomb Group said: *"To lead you have to be in the air and in front. You can't run a flying outfit from the ground or from the rear with the beer."* There was a gulf between combat crews and "paddle feet," spectators who milled around. Intelligence and prudence were prized. Aggressiveness was important, but not if it became rash. Flying was risky, even in training. By the time you reached combat several of your buddies had been killed in training. Statistically, air crews had the least chance of survival. At first, less than half finished their tour. Some missions sustained 20% casualties. Bomber crews were very close. They were family, men who had nothing in common from the past, but who, in their shared deadly present, had everything in common. We were probably the last flyers to actually see enemy faces. There's an element of fairness in one pilot fighting another because each had a chance. Today's aerial warfare toggling a switch and launching a missile against a pilot miles away that you can't see, seems detached and vicarious.

The Pacific air war was not a spit and polish operation. There was no needless display of authority. Rank wasn't emphasized in the air, where much depended on chance, little on rank. We didn't wear insignias on our flying suits. Perhaps the Jap sniper's affinity for officer insignia influenced our strip act. There was no such thing as "proper dress." I have a picture of an awards ceremony on Morotai where maybe twenty guys were lined up to receive whatever they were receiving. No two were dressed alike. Funny thing about medals. You got one because somebody saw you do something. Most courage went unseen and unreported.

Because depression times were hard, the Air Corps attracted young men. It was a way up and out. It was exciting, required higher skill and was very demanding. Initially, two years of college were required for admission to the Aviation Cadet Corps. War knocked down that barrier, but training to earn those silver wings remained rigorous, mental and physical. Upwards of two years of intensive and specialized training was required to become a pilot, navigator or bombardier.

To be accepted as an aviation cadet required passing tests for physical, mental and motor skills, and such traits as hand-eye coordination. Academics covered diverse but useful topics like math, physics, meteorology, Morse-code, astronomy, firearms, parachute training survival and navigation. Ground classes encompassed a wider curriculum than merely getting airborne. Fifty percent had not finished high school and only ten percent had been to college. Training was vigorous and non-forgiving. When the squadron first assembled, cadets were told: "Look at the man on each side of you, because one will be washed out." Discipline was stern and severe. For the first six weeks, cadets were confined to base. Even a mild rupture of rules earned the offender "gigs," redeemable by walking four-hour tours on guard duty, usually at night. Everything was hubba-hubba and instant response. Wellington's line about Waterloo being won on the playing fields of Eton, resonates with training we received as cadets. There was a dignity and pride instilled amongst Aviation Cadets that perpetuated itself in their squadrons, their planes, their crews and, in many cases, the remainder of their lives.

The Air Corps determined that its airmen were to be trained for combat better than their foes. Physical conditioning was superb, honing the body into its best ever condition. Every cadet activity was competitive against members of your own squadron and inter-squadron. Who had the neatest footlocker, the cleanest barracks, the snappiest formations? The E-Flag was proudly carried by the highest achieving squadron on Saturday review. Cadets were fattened up. Malnutrition rejected many draftees. The chow was exceptional. All you could eat, meat and milk, eggs and fruit. For the first time, many cadets tasted steak. That competition and conditioning saved countless lives from the fiery hell of, and physical exhaustion from, air combat.

A letter I mailed home in 1943 records my surprise at cadet cuisine: *"You wouldn't recognize me now. I weigh more than I ever have. We have roast beef, steak, milk and butter. A real relief after greasy mess sergeants. Drinking two quarts of milk a day keeps me in fine form. We must eat with one hand in our lap and no part of our hand may touch the table while eating. They teach officers of the future how to conduct themselves."*

Pacific operational problems were pervasive, compounded by hand-me-down equipment surplus to Europe. Radios were a new technology plagued by gremlins and mildew. Sometimes pilots sent messages by hand, sometimes by waggling wings. Sometimes a mike button stuck, creating a one man circuit. Radio mikes that fitted around the throat made blisters. Nor was radar effective, because mountains interfered with radar beams, letting enemy planes sneak in undetected. Runways never seemed lined up with prevailing winds. The Seabees were great guys who laid down those strips, but we wondered why they had to build every runway cross wind.

Air battles were chaos and confusion at top speed. What began as a formation quickly scattered across the sky. Pilots' heads constantly swivelled, looking for friend and foe. Spotting an enemy before he sees you is critical. New pilots look for planes. Experienced pilots look for glints flashing off canopies, a significant tactic under tropical sun.

The line squadrons had one chaplain to accommodate all faiths. Ours was a Catholic priest from Chicago known to his flock as "Padre." A swell guy who handled spiritual duties like a chameleon, adapting to the background in which he worked. There were no regular services that I remember except on holy days, but that there was a God above harbored every mind. Because of our odyssey existence, we were never in one place long enough to build a chapel, nor were we ever at a place where one had existed before. Chaplains generally weren't overworked, although there was usually a lot of praying around mission time. It was said that if you weren't a religious person on the way to a target, you would be by the time you returned. We all prayed to the universal God: Going Home! I remember chaplains more as a personal sanctuary than a structure. The emotional problems of loneliness, family and "Dear John" letters kept them busy. A prevailing belief was superstition. Everybody had their own talisman—lucky days, lucky charms, lucky numbers. I was very much attached to my St. Christopher medal. One time I couldn't find my medal. I did not fly that day.

Bomber crews were a disparate group. My crew came from Idaho, Minnesota, Texas, Philadelphia, Salt Lake City, Pittsburgh and Brooklyn. Seven men flying an aluminum cigar whose lives depended on each other. There was good-natured kidding about accents, but the common denominator was Americans fighting for our country. Sounds quaint today, but our patriotism was fierce, our country respected, our flag revered. Our values were defined by Pericles two thousand years ago: "For it is only love of honor that never grows old." There was seething hatred of the Japanese. The language du jour about the enemy would now be disparaged as racial slurs. The idea of "sensitivity training" would have been greeted with guffaws since we were trained to kill people, not socialize. Our war was not a spectator sport, it was a deeply shared national experience.

The isolation of Pacific combat and its estrangement from sights and sounds of our own civilization conjured images of home. People left behind were fondly remembered. Home seemed a magic fairyland. (Today's ilk who accuse America of empire building are historically deaf, dumb and blind. All American soldiers want to do is come home.)

Letters are an insight into the reality of those times. I cite just one from a young man who worked at the Dallas Morning News (then the media was on our side) who was killed by kamikazes. Orvill Raynes married Ellen Grimes in 1940, when his salary was raised from $18.00 to $23.00 a week. His letters to his wife were published in *Good Night Officially*, a touching book. From his last wrenching letter:

> *The separation when I left you in San Francisco is the most severe blow I have ever known. The way you clung to me is the sweetest thing that ever happened... I hope you never have to read this because it means the blow has been struck.*
>
> *When we parted, for the first time in my adult life I cried. My soul has been disintegrating within me. I live only to get back to you. You will know by this letter that my life span has been completed and our four wonderful years together will have to do us.*
>
> *Now for the difficult part. It approaches a last will. Now, everything I own belongs to you... By everything, I mean the car and my pipes, the house shoes and everything else that I got together to make*

do until I was able to get you 'anything that money could buy'. I am gone, Baby Darling, I am no longer in your life...

I guess that is all my Darling. If God will be gracious and allow my presence in that place where only people like you can go, I will see you again.

Goodbye, My Darling Baby ... I go feeling thankful that God's miracle created you for me. Had I not had you, I would have cause for remorse, but as it is, I thank you and God for a very wonderful life...

All the love, devotion and worship that any man can give a woman, I give to you in this, my last "Good Bye Officially."

Your devoted husband

Orvill

CHAPTER EIGHTEEN

Diary Speak

Although there was a "mickey-mouse" regulation against keeping a diary, some did. Too bad more didn't, because real-time events told in real-time rhetoric capture reality eluding latter day recollections. William Gaskill, a 13th Air Force pilot kept one. His unadorned notes make good history:

"April—1944
We would take a small area, establish a perimeter, and bypass the rest of the island. We would hold only the airfield. Sometimes we flew so low the props made little whirlwinds off the ocean water.

"12 May—Best mission yet!
Strafed Simpson Harbor at Rabaul. We must have come in at 380mph. I throttled back to about 300 mph, and dive bombed. Diving from 13,000 to 1,000, the cockpit fogged up. As I pulled off the target a stream of bullets whizzed past. Lts. Hackbarth, Swanson and Comstock met tragic endings.

"10 June
Worley motioned for me to get rid of my bomb that I thought had dropped, but he kept motioning so I thought I still carried a bomb. I yanked back and went into the skids and slips. What a joke. I wasn't carrying a bomb, but you can't tell from inside the cockpit.

"14 June
Capt. Stege asked Cunningham to take the jeep to the flight line. Junior said: But, Sir, I don't know how to drive. Capt. Stege spent the afternoon showing him how to drive a jeep. Junior was one of the best fliers I ever knew, and he had not yet learned to drive a car. Sgt. Gerhardt told his driver to take the mission papers up the hill. He didn't know you could shift gears with the engine running.

"14 June
Sometimes we were attached to different outfits for chow and quarters. The navy fed us well. While with the Australians, I started for the mess hall; I could smell it from way off. I faced a tub of sheep's tongues about half cooked. I couldn't take that.

"25 August
Lt. Kelly undershot and plowed off into airplanes beside the runway. It exploded. He never had a chance. He was a swell fellow and was soon to go home. He was talking about the wedding he was going to have. I am going to close this diary tonight with Joshua 1:9 which Mother wrote in my Little Testament—'Be strong and of good courage: be not afraid, neither be thou dismayed for the Lord thy God is with thee.'

"2 September
Ten B-25s on a tough mission. Four were shot down, three damaged. A coastal gun fired right between my booms.

"1 October
Air raid last night—two officers and one enlisted man killed.

"3 October
B-24s got it again when they went to Borneo and nearly 30% were lost! Golly, I feel sorry for those fellows."

"6 November—longest mission yet
10 hours to the Philippines. We hate to go to Leyte as they are trigger happy. Some joker on the ground shot out Norm's engine. When he attempted to land on the other engine with wheels and flaps down, they shot out his other engine. He went in the drink. I hardly feel like protecting someone as ignorant as that. They have shot down many of our own planes, including two PBYs on yesterday's mission. We heard the distress call from Lt. Owens, 'I am hit, I'm going in.' He water landed, got into his raft and got to shore. I went to Col. Ford at the Second Air Sea Rescue Squadron at Morotai. He told me if I'd cover them, they'd pick him up. He said, 'We have sixty crews out there to pick up.' We were searching when Owens fired his flare pistol. I wrote a note, put it in my canteen and dropped it near him. Col. Ford said he would pick up Owens if we would rendezvous with him the next morning.

"Next day, we broke out of the weather and there was Playmate 22—our PBY angel of mercy. There was Owens on the beach. The PBY landed while we circled overhead. The Japs were nearby. Filipino natives rowed Owens out to the plane where the PBY boarded him and took off to pick up somebody else.

"26 November
Raids on Morotai have been pretty severe. The Japs got 20 planes on the ground one night.

"11 December,1944—Lt. Raymond is lost. The direction finding station gave him a wrong reciprocal course. He was low on gas and tried to ditch. To ditch a P-38 at night is out of the question. Operations in Biak screwed up when they let B-25 boys ferry three new P-38s. They all went in the drink.

"17 March,1945—42nd Bomb Group lost their Group C.O., Deputy C.O. and Group Navigator in a plane crash. Also several planes have exploded on takeoff lately.

"14 April, 1945—Target was Saigon. The 347th Fighter Squadron had flown P-38 and P-39 missions from Guadalcanal, New Guinea and the Philippines, over the Coral, Bismarck, Celebes, Sulu, Molucca, Ceram Straits and South China Sea—ninety-nine percent of them over water. Fighter Command decided the flight to Saigon should have a lead navigation plane. A B-25 was assigned to lead us. The flight would be 850 miles over the South China Sea and back, entirely over water. The B-25 flew a northerly heading. I moved in behind McBride, held up my map, pointing to the B-25 and shook my head. Texan McBride broke radio silence: 'Ahh know, ahh'm gonna' give him five more minutes.' The B-25 pilot also broke silence: 'Is there a problem?' McBride: 'Yeah, you're off course.' B-25 pilot: 'Minute, please.' Shortly, the B-25 pilot radioed: 'Our navy says we're okay.' McBride looked at me. I shook my head. He nodded and our six P-38s banked left and we rolled out on a new heading for Saigon.

"A Japanese destroyer in the Dong Nai River was firing at us. We made a strafing run, pulling up and over the destroyer. We kept below the treetops, heavy artillery and intense ground fire came from the river. McBride nearly flew through the hangar while blasting it. There was a large fuel tank which I punctured. Our P-38s sunk a freighter, damaged four others, destroyed a hangar, gun positions and fuel storage tanks.

"Red leader called out, 'Look who's here at 10 o'clock!' Approaching us at 5,000 feet was the B-25 navigation plane. McBride couldn't resist, 'You missed the show, Baker Fox!' No response. That was our last contact with the B-25.

Arthur J. Finnell gave me his action report on the longest bomber mission at that time, a thirteen-hour flight to the great naval base at Truk. So successful was the mission led by Finnell, it received a Presidential Citation:

"I had flown 40 missions, some with rough experiences over Rabaul. Truk was a giant atoll 50 miles across with a number of fighter strips. The area was loaded with war ships and aircraft. Our bomb load was eight 1000 pounders. The 23rd squadron was the lead squadron and I was group leader. We took off from Los Negros. Our troubles soon began. We ran into heavy weather. After we were in the clear, my tail gunner, 'Goldie', reported we were missing one squadron. They aborted. There we were, three squadrons continuing toward Truk.

"We soon were flying through another front. When we came into the clear, another squadron was missing! That left just two squadrons to complete the mission. Another front was looming up, but we flew on.

"Finally, we got through the violent weather. The third squadron was now missing! There we were, one squadron of B-24s flying into a Japanese stronghold. We went on oxygen and climbed to 20,000 feet. Lady Luck smiled. When we reached the I.P. my bombardier, 'Will' Snodgrass, took control. We dropped our thousand pounders right on target. We went into a descending turn to get the hell out of there. We caught the Japanese by surprise. As we were leaving, a swarm of Zeros caught us. There must have been 30 of them, and if they had been experienced, they would have ripped us to pieces. Instead they lined up just out of range of our .50 caliber guns. One by one, they peeled off, shooting in our general direction! 'Aviation cadets' my nose turret gunner, Scottie, called them. We settled down for our long flight back to base. We broke out our sumptuous lunch of D-rations. After a few hours sighted our base at Los Negros. Home again—mission accomplished!"

During the protracted genesis of this book, I corralled some legendary fighter pilots of the 13th Air Force to wring recollections from them. Rex Barber, Bill Harris, George Chandler, Doug Canning, Bill Starke, Art Finnell and others once blazed across the Pacific skies like avenging meteors. They were Aces, squadron commanders and decorated heroes. Their vignettes are an insight into a war not likely to be seen again, when the nation was fired by patriotism and its enemies, in or out of uniform, marked for destruction.

"Japan used phosphorous bombs which were disconcerting. They would fly above us and drop torches which looked like Roman candles shooting through our formations. During their raids on Morotai, phosphorous fragments burned holes right through our planes parked on the ground. These fireballs looked like blazing bullets. They worked on your mind."

"Formosa was all steep mountains and canyons. The Nips hid their ack-ack guns in caves in the canyon walls, so to strafe them we had to fly deep inside canyon walls. They got smart and strung steel cables dangling with mines between the sides. That put an end to our canyon shoot-outs."

"I came straight from Hamilton Field in California, which was the country club of the Air Corps, so Guadalcanal was a shock. Everybody had dysentery, and mosquitoes were thick as blankets. We had Spam three times a day, if you could stand it. During air raids the shrapnel rained down on the tin roofs over our foxhole sounding like a death rattle. We were an army squadron in an area run by the navy, meaning we only got what the navy didn't want."

"Our combat tactics were fashioned by our plane's performance, the opposition and the mission. Escorting bombers wasn't much fun because we were tied to them for the entire mission. Once on a bomber escort mission, a P-38 pilot peeled off to attack a Zero. Although he shot it down, it was an unauthorized act and he was severely disciplined. Fighter sweeps were wonderful because we could freelance on targets of opportunity. On those sweeps, we never brought any ammunition back."

"Speed was critical because you could force a fight, or get the hell out. The flight leader sets the speed and the elements fly on him, thereby eliminating throttle jockeying which wastes fuel. Sometimes drop tanks wouldn't drop, increasing drag and lowering speed. Sometimes bombs wouldn't release which was a problem since we weren't paid to bring bombs home and nobody wants to land with a full bomb load."

"We were intolerant of any pilot turning back with a 'rough engine.' A plane that aborted a mission was grounded on its return, and nobody could touch the plane until the commanding officer test hops it."

"There were five airports around Rabaul, all swarming with Zeros flown by experienced and bold pilots. Whenever we reduced their numbers, they'd fly in a new squadron from Truk."

"We tried to get our P-38s over Rabaul at dawn and dusk, but on night flights the return was 300 miles over open ocean with no landmarks or radio signals. Sometimes on the way home a PBY would orbit half way and shoot star shells, which was the greatest sight in the world."

"A bottle of bourbon was highly prized and worth $100. Shipped in from New Caledonia, it was hard to hide from the ship crews. We tried everything. We hid bottles in gun belts, but the navy found them. Once we hid a bottle in a container and welded it, but the navy stole the whole container."

"Parked on the ground, planes got so hot touching them would sear your skin. Since heavy flying gear could not be put on, by the time we reached altitude the air was freezing. You'd shiver the rest of the mission."

"During the invasion of Munda, we had a very tough battle with a Jap cruiser. We lost several B-25s and P-40s. We went home, got drunk and tried to forget."

"We were flying combat air patrol over the Solomons from thirty minutes before dawn till dark. We'd come back, land, eat something, sleep on the flight line and five hours later take off again."

"We were on a mission to Rabaul and the Zeros were going up and down like yo-yos. Two got on my tail and some P-38s scissored to knock them off. A shell hit my engine and set it on fire. I rolled over to bail out and saw I was in between two gun batteries. I knew I'd never get down alive, so I rolled back over, cut the fuel and the fire blew itself out. I feathered my props and here came two Zeros to finish me off, but P-38s shot the Zeros off. I bailed out and landed in Simpson Harbor, where I knew my goose was cooked. Suddenly a PBY came skipping across the water, snatched me up and took off without stopping. How any of us got out of that was a miracle."

"I had eight kills, but got shot down in four different planes: P-38, P-39, P-40 and P-400E. One more and I would have been a Jap Ace".

"When Navy planes came in, we'd stand around and watch because they were used to tail hooks to stop their roll. On our strip they all ground looped trying to stop, and we laughed like hell."

"One day we got a call for help from a coast watcher who said the Japs were hunting him with dogs. These guys were valuable because they'd radio, 'there's forty Jap bombers headed your way.' This gave us time to get airborne and intercept. No way could we see him or Japs in that jungle, but we knew about where he was. We loaded empty beer bottles in a B-17 and scattered them over the area. They sounded like bombs. Next day he called and gave us a 'well done mates.'"

"One day two Jap transports ran aground off Guadalcanal. They were loaded with troops who jumped overboard trying to swim to shore. There were so many of them the water was black with soldiers. We flew back and forth lacing the water with our machine guns. Later somebody asked me if I felt bad doing that? Yeah, but only because I couldn't kill more. How can you feel bad about killing guys who are trying to kill you?"

A couple of personal anecdotes stick in my own memory:

We took off for combat duty from Mather Field in Sacramento at midnight so as to hit Pearl Harbor in daylight. We were given sealed orders to be opened when we landed. Our last sight of home was the Farallon Islands off the California coast. As those lights slipped behind, we furtively faced the oldest and greatest of oceans. Its sheer vastness made me uneasy. The stars would be our guide. There were three picket ships stationed en route to send radio signals, but we never raised one. That left little room for error. Sometimes planes attempting that long hop never made it.

Seventeen hours later, we landed, tired, hungry and apprehensive. We made a bee line for the officer's dining room in our sweaty flying suits. At the next table marked "Field Grade Officers Only" (a sign I had never seen before). I overheard a major decked out in a crisp, starched uniform complaining "I never asked for this overseas duty." That was my first experience with rear echelon service officers. It made a lasting impression!

Another ignoble memory etched in time involves covering bomber strikes against Borneo. To orbit over the target at noon meant a wake up call from the CQ at 0300, jump into flying suits and mush through mud to the mess hall where awaited a plop of powdered green eggs, stale bread and bad coffee. Occasionally there'd be an "intelligence briefing," simplistic of detail such as "any fighter planes seen over the Celebes will be bogeys." There was no weather information because the enemy neglected to broadcast their local weather. Then we'd scramble into an open weapons carrier for the ride to the flight line in a refreshing rain storm, pile out at the parachute tent and pick up a Mae West. The mission began with the crew wet and cold with no means to dry off or heat up. Crossing over the high Celebes mountains guaranteed additional refrigeration. Then it was drop down to the deck in the Makassar Straits astride the Equator where temperature was so intense steam rose from the jungle and heat waves shimmered off the water. Those missions were fourteen hours of bone-cracking cold and suffocating heat.

REFERENCES

Gaskill, William M., *Fighter Pilot in the South Pacific*, Manhattan, Kansas, Sunflower Press, 1997

CHAPTER NINETEEN

Waltzing Matilda

September 1, 1939, Germany invaded Poland and World War II began. Australian soldiers were stripped from their homeland and dispatched to protect the Empire's bastions in Suez and in Singapore. Two months after Pearl Harbor, the "impregnable bastion" of Singapore surrendered to General Yamashita who bicycled down Malaya and spoofed Singapore with fewer troops than defended the city. The Japanese then headed to Australia, who demanded their troops in North Africa come home. They did. By 1945, they were on the offensive in Borneo, capturing Borneo's oil producing areas at Balikpapan, Tarakan and Brunei. The campaign was commanded by Sir Thomas Blamey, Commanding General of Australian Armed Forces. His strategy was simple: "We should leave only ashes where Japan's cities stood. Survivors will be nomads."

The Aussie operations were supported by our surface navy and army air forces. The PBY was the only plane capable of interfacing with the Celebes Sea, Sulu Sea and Makassar Straits which encapsulate Borneo. My squadron, the Second Emergency Rescue Squadron and its amphibious PBY5-A Catalinas were awarded the exclusive franchise for Borneo. A duke's mixture of unusual missions were flown in this campaign, two of which I flew.

During the Balikpapan invasion in July 1945, the Aussie medics ran out of blood. Urgent requests could be answered only by PBYs since the Japs held the runway. The Aussies were supposed to fly the blood in, but they ran out of "Cats." My Squadron was ordered to bring the "Blood to Balikpapan." That blood saved a lot of lives. Getting it there cost some, too. Captain Harry Remington landed off Balikpapan under enemy fire. The Aussies scooted out in a rubber boat and retrieved the blood. Before Remington's plane could take off, enemy shore batteries capsized it.

This mission was mentioned in a Presidential Citation awarded in 1945:

"Although the total strength of the squadron was only three hundred seventy (370) men and twelve (12) airplanes, their combined efforts resulted in one of the most amazing combat serial records of the war. In addition to

Downed PBY in bay of Balikpapan

these open sea res-cues, twenty four (24) personnel were evacuated from danger areas. Since the PBY was designed for smooth water, the hull of these ships is only .064 of an inch thick. Every time an open sea landing was made the crew was confronted with ocean swells, winds, currents and ground swells, each of which was conflicting and added to the danger of the opera-tion. On these landings, often as many as seventy (70) rivets would be knocked from the hull necessitating the utmost skill to prevent the ship from capsizing in the running seas before completion of the mission.

"The mission which carried the blood to Balikpapan was flown on D-Day plus one (1) to the beachhead. With eighteen hundred (1800) pounds of blood on board for the wounded on Borneo, a forced landing was made in the heavy swells of the Makassar Straits. Immediately upon landing the swells began to smash the ship to pieces. Yet the entire crew stayed with the helpless plane and transferred the precious cargo to waiting craft in perilous waters and under enemy fire. This exploit drew the commendation of the Australian Military Forces which on 14 July 1945 published a citation as follows: 'Immediately after the 7th Division landed at Balikpapan an urgent signal was sent to Morotai for eighteen hundred pounds of fresh blood. How Capt. Remington of the 2d Emergency Rescue Squadron got it ashore in a Catalina through the tremendous seas which rage off Balikpapan can now be told. A sea plane was the only way of getting the blood ashore. The RAAF Rescue Group had already lost two Catalinas in an attempt, and had no planes available. So it passed the request on to the 13th Air Force. Seas with waves 15 feet high were sweeping the entire bay as Capt. Remington reached Balik-papan with his loaded airplane and one look showed him he would never get his plane down safely. But he put the Cats nose down. She struck the crest of a vicious wave and bounced drunkenly on to the next. The impact split the entire seam running along the hull and smashed out the rivets. With the crew frantically bailing amid crashing waves, the pilot tried to steer the plane

toward shore. A U.S. crash boat sped to their aid, but a tremendous wave hurled it against the Catalina's tail and smashed the tail to matchwood. Remington was now unable to taxi. The plane was rapidly filling with water. Tide and sea began carrying her swiftly along the coast where the Japanese shells were falling. Buffeted incessantly, she drifted for four miles before another navy boat reached her and took her in tow. Just before dark she was caught and wrecked on a reef thirty yards from the beachhead. But an Alligator came alongside and the blood was delivered intact.'

After the Aussies captured Balikpapan's airstrip, my plane was the first to land. That mission was captured by official 13th Air Force photos. That was the biggest media event I saw during the entire war. Actually, it was the only one. In the "official" photo, your humble author is the guy with a baseball cap flipped up, a .45 strapped on, announcing to the massed

Author David Witts, fifth from right, being interviewed by Aussie reporters

media (two Aussies with note pads) that it was a piece of cake. The air force video "13th Air Force Report" shows the first plane to land at Balikpapan. It lumbers down the strip. It stops. Climbing out the blister, our crew is seen claiming Balikpapan for the 13th Air Force.

While waiting to get off that combat active strip, we quickly bonded with an Aussie patrol whose job was to keep the strip and its new occupants Jap-free. Those Aussies were fearless. They were the "Rats of

Tobruk." Rushed home, they faced down the Japanese army on the Kokoda Trail in New Guinea. As the enemy withdrew, the Aussies continued attacking, supported by our air force. Refusing to surrender, the starving enemy was reduced to cannibalism. A Japanese medical officer sliced flesh from wounded Aussies. Human flesh was found in knapsacks of dead Japanese. Aussie rage never stopped boiling.

The Aussies always had time for a "spot of tea." They also practiced combat dentistry. Rounding up a Jap soldier, they displayed team expertise. One Aussie stood on the patient, feet planted on chest and head. With pliers, the other Aussie removed the patient's gold teeth, plus others nearby. It was not a precise extraction. We rewarded the demonstration with cigarettes.

I saw refinery workers hobbling around with Dutch engineers who came ashore to survey the refineries. Their achilles tendons had been cut so they could work, but not run away. Four years before when Japan seized Balikpapan from the Dutch, they massacred the entire white population. Some had arms and legs chopped off with swords, others were driven into the sea and shot. Wives and daughters were repeatedly raped, and then became comfort slaves.

Tarakan was another oil facility in Borneo near the Sulu Sea. General Matheny of the 13th Bomber Command reported the Japs did not believe we would strike Tarakan after our heavy losses at Balikpapan. However, on November 18, 1944, 13th Air Force struck. Tarakan and its oil were snuffed out from the air.

The Presidential Unit Citation was awarded my squadron for its Borneo campaign. The Commanding General XIII Command cited service from 13 June 1945 to 4 July 1945:

"This squadron completed one of the most amazing combat records of the war. Each day these crews flew through adverse weather, alone and without fighter protection in slow, vulnerable and practically unarmed aircraft flying strike protection, search, ferry, evacuation and airborne supply missions throughout a vast area including New Guinea, Netherlands East Indies, Borneo, Philippines, Indo-China and the China Coast.

"During these three weeks of accelerated action a total of 89 combat missions averaging ten hours each were flown. Crews flew their plane into the sea 21 times, in the face of manifold dangers, which resulted in loss of planes, injuries and death to crew members. Twenty-one hazardous open sea landings were made, often in the face of mountainous swells and enemy fire. Sixty airmen were saved.

"It was instrumental in the successful invasions of Tarakan, Brunei Bay

and Balikpapan, flying in personnel, vital supplies and dispatches. Sea planes were the only way of accomplishing these missions.

"In the invasion of Brunei Bay, the first plane to land was a PBY5A which carried General Sir Thomas Blamey, Commanding General Australian Military Forces and staff to the beachhead." (Author's note: I flew that mission reported in the chapter Mission to Borneo.*)*

"In two (2) open sea landings in the Makassar Straits, the Borneo invasion convoy, spearheaded by the Seventh Fleet, was intercepted to place important naval and army personnel with secret invasion plans on board the war ships to preserve radio silence." (Author's note: I flew one of those missions)

"The first plane to land on the mainland of Borneo was a PBY5A which landed on Balikpapan and evacuated Colonel Staklin and four other personnel of the 13th Air Force." (Author's note: That was the mission recorded in the video 'The Thirteenth Air Force.')

"Frequently ground crews worked all night long by the light of Jeeps so every fighter and bomber strike in this vast area would be assured of daily rescue cover and protection, in addition to supporting three Australian invasions.

"Air crews demonstrated great courage in flying unescorted long and hazardous missions far behind enemy lines, often through violent weather and in the face of ack-ack and enemy fire. Yet no crew from this squadron ever turned back before the successful completion of every assigned mission."

> *Paul J. Yurkanis*
> *Lt. Col., Air Corps*
> *Commanding*

REFERENCES

Smurthwaite, David, *Pacific War Atlas*, Mirabel Books, N.Y. 1995

CHAPTER TWENTY

General Sir Thomas Blamey and the Sultan of Sarawak

The Commanding General of Australian Armed Forces, and MacArthur's Deputy Commander, was a burly Aussie respected by his countrymen, General Sir Thomas Blamey. He understood the enemy: *"The enemy is a curious race—a cross between a human and the ape. Beneath the thin veneer of a few generations, he is a subhuman beast, who fights by the jungle rule of tooth and claw, who must be beaten by the jungle rule of tooth and claw. Kill him or he will kill you. We must exterminate these vermin."*

In a bizarre episode, my crew was picked to fly the Australian General into the invasion of Brunei Bay, the giant oil province on Borneo's west coast. Its harbor provided shelter for Japan's fleet and oil for its ships. Brunei's capture was assigned to the Australian Army with on-site support from our air and naval forces.

Brunei is now called Sarawak, ruled by the Sultan, whose profligate playboy brother, Prince Jefri, squandered $15 billion of the nation's capital. Not an easy task. It required luxury hotels, thousands of cars, dozens of aircraft and hordes of entertainers. I recently saw his yacht in Monaco. Unforgettable. Sleek as a black panther, with an intriguing name, "Tits." That cornucopia of extravagance recently imploded in a six-day auction of Rolls Royces, Mercedes and gold-trimmed Jacuzzis.

In July 1945, ferrying General Blamey to Brunei was assigned the amphibious PBY5A since arrival might occur on water or land, whichever was appropriate on arrival. My squadron drew the duty. General Blamey gave me a hat as a souvenir.

David Witts with Aussie hat

So many goofy things happened on that mission, the squadron c.o. asked me to report it. Using the rickety squadron typewriter, I chronicled the mission. The original 1945 script is in the Hoover Archives. The breezy and sophomoric rhetoric was not in keeping with the gravitas of the mission, but I was so glad to get back, rhetorical exuberance followed:

Mission to Borneo—July 1945

The Operations Officer alerted our crew to stand by for a secret mission. Four hours later we were in the briefing room when in walked two Australian captains. We were briefed for a flight to Brunei Bay, strategic base on the west coast of Borneo, the invasion of which was then underway. Our mission was to carry VIPs. Although their identity was not disclosed, that we were told to leave our moldy flying suits in favor of less moldy khakis tipped the mitt we would be hauling wheels of no trivial diameter. Route and code data arranged, take-off was set for 0600 the following morning.

"A five o'clock air raid found us burrowing mud at the nearest foxhole. Since Morotai was the most bombed island in Pacific, I departed my cot without bothering to disengage the mosquito net. Ardor for this mission was dimming.

"Take-off was upped to 0800. That hour revealed a curious crew standing alongside our Catalina watching the engineering officer personally supervise the pre-flight. Suddenly hitherto ignoble taxiway "C" of ignoble Morotai gave way to heraldry. A staff car resplendent with four stars and flanked by lesser vehicles roared up to our astonished group. The convoy gushed brass. The door of the staff car opened and the occupant turreted his bulk on us, we recognized him from pictures to be General Blamey. The Australian Commander shook hands with seven gaping Americans. Until then, the highest rank I ever encountered was our Squadron Captain 'Jungle Jim' Jarnigan.

"After an orderly loaded a trailer of baggage, the portly General was hoisted and/or climbed aboard. As we taxied out of the revetment, an Aussie Lieutenant leaning into the prop wash pounded on the port blister, struggling with a cumbersome object. It seemed the General forgot his medicine ball.

"We set course and commenced to climb, when I ambled back to the blister to see that all was well. While I ogled the General's ribbons, Sir Thomas barked, "my case!" A brigadier flailed baggage and produced a handsome leather case with locks. The General cooly selected a book. The cover rang a note. It displayed a tasty portrait of beauty contest legs. Preparatory to the

invasion, the General was reading Perry Mason's The Case of the Lucky Legs.

"[At] 8,000 feet above the Molucca Passage, the starboard engine began cutting. We turned back. The weather at base, as always, was terrible, so the only thing left to worry about was a landing in a rainstorm with our overloaded ship carrying Australia's top brass and 1800 gallons of gas. But we made it and the only thing that bounced was the medicine ball.

"Takeoff was reset for 2400 hours. The engineering officer and ground crew swarmed in spasms of parts and profanity. At midnight we took off and set course for the South China Sea. The grey hour preceding the tropical dawn found us sneaking along the northeast coast of Borneo near the big Japanese base at Sandakan. This reverie was disturbed by the swish of an airplane past our tail, a meatball on its wing. We hit the cloud deck.

"By mid-morning, we passed the Japanese garrison at Jesselton and were approaching Brunei Bay. Those who have tried to explain to a Chinese laundryman to starch the shirt but not the collar will appreciate landing instructions from an Aussie controller over a tired VHF set. Putting a Mae West on Sir Thomas was a joint operation of the Australian general staff and our radio operator. Wing floats down, we were on the final approach to Brunei Bay when the Aussie controller with sudden clarity advised caution in landing because of mines floating in the Bay. We finally rocked to rest without irritating a mine. The General ceremoniously transferred to a crash boat sprouting dignitaries. We were ordered to await instructions.

"Anchoring the good ship Playmate 43, we went ashore. There we bummed chow from engineers working on the airstrip. The meal was uneventful until the cook pulled lumber off a woodpile exposing an antagonistic Nip who scurried out shooting at citizens in the area. Japs would lie like rats in the swamp and suddenly pop up distributing hand grenades, or hide in the kunai grass and snipe with 'woodpeckers.' His desire to join his ancestors was facilitated by Aussie burp guns.

"We received a message to return to the plane, take off and land on the strip, which the Aussies had thoughtfully acquired. We pulled anchor, skipped across the bay and took off. We were about to become the first Americans to land on Brunei, when the engineer dropped into my compartment and croaked, "Lieutenant, Lieutenant, there's a snake in here!" I patted him and said, "take it easy Hermann, we've been flying too much; you'll feel better when we get on the ground." He gazed at me with the eyes of man who had just looked on things best kept from view and thumbed toward the compartment he was evacuating. To humor the man, I wheeled and looked over the bulkhead into the engineer's compartment. To my abysmal distress,

I was staring into the dark eyes of a snake, likewise peering over that same bulkhead six inches from my nose. Two compartments were now evacuated.

"After we landed, the Aussies clustered around our plane ready for cigarettes. Now only slightly unhinged, I casually announced there was a snake in the plane, but assured them from snakes I have known it wasn't poisonous because his head tapered into his body, unlike that of the rattler. These guys were the "Rats of Tobruk." One of the "diggers" picked up a stick, strolled into the ship and flicked Mr. Snake outside, where he clubbed it. It had crawled aboard while we were anchored in the bay. One of the Aussies gave me sly grin and said, 'so she ain't poisonous, eh mate? That's a bloody coral snake. You'd be good for about thirty seconds after that bloke had a go at you.'

"The cigarette loving Aussies offered to show us scenes of local interest. A barbed wire enclosure held some captured Nips. Standing guard over these sons of Nippon were bearded Sikhs who had survived Japanese prison camps and were liberated the previous day. Because of their size, the Nips accorded them brutal treatment. The Sikhs had their former torturers doing close order drill and saluting. One had the Japs line up and 'count-off,' a meaningless ritual constantly conducted by Japs on prisoners. The Sikh faced his command and ordered 'count off.' The recruits were unable to cope with the mutating mathematics. Whereupon the Sikhs gleefully proceeded down the line administering academic instruction with rifle butts, seriously rearranging profiles. This open air lecture was a joy to behold.

"By nightfall, the strip was secure, we thought. The Nips and all hell simultaneously broke loose. A night battle when the enemy has broken through the perimeter produces considerable confusion and stray lead. A small fire came to life in the clearing. Those familiar with the Aussies can guess the rest. An Aussie was warming his billy for a bit of tea.

"Eventually, the fire-fight subsided and we received orders for immediate takeoff. The P-40s along the strip began to blow up. In violation of the Geneva Convention, the Nips had strapped 30-pound demolition bombs to their backs and were running at full speed into the parked aircraft. Just before they got to our revetment, they either ran out of halfbacks or bombs.

"The General and his staff arrived under heavy guard and we unceremoniously took off with no regrets. Dawn found us winging our way in the opposite direction from Borneo, land of tropical enchantment and paradise. Personally, I'd give Borneo back to the National Geographic."

CHAPTER TWENTY-ONE

Eyes in the Sky—Air Navigation

Incredible as it now seems, with global position gadgets in everything that moves, our air navigation was little different from the ancient mariners... stars and sextant, clock and compass. Since oceans have no landmarks, our aerial navigation was graduated guessing, and find your way home by guess and God. I know, I was a navigator. Operational losses because of navigational errors often exceeded combat losses. On 1,000-mile missions over water without landmarks, the slightest navigational error was magnified, often fatally. Tumultuous weather made just flying from one place to another hazardous. Each plane had to do its own navigating. Along the equator, great masses of black clouds and enormous storms disabled planes and disoriented pilots. Lacking forward meteorology, pilots flew on what they could see from the cockpit. On April 22, 1944, known as Black Sunday, the 5th Air Force lost thirty-one aircraft in a fierce storm.

We used sextants to take "fixes." This was a complex procedure in which a hand-held bubble sextant took a bearing on a celestial object. When turbulence jiggled the bubble and clouds obscured the stars, bearings were suspect and accuracy defeated. Sights were plotted on three stars at different locations in the sky and, where those three bearings crossed, marked the plane's location at that moment. It was a chancy procedure, the individual skill of the navigator being decisive. He had to identify various navigation stars by sight and then interpret bearings timed by Greenwich Mean Time and astronautical tables. Since there were no time check facilities, each Navigator carried a Hamilton Watch Company Chronometer, an accurate pocket-watch, reporting G.M.T. If everything worked to perfection, the fix told you where you were fifteen minutes ago.

Brilliant stars, such as Polaris, Sirius, Vega and Antares, were used for navigation in the northern hemisphere, but were not always visible south of the Equator. Where the constellations were strange, we tried to identify stars by sight and from diagrams. They would arise one by one, and soon the sky was crowded. Most had weird names, Imagine Bostonians,

Navigating in the air

Crackers and Texans speaking names like Betelgeuse, Fomalhaut, Procyon, and Aldebran. A pronouncing guide used by air crews was our "diversity training." The Big Dipper always pointed to Polaris, the North Star, which, for reasons I never understood, did not rotate around the sun. The Southern Cross was not functional for navigation, and we were not familiar with other stars in the southern hemisphere.

Navigating over the ocean with no landmarks was dicey. Eddie Rickenbacher, America's World War I Ace, was flying a B-17 from Hawaii with a secret message from Secretary of War Henry Stimson to General MacArthur in Australia. His plane missed Canton Island, got lost and ran out of fuel. The plane ditched, and Rickenbacher along with seven crew members, scrambled into life rafts. Despite intensive searches, it was three weeks before they were rescued. That high profile search revealed the intolerance of the vast Pacific, where a slight error became an unpardonable sin.

Navigation was basically "dead reckoning" by compass course, air speed and wind direction. Winds aloft are constantly variable. Calculating wind direction and velocity, with no landmarks along the way and fuel calculated in minutes, kept navigators alert. At low levels we calculated wind direction from waves sighted along the drift meter's grid, which indicated wind direction. Velocity was estimated from the ocean's surface condition, e.g., oily calm meant a wind speed of 0-8 knots, white caps calculated by size indicated velocity, such as 12-20. Blowing spray and wind streaks upped the scale to 30-40 knots. Winds changed velocity and direction at different altitudes, adding further mystery. Sometimes waves of heat would dance off the water. Winds often drew fine lines on the sea. One pilot whose air speed indicator malfunctioned estimated his speed by pulling the canopy back and judging speed by sound and wind.

There being no radio beacons, airplanes in the Pacific relied on magnetic compasses which are subject to both deviation and variation. To obtain the compass heading to be flown, these two variables must be factored. Determining the compass heading required three steps.

1. True course was determined by a specialized ruler called a Weems Mark II Plotter. For instance, true course from Dallas to Chicago would follow a plotted course of, say 20°. But you would not steer 20° by the compass, because of Variation and Deviation.
2. Compass needles point to the North Magnetic Pole, which differs from true north. That angle between true north and magnetic north is called Variation.
3. Deviation is the influence metal objects (engine, guns) near the compass exert on its magnetic needle. TVMDC (True Variation Magnetic Deviation Compass) was the formula to determine compass heading. True course was determined by plotter. Variation was applied to obtain magnetic course. Deviation was then applied to obtain compass course. Aviation cadets would never remember this mantra, so TVMDC was taught as: "True Virgins Make Dull Company." No flyer ever confused this formula. My handwritten notes in the Hoover Archives show how we computed deviation, variation and relative bearing. Such hands-on navigation was all we had.

A pocket notebook embalmed in my footlocker contains an odd miscellany of penciled notes in contrast to today's structured flying:

Mission:15 July—Balikpapan.
Pick up Col. Stehlin, 13th AF PR officer. Magpie is control. Fighter sector Tespire. Allow 45 min. for transfer and then chop hell out of it.

Mission:12 July—Search for Bogey RDF stn. in Halmaheras. Skirt coast at five angels. Caution AA. Any fighters seen will be bandits.

Mission 11 Aug.—Formosa.
Cover 4 Sqdns. Hellcats from Samar hitting Hesto Airdrome. Orbit in Takao Harbor 1130 -1200.

Mission 19 Aug.—Orbit 1200-1300 Pratas Reef.

Cover Navy sector search.

Code Messages:
Rainbow—P-38 cover
Cream Puff—hit by ack-ack
Red Devil—hit by aircraft fire
Salt Lake—landing in sea
Half-baked—may have to land, escort me
Yellow Jacket—survivor in Mae West
Goodyear—survivor in life raft
Davy Jones—survivor in water without life raft

Code Identifications:
Easy—Catalina
Fox—F6F
Love—B-17
Mike—B-24 or PB4Y
Peter—P-40
Queen—A-26
Roger—B-25
Victor—P-47
X-Ray—Spitfire
Zebra—P-51

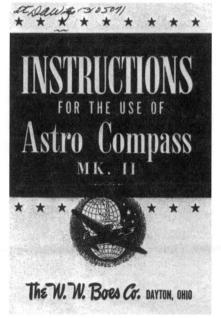

Obtaining Longitude By Sunset: Find GCT of sunset at Greenwich at DR latitude. Correct for altitude and subtract that from observed time. Convert difference to degrees and minutes. That = West longitude.

Instructions for the Use of Astro Compass M.K.II is the manual for navigators. It says the Astro Compass is designed to provide: (a) true heading of the aircraft; (b) true bearing of a distant object; and (c) relative bearing of a distant object. Specific instructions apply

Astro Compass—the book

to specific functions. To find true heading by the sun:

1. Extract the GHA Sun and Declination against GCT and date in Air Almanac.
2. Compute LHA Sun by: LHA Sun=GHA Sun +E Longitude–W
3. Set DECLINATION.
4. Set LHA.
5. Set LATITUDE.
6. Rotate Azimuth Circle until shadow appears on shadow screen of Sight.
7. Read TRUE HEADING against lubber's line.

The Astro Compass

Today's instantaneous communication and information, makes our Pacific navigation positively primeval. Pilots and navigators had to calibrate compasses, repair radios, estimate winds by reading ocean waves, compute load factors for weight and balance, communicate by Morse Code, and use strange formulas to determine moonrise, sunset, latitude, longitude and other crucial facts. Instruments were crippled by tropical humidity, radar and Loran were experimental, terrain and weather blocked out transmissions. Note the printed instructions on our Aussie

A Dutch navigational map

maps: "All service users of this map are requested to indicate necessary corrections hereon and return to RAAF Headquarters through the usual channels." Some maps we used in New Guinea and Netherlands East Indies were written in Dutch.

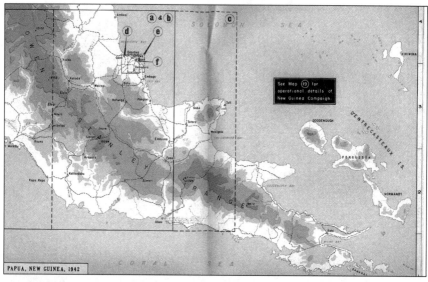

WW II era Pacific map which demonstrates the lack of detail with which pilots had to contend.

CHAPTER TWENTY-TWO

High Jinks and High Flying

One war-taught axiom is that all that careful planning goes out the window when the first shot whizzes by. Instinct and survival take over. Departure from standard operating procedures hatched regularly in the Pacific Paradise.

Strategic Bombing.

Before the war, Army Air Corps brass claimed their Norden bomb-sight so accurate that bombing was like "shooting fish in a barrel." Aerial warfare would become "strategic bombing." Like so many Washington strategies, it didn't work. Pacific winds aloft were sometimes so fierce jet streams whipped bombers across the sky. Occasionally bombardiers reported their bomb-sights were unable to keep the target in sight. "We were up about as high as you could go," recalled one crew member; "practically in a stall at 30,000 feet. We were going so fast downwind there was no way the bombardier could hold the target on the bomb sight. Another time, the damn target backed right off the radar, we were going backward over the ground."

High Level Bombing.

Pacific targets were not fixed such as cities, factories and airdromes. The targets were tiny, obscure, camouflaged and often in motion. High level bombing was ineffective against moving targets. At 10,000 feet, a moving ship will travel 1/4 mile between time of bomb release and impact, infecting the bombsight with inaccuracy. I never saw a high alti-tude bomb hit a ship. High level bombing was not a precision tool, but a sledge hammer. Japanese sailors learned to watch our bomb-bay doors yawn open at high altitude and, as soon as bombs were toggled, they wheeled their ship hard. Our crews wised up and countered by first drop-ping sand bags, which, from the surface, looked like bombs. The target ship would turn on a new heading. So would the plane. Bingo!

Skip-bombing.

Since high altitude bombing meant low percentage hits, conventional wisdom was "fly high and miss, or low and get shot." Pacific flyers developed another strategy. Instead of trying to hit a match stick from 10,000 feet, medium bombers attacked ships coming in at mast level and dropped bombs aimed amid ship, a broadside target. Dropped at low level, the bombs skipped along the surface, like rocks skimming across a lake. Sometimes the planes came in so low the ship guns couldn't depress that low. Delayed action fuses allowed the planes to release bombs and skip away.

Parafragging.

Unlike Europe, there were no great airdromes which could be bombed from 20,000 feet. Pacific airstrips were tiny targets, hacked out of the jungle and obscured by it. Bombing a jungle strip demanded visibility and accessibility, which factors converged at low level. Bombs dropped at low level exploded before the messenger got away. So, bombs were rigged with parachutes. The bombs drifted down, giving planes time to hit and scoot. These low level attacks took the enemy by surprise. They had no time to get their planes in the air. Low level bombing was destructive and concentrated. It put holes in everything on the ground—buildings, planes and people. The 42nd Bomb Group flew the first "parafrag" missions.

Leaflet Drops.

Another high level trick involved dropping leaflets warning the target of an attack, a seemingly humanitarian gesture to those far removed from the front. Tipping targets in advance invited flak from an ungrateful enemy, making no sense to airmen. These leaflets were in heavy packets bound by tape. Crews were supposed to cut the tape and salvo the scattering sheets. Many felt the message would have greater impact if delivered in bound form, thereby giving the message maximum focus.

Weight and Balance.

These procedures were a constant problem for flights which required a maximum of aerodynamic efficiency and a minimum of drag. The weight and balance slide rule was a fancy contraption designed to arrange load for trim, balance and safety. It was complex. Our B-24 crews trumped technology with simplicity. An empty ammo box was placed under the tail skid. The plane was then loaded until the weight shifted sufficiently forward to tilt the nose wheel to the ground. That signaled the plane was balanced and ready to fly.

Field Requisitions.

Paper work was anathema to line squadrons, always frustrating, seldom productive. It was required by rear echelons, variously disdained as "paddle feet" and "ground pounders." Ingenuity overcame paper every time: "Our squadron ran out of ethylene glycol. My crew chief said he knew where we could get some. We took off in a P-38 with a 300-gallon belly tank. He rode piggy back, hunkered down across my shoulders without a parachute. We flew 200 miles to a supply base. My chief said: You keep the man at the front desk talking, I'll tell you when we're ready. He somehow got his hands on antifreeze and filled the belly tank. He soon returned and said our plane was ready to go. And so it was."

Flying Artillery.

Another Pacific innovation was mounting a .75mm cannon in the nose of a B-25. When that cannon hit a target it ceased to exist; however the recoil was dramatic. One crew said when they shot the cannon the plane literally went into a dead stall. Since this modification was not extensively used, little is known about it. Michael John Claringbould, the Aussie historian who has written extensively of the Southwest Pacific air war, sent me this episode about one of those cannon-toting B-25s:

"It was late 1944 and Japan's isolated forces were struggling. Scattered garrisons had their supply lines cut. The garrison at Paimaimal on New Britain was radioed from Rabaul a string of barges carrying food, fuel and bottles of sake was being towed there by tug. It dared moved only at night and hid during the day.

"The last day, the flotilla was ordered to proceed during daylight. At the same time three 13th Air Force B-25s were warming up on Stirling Island to search the coast for targets of opportunity. One plane was equipped with the cannon. Lt. Wolfendale spotted a string of barges. Caught in the open, the tug had only two machine guns. Before they could shoot, the first B-25 started chewing on the barge with its ten .50 calibers. Wolfendale was the second ship. His gunner loaded the .75mm cannon. Wolfendale gave the order to fire. The tug disappeared in a shattering explosion as it was lifted out of the water. As he passed over, the tail gunner reported the tug had disappeared. The entire string of barges were splintered by the cannon and machine guns of the B-25s.

"As a footnote to this mission, Wolfendale's plane lost an engine and landed on a short emergency strip. The rough surface blew the nose tire, collapsing the nose gear. The plane skidded off the strip. It lies there today, overgrown with jungle. Parts of the numbers are still visible. One can still clamber up thru the tail gunner's hatch and see its solid .75mm cannon."

Jungle Juice.

     Real booze was non-existent, except for the two ounces of good stuff doled out by the flight surgeon to air crews returning from a mission. Ingenuity omnia vincit. "Jungle Juice" was created from various weird substances by creative alchemists. Sometimes its base was alcohol strained from torpedoes. Sometimes it was canned peaches or plums. Remember, this generation grew up during Prohibition when home stills produced "home brew." A five-gallon tin, heavily sedated with sugar for fermentation, parked in the sun and covered with mosquito net soon rose to the occasion. The product smelled awful, but a dedicated drinker who could get enough of the potion down and keep it down, soon departed reality.

Fuel Conservation.

     Unforgiving Pacific distances necessitated new techniques to stretch fuel supply. Bill Harris told me of his group's success with fuel experiments. Bill Harris was Deputy C.O. of the 18th Fighter Group when it moved to Lingayen. He said that Colonel Milton Adams, the C.O., and Captain Joe Gunder, the group engineering officer, perfected this tactic for their P-38s. They tested low rpms, high manifold pressure settings and fuel mixtures. Fuel conservation gave them range to fly the longest missions ever flown by fighter planes. From Morotai and Palawan, the 13th fighters flew 2,000 mile round trips to Java, Borneo, Makassar and the China Coast. George Chandler told me he learned such measures during his first tour when he became a P-38 Ace. On returning stateside, he instructed in these techniques.

Fresh Coconuts.

     The mania for fresh food was so overpowering that coconuts were attractive. Problem was lack of coconut pickers who could climb fifty-foot tall trees and pluck the coconuts from their testicular hang. Squadron behavioral experts figured out that throwing things at monkeys made them mad and exacted a reprisal. Their artillery was coconuts which they hurled with noisy chatter. The downside was that you never knew just when they would retaliate. One pilot was beaned so badly a concussion sent him to the station hospital.

Fresh Water Well.

On Mindoro the surface was hard rock. There was no fresh water. The supply officer tried to get a drill bit to drill a water well, but none were to be had. Bill Starke of the Vampire Squadron invoked self-help. He laid hands on several bottles of whiskey, stacked them in his parachute bag, fired up his P-38 and headed for the big army supply depot on Leyte. With such compelling currency, he acquired a drill bit. A few days later, air crews on Mindoro had fresh water.

V.D. Officer.

Our engineering officer, competent in his job, was forever scheming to hitch a ride with an air crew on rest leave to Sydney. He was a constant caterwauler about his vital importance to the squadron, without whose dedication the planes would be neither safe nor flyable, and blah, blah, blah. Finally our C.O., "Jungle Jim" Jarnigan, succumbed to the noise and designated Lt. Fisher as venereal disease control officer, which designation, by extrapolation, could justify a Sydney mission. Deeply grateful of the appointment, I heard Fisher thank Jarnigan, asking how it was he was so recognized. Straight-faced, "Jungle Jim" replied: "because you're the best man for the job."

Buzzing a Carrier.

"Dewint Zericor and R.S. Corbett were towing targets in P-40s. After dropping the target sleeves, we spotted the carrier Bunker Hill where navy pilots were shooting landings. We thought it would be fun to see if we could land on that small carrier deck. After attempting to land three times, and disrupting the entire carrier operation, we buzzed the flight deck and then flew back to Fighter II. General Barnes and Colonel Westbrook were the welcoming committee. We were summoned before General Barnes and Colonel Westbrook in full Class A's for a hearing. We stood at attention and got a royal dressing down. Then we saluted, about faced, and marched to the door. When we reached the door, Westy said 'just a minute'. Both of us froze and thought the worst was about to happen. Westy said: 'Did you guys have fun?' We said, 'Yes sir', in unison. Then Westy smiled and said, 'Damn, I've always wanted to buzz a carrier'."

The 13th constantly devised new techniques. Doug Canning of the

339th Fighter Squadron (P-38s) on Guadalcanal, provided this:

"*We were briefed that six marine Corsairs (F4Us) found a freighter in Vella Lavella. They strafed it but had been unable to sink it. Our mission was to go up there (seven P-38s) and see what we could do.*

"*We tried McClanahan's special fire bomb technique by dropping our belly tanks on the ship, and then torching it with incendiary bullets. We took off with Captain Tom Lanphier leading the flight with wingmen Lts. Rex Barber and Joe Moore. We found the target and dropped our tanks on the ship. I came in low and my belly tank hit the bridge. Del Goerke came in behind me firing at the gasoline-drenched ship and it began to burn fiercely.*

"*We flew back to Guadalcanal and reported our success. Marine operations sent a Black Cat PBY back to the scene. They saw the ship explode with a tremendous fireball. Evidently, it was a munition ship.*

"*Admiral Halsey sent this message to each of us—'COMSOPAC SENDS PERSONAL CONGRATULATIONS TO CREWS OF LIGHTNINGS FOR INGENIOUS INITIATION OF BOMBING WITH BELLY TANKS… 4 April 0515.' Admiral Halsey delivered to us a case of fine whiskey. After the Yamamoto mission, he sent us two cases.*"

The mean and thankless jobs of keeping those planes flying fell to unsung ground crews. Robert Pappadake of the 70th Fighter Squadron wrote a tribute. He called it *Aircraft Mechanics' Lament*:

> Out in the morning, when it's still dark
>> Out to the line where my plane I did park
> with the litheness of youth, I climbed on the wing,
>> ready to start, to hear the engines sing.
> To energize, engage, how I loved that whine
>> I sat like a king, this plane was mine.
>
> Now I got serious, I had things to check out
>> That I knew what I was doing, there was no doubt
>
> The pilots came out, mine seemed happy
>> I helped him with his chute, he said thanks "pappy"
> I pulled the chocks and signaled okay
>> Out went my plane, to the runway
> He gave her the gun and took off with a roar
>> Into the wild blue yonder he started to soar.

Now those of you who are still around, how does
it feel with both feet on the round.
Although most are one pill or another, we did earn
those pills, know what I'm saying brother.

So, to the men of 13th and your dedication
for a job you did so well,
God bless you all for your participation
that someday history will tell.

After twenty-five missions, crews were given rest leave in Sydney. It
was an exponential opportunity. There were very few men in Sydney,
because in 1939 the Aussies were shipped off to Singapore and North
Africa. Sydney was off limits to our army, which got no further south than
Brisbane. The navy mostly operated out of Melbourne and Perth.
Therefore, by 1945, when our enthusiastic rest-bent crews hit Sydney, it
was a match made in heaven. Flush with cigarettes and combat pay, "controlling legal authority" dictated quick integration. Reciprocity was in order.

Before their first rest leave, crews about to embark on the unknown
for the first time, collected phone numbers and related intelligence from
those who endured the journey before. So as not to waste time, phone
contact was initiated from Kingsford Airdrome the moment we landed in
Sydney. Once contact was established, the happy warriors proceeded to
Bernly Hotel, the downtown BOQ, from whence operations emanated.
A scrub, shave and taxi ride delivered the deserving to Rendezvous
Number One. The first hour or so involved a meal, or a dance or a song.
Formalities dissolved. It was war time. Everybody was clock conscious.
Sydney's eight-hour wartime shifts were readily assimilated by the warriors. As one shift of lassies went to work, relentlessly pursuing happy
warriors worked the clock. Those lassies focused on one man and his happiness, unlike American girls who operate under a reverse philosophy. We
identified "irrational exuberance" fifty years before Greenspan stumbled
across it.

A 1946 *Pictorial History of the 13th Air Force* contains a chapter on
Sydney which causes me to question its authenticity. It asserts:

"Bondi Beach, known for its feminine beauty, is popular in Sydney. The
Bondi Officers Rest Home was a rendezvous for officers on rest leave. It was
suited to afternoon get togethers, when coffee and cookies were served with
symphony music."

REFERENCES

Lippincott, Ben E., *From Fiji Through the Philippines*, U.S. Air Forces Aid Society, Washington, D.C 1948

CHAPTER TWENTY-THREE

Charles Lindbergh—"The Lone Eagle"

Another little known chapter in the South Pacific Air war is the involvement of Charles A. Lindbergh, the American who flew non-stop from Long Island to Paris in 1927. Flying alone, in a single engine plane, navigating by dead reckoning he landed in Paris to the tumultuous welcome of 150,000 people. His solo flight across the Atlantic stunned the world. Lucky Lindy became an American icon. "The Lone Eagle" was probably America's best known hero. Americans love heroes and none was bigger than Lindbergh, not even Babe Ruth or Jack Dempsey.

Prior to the war, he visited aircraft factories in Germany where Goering himself showed off the Luftwaffe. Lindbergh recognized Germany was the world's premier air power, and although his observations were accurate, they were not popular in Washington.

Lindbergh played a pivotal role with the Army Air Force in the South Pacific, but, being a civilian, his military role was hushed up. He wangled his way into MacArthur's New Guinea campaign as a 'technical representative' of an aircraft company. He met MacArthur who was impressed by his quiet determination that he could increase the range of our P-38 fighter planes several hundred miles. MacArthur said it would be "a gift from heaven and go out and try." Gen. Kenney said if anyone could fly a little monoplane from New York to Paris and have gas left over, he could teach our pilots how to squeeze more range from their planes. Kenney did not want Lindbergh in combat, but Lindbergh talked his way into the air, saying he had to go along to check performances.

In July 1944, Lindbergh came to the 475th Fighter Group in New Guinea. By experimenting with the manifold pressure, fuel settings and carburetor, he reduced gas consumption to such an extent that range was substantially increased. To demonstrate, Lindbergh flew missions bringing back enough fuel to fly a return mission. He taught his techniques to squadrons at Biak and Hollandia. The pilots stretched six hour missions to ten hours, doubling their range. The increased range completely surprised the Japs who suffered devastating surprise attacks.

He flew fifty missions and was "shot at by every anti-aircraft gun in

New Guinea." On July 28, 1944, he got in a fight over Ceram. Lindbergh wrote in his diary: "We jettisoned our drop tanks, switched on our guns and attacked. I started firing, but this Zero flew directly at me. I held the trigger down with my sight on his engine. We approached head-on. My tracers and .20s splattered his plane. We're close, hurdling at each other at 500 miles per hour. His plane suddenly zooms upward. I pulled back with all the strength I had. A second passes, two or three, I can see his engine cylinders. There is a rough jolt of air as he shoots past me. He starts down in a wing-over. His nose goes down. The plane picks up speed, down, down toward the sea. A fountain of spray-white foam on the water—waves circling outward as from a stone tossed in a pool, the waves merge into those of the sea, the foam disappears, the surface as it was before." At the debriefing session, he was non-committal about his victory. He said only that he fired in self-defense and then droned on lecturing about throttle settings and rpms. The impressed fighter pilots joked that he was so smart he could do crossword puzzles in ink.

Lindbergh, a throw-back to the chivalrous tradition of the warrior who respects his adversary, found no such sentiment in New Guinea. His diary detailed how our soldiers cut a Jap prisoner's throat in a demonstration of how to kill. "Our men think of nothing but shooting a Jap. They look on them as animals. It is well known that Australians when flying Japs to prisons would throw them out of the plane. Nevertheless, the Japanese atrocities are worse than ours."

CHAPTER TWENTY-FOUR

Kissing Cousins

There was a naval air squadron which flew in our operational area at the same time as we, and whose history so parallels ours, it deserves inclusion. The saga of VPB-104 (Patrol Bomb) was chronicled in a remarkable book, *Low Level Liberators*, by my friend Paul F. Stevens.

I met Paul Stephens during a symposium at the Nimitz Museum and learned we flew comparable missions at the same time from the same airstrips. They flew single plane missions as did our Squadron. Their mission was search and destroy. So was ours, except we were more search and less destroy. Paul sent me his remarkably well written and illustrated book, whose theme is the same as mine: "This book is a record of achievements rather than a scholarly history or empty statistics from action reports. It is a story of what we did and how we did it."

PB-104 was a navy squadron flying army B-24 planes. It was a stud horse of a plane sprouting ten .50 calibers and carrying a ton of bombs of all sizes and functions. The navy designation was PB4Y-1, indicating single, rather than twin tail. Flying from army airfields, they received the same treatment the 13th got from the navy: "This land-based navy squadron was reported by the 5th Army Air Force. Our kills were credited in the news as "MacArthur's Bombers." They enjoyed the same Morotai amenities: "Our recreation was digging foxholes. The population of pythons and boa constrictors was unsettling. Japanese breakthroughs were ever present. We conducted patrols regardless of weather." On one mission, Stevens shot down Japanese Admiral Yamagata enroute to Tokyo for an audience with the emperor and promotion to secretary of the navy.

An interesting vignette is how the navy came to fly the army B-24. Early on it was apparent the PBY Catalina could barely survive in a hostile area during daylight hours. A deal was made. The Army Air Corps gave a number of B-24s to the navy in exchange for the navy relinquishing a Boeing production facility designed to produce an advance seaplane to replace the PBY. This facility produced the B-29.

We both moved up from Morotai to the Philippines where we began choking enemy shipping in the South China Sea. Japanese shipping along the China coast had been attacked by General Chennault's 14th Air Force early in the war, but after over-running our bases in China, Japan enjoyed a two year holiday until the Southwest Pacific planes took over the job. It was a combined operation. Navy Liberators flew daylight search missions as far north as Shanghai, joined by 13th Air Force planes from Morotai and Palawan. The surface navy could not blockade the China Sea without smashing enemy air bases along the coast that protected their convoys. The heavily defended harbors were a refuge for shipping. In addition to ships, our targets included air bases along the China and Indo-China coast and Hong Kong, Saigon and Canton. The air campaign against Saigon began when 13th Air Force B-24s bombed the harbor.

From Philippine bases we both flew against enemy operations in Mindanao, Leyte, Ormoc, Lingayen, Palawan, Cebu, Luzon, Negros, Mindoro, Panay, Borneo, Celebes, Makassar Straits, Balikpapan, Brunei, Sandakan, Indo-China, Hong Kong, Swatow, Okinawa and Formosa.

Once his damaged plane was repaired by replacing its entire empennage with a tail taken from one of our damaged PBYs. He flew the rest of his tour in a navy plane with the tail adorned with 13th Air Force markings. For sure that qualified us as kissing cousins.

REFERENCES

Stevens, Paul F., *Low Level Liberators*, Markville, Tenn., 1997

CHAPTER TWENTY-FIVE

Bill, A Fighter Pilot

There were two Super-Aces in the 13th Air Force. I have the good fortune to know one of them. He collaborated enthusiastically in the development of this book, giving suggestions, references, and always encouraging the project. His name is Bill Harris. Today he is the greatest living

Lt. Colonel William Harris

Ace of the 13th Air Force. This chapter is sourced either from a book about Bill, or what he told me personally.

Sometimes our paths crossed. His last mission landed at Balikpapan. My plane had flown the first mission to land there. On August 1, 1945, Bill led a flight of seven P-38s on a sweep to Java. They refueled at Balikpapan and flew on to Java where they encountered the greatest concentration of trains ever encountered in Indonesia. Their bullets ruptured the boilers, and by the time they turned for home thirty-seven trains were destroyed. Bill opines that was probably the most locomotives ever destroyed by a single fighter strike. When they returned, they had been airborne eleven hours and forty minutes and covered 2,500 miles. With typical European gratitude, the Dutch government filed a complaint for damaging their property.

With this mission, Lt. Colonel Bill Harris ended his military career. General Barnes offered Bill a full Colonel's rank on the spot if he would remain. Bill said, "General the war is over for me. It's time to go home." The General held out his hand and said: "I'm sure Colonel Harris that you are a chosen man of God. He has been visible through you and your conduct. He has given you ability and skill far beyond the average pilot. Your fellow pilots and the Americans you served with as well, recognized this and felt more serene in your presence. There is no greater honor that can be bestowed on you. May God continue to be with you."

I recognized Bill Harris as a remarkable example of what were once called "gentlemen flyers." Nor am I the first to do so. Brooklyn Harris, no relation, was Intelligence Sergeant of the 339th Fighter Squadron on Guadalcanal. Brooklyn was so taken with Bill he wrote an intimate book called Bill, A Fighter Pilot. "There was something different about this quiet young man. He was a combat Pilot's Pilot. His 339th Squadron was one of the most effective squadrons of World War II. If Bill had been ambitious, he could have shot down many more enemy planes. Concerned with the safety of his pilots and protecting the bombers, he was more concerned with saving American lives than destroying enemies. This kind, gentle, Christian, God-loving man would become the top Ace of the 13th Air Force by the end of his first tour of duty. On a list of a few great Americans, Bill Harris would head the list. Bill's life is living proof that love and respect are more powerful weapons than those used in war. Without these, civilization succumbs to slavery and tyranny."

Bill was the first 13th Air Force pilot to use napalm. General Barnes of the 13th Fighter Command learned that the 5th Air Force received a lot of napalm, but didn't want it. He asked Bill if he could get some. Bill says: "I contacted Dick Bong on Morotai, who said if I sent a cargo plane to Morotai, he would get some. We got a full C-47 load. I set up test targets and destroyed them completely with the napalm. General Barnes flew above me as I destroyed the targets. We used low-level attacks carrying napalm in 310 gallon belly tanks. When released, the tanks tumbled end over end, then slammed into the supply sheds. The tanks burst, throwing searing flames to each side, leaving an area of total destruction. At last, we found a weapon fighters could use against surface targets. We napalm-bombed Mapia, where the Japanese had a radio station. We hit the barracks and radio station from 100 feet altitude. Next day the Navy sent a landing force to Mapia. The installations no longer existed. The Japanese gunners were still in their gun positions, but were burned to a crisp!"

In July 1945, Bill led eight P-38s on a mission to Surabaya, Java to dive bomb shipping: "I saw a large merchant vessel. I peeled off and dove on the ship, but the bomb did not explode. I was at 6,000 feet descending at 550 miles an hour. As I tried to pull the plane out of the dive, it did not respond. I was in compressibility. As the air got more dense closer to the water, the trim started the nose coming up so suddenly that I blacked out. When I recovered, the plane was flying straight and level. I gathered the scattered Flight and returned to Balikpapan. Back at base my Crew Chief informed me the wings were bent up eight inches and would have to be replaced."

George Chandler, himself an Ace, told me about Bill in respectful tones. *"Bill Harris was and is a unique man. He is an exceptionally skillful pilot, but his skill as a shooter was almost unbelievable. On one mission Bill climbed into a circle of Zeros, shot down one and then, whipping back, got another one. Keys to Bill's success are confidence and knowledge. He knew when he fired at a Zero, he would hit it. I could not shoot a 40 degree reflection shot and hit anything. I had to come up straight behind the target and shoot it dead ahead. I know that the 13th Air Force command wanted to develop Bill as their top Ace who could outshine Richard Bong of the 5th Air Force. They offered him all kinds of special missions like Bong was flying. A skilled pilot with a good wingman can find planes to shoot with little risk. With gun cameras to prove his victories he can run up his score. It aggrandizes a particular pilot. It tells you about Bill Harris that he declined, concentrating on protecting the bombers and training young pilots. His conduct was great for pilot morale during these times of heavy losses. On four different times over Rabaul, he came home with an engine shot out and a plane riddled with bullet holes. He is a Pilot's Pilot, and a great leader."*

George Chandler told me that Bill Harris is a real life story of the values of a man who loves his family, his country and his God. These traits are not unique in America, but are the substance of it. He was a pilot who pre-thought risks and was ready for the unexpected because if you were unprepared that was not the time to begin solving a problem. From the moment a pilot released his brakes and accelerated for take off, his odds of living lowered and those of death increased. A tire blown, a collapsed landing gear, an engine stall during take off probably meant instant death by fire.

This episode demonstrated his super-human flying skill: *"February 19, 1944, was a particularly difficult mission. I was leading a flight of 16 P-38s protecting a low-level B-25 strike against Vunakanau. There were about forty Nips in the air. We kept the Zeros from diving down on the bombers. But they got my right engine. I managed to shoot one down. I decided I could lead the Zeros off if I dived for the deck. Several followed me down. I had to shut my right engine down. I beat them to the deck by about five seconds. There was a heavy sea running. This permitted me to get down in the trough and have the waves above each side of the plane. This made me a difficult target from the sides. The Zeros took turns trying to get down in the trough behind me. When the tracers flew by, I pulled up, slid over a crest and got down in the next trough. My thoughts were on a higher authority than man, and I said: 'Lord, if you have anything more for me to do, you better give me some help. I'm about at the end of my rope.' Suddenly the Zeros pulled up. I turned and saw a P-38 which knocked them off me."*

Fighter pilots by their nature are aggressive and often loud. Bill was never loud or profane. His strongest denunciation of the Nips was "rascals." Bill was loved by his crew chief and the admiration was mutual. Bill apologized for all the extra work he caused plugging bullet holes and changing engines. The crew chief said: "Captain Harris, its easier for me to fix them than for you to get them. Your plane will be ready for you tomorrow." And it always was.

Shortly after the Leyte invasion, the 18th Fighter Group was sent an urgent request for help from Admiral Halsey, who had been decoyed north chasing Ozawa's bait. The Japanese were closing in on Leyte from the rear at Ormoc Bay, with a convoy of four troop ships and four destroyers that could decimate our landing force. The 18th found the convoy and sank all the transports so that no soldiers landed behind MacArthur's forces. They earned a Presidential Citation for that fire drill.

One mission Bill speaks of is the one that saved Cabantuan prison camp and the Ranger Battalion that parachuted in to protect it. The Japanese planned to kill every prisoner. A Japanese force of 6,000 men which would have overrun the Rangers and the Prison was intercepted on emergency orders. Bill reported: "We were told to get all the explosive power we could muster. We rushed 21 planes into the air with two 1,000 pound bombs on each. In ninety minutes we were airborne. We caught them and obliterated 5,000 Japanese, their trucks and tanks. Our strike saved hundreds of prisoners and the Ranger Battalion. I don't know of another mission in which a squadron of P-38s did more damage to the enemy or saved so many lives of our own."

One of Bill's closest friends was Colonel Robert Westbrook, who along with Bill comprised the two top fighter Aces in the 13th. "Westy" Westbrook shot down twenty planes and was the 13th's leading Ace. From Hollywood, he was movie star handsome. His six-foot-two-inch frame and blonde hair made him the model for the fictional Steve Canyon.

Flying a great many missions in several tours of duty, he rapidly rose from Second Lieutenant to Lieutenant Colonel. Along the way he was awarded the Distinguished Service Cross, Distinguished Flying Cross, Silver Star and Air Medal with fifteen Oak Leaf Clusters. Westbrook of the 347th Fighter Group was shot down attacking a "Flak Trap" ship in the Makassar Straits near the Celebes, 900 miles from his base at Middleburg. A "flak-trap" is a transport ship whose deck is covered with guns that throw up blankets of fire. This loss stunned the entire Fighter Command. It put a heavy burden on Bill, who wrote: *"When I was alone, I prayed for spiritual strength to withstand the loss, for his family, and for assurance that his heroic deeds, for all of mankind, would confirm final victory in this war, and that he would be remembered for eternity."*

Colonel Robert Westbrook

In my interviews with Bill Harris, I found him every inch the true-blue American Brooklyn Harris extolled. We produced a stream of correspondence as he encouraged me to write this history. His own words are a window on this remarkable man and his flying machine:

"Your questions remind me of things that I had completely forgotten, of interest probably only to me, but maybe they save our history.

"What a wonderful feeling it was after coming off the target and seeing the Cat down there ready to pick up a downed pilot or crew. I have flown cover on those Cats when we had men in the water, and how the PBYs stayed alive on those pick-ups I will never know. They used to go right into Simpson Harbor at Rabaul and pick up our downed pilots while the shore batteries were firing from every direction. That Cat would hit the water, throw out a life preserver, drag the guy in while picking up speed to take off. I still get tears in my eyes just remembering the chances they took to save one or two. In the Sealark Channel, they picked up three downed P-38 pilots on one mission. One mission to the Celebes they picked up Strader right out of the bay. To me they were the real heroes and anytime they wanted a cover flight our outfit was sure ready to go.

"There is a parable in the bible about a landowner that was to be gone from his place for a time and he gave five pieces of money to one of his laborers, two to another and one to another. When he came back he got his laborers together and asked the one with five pieces of money how he did. The laborer had doubled his money, and he said 'Well done'. The one with two pieces also had doubled his money and he said 'Well done'. The one with one piece hid his and was useless. He was like the pilot that would always have a rough engine when we had a tough mission and would return to base. After a few of those, I would see that they were sent back to the states. They were a danger to everybody in the flight.

"I used to fly the mail on my off days to Munda and the Russells in an old Norden Norseman and had to know all the places the Japs had guns so I could go around them. It kept me watching all the time so I could do evasive maneuvers when their guns started blinking at me.

"After Munda was taken and the Seabees repaired the strip, the Marine F4Us were supposed to be first to land with pictures taken and all that stuff the big heroes get. Two of our P-38 boys found out about it and just before the F4Us were to fly in formation over the field and land, one of the P-38s called a May-Day, cut his engines and landed, followed by his wing man. It caused confusion and messed up the whole situation. I am sure the Marines smelled a rat but never could prove it. The pilot that did that was later shot down over Rabaul."

This is the prayer, author unknown, Bill carried with him and shared with pilots in his squadron.

A FLYER'S PRAYER

Dear God, give us strength to beat the foe,
Refresh our courage as we go
Instruct our leaders from above
And shelter those at home we love
Dear God, protect us as we fly,
Oh grant us mercy, should we die,
To fight and conquer, Lord, we must,
Be with us, for our cause is just.

The stories about this legendary Ace remind me of Michener's line about Lt. Brubaker in *The Bridges of Toko-Ri*—"Where do we find men like these"?

REFERENCES

Harris, Brooklyn, *Bill, A Pilot's Story*, Klamath Falls, Oregon, Graphic Press, 1995

CHAPTER TWENTY-SIX

Philippines and Clark Field

The 13th Air Force supported MacArthur's return to the Philippines, whose pleasant islands were welcome from the fetid, fever swamps of New Guinea. The Philippine archipelago runs north-south for a thousand miles. Its 7000 islands are rich in lumber, minerals and food. The Philippine people, unlike other Asians, did not regard Japanese as liberators. Instead, they fought the Japanese and were always friendly to us. Tagalog is the native language, but they also spoke English and Spanish, Spain having occupied the islands for 300 years. Although little known, the savagery of the Philippine campaign is shown by a single statistic: Japan lost 400,000 soldiers there, more than they lost at Guadalcanal, Iwo Jima and Okinawa combined. The fight for Leyte alone cost Japan 70,000 casualties against our 15,000. At various times I flew missions from Leyte, Mindoro, Cebu, Palawan, Panay, Luzon, Mindanao and Cuyon, the Leper Colony. At that time, I knew Philippine geography better than Texas.

We staged missions from Zamboanga on the savage southern island of Mindanao. The Operations shack had a sign reading: "They have no tails in Zamboanga." Mindanao is second in size to Luzon. The mountains are rugged and remote. They became the sanctuary for Colonel Fertig, the colorful U.S. Army officer who refused to surrender and took to the hills. He surrounded himself with a band of guerrillas who bedeviled the Japanese with raids furtive and deadly. The frustrated Japanese were never able to put him out of business. MacArthur kept him supplied with the toys of war. One such mission was flown by our PBY landing on Lake Lanao in remote mountains to deliver radio equipment to his guerrillas.

What sticks with me about Mindanao are the Moros, descendants of African Moors. They are Muslims and very different from other Filipinos. They were wild-looking, mean and spoke no English. They had names like Abdul and Mohammed and were as ugly as Yassir Arafat. Moros don't like anybody, but preferred us to Japanese. The fierce Moros forced the U.S. Army in the Spanish-American War to adopt the .45 caliber pistol because the .38 would not stop a charging Moro. Moros are the epicenter of Islamic militants now fomenting trouble in Southeast Asia.

A personal scalp-lifting experience with the Moros is unforgettable. For our entertainment and cigarettes, the Moros tied a captured Japanese to a tree, cut the skin across his shoulders and skinned him alive. I had skinning experience with rabbits, they being a Depression delicacy served with dumplings. Those rabbits however were deceased prior to the procedure. Moro skinning was a more lively operation. For cigarettes, the Moros traded me the kris knife used for skinning. This kris, with black bone handle and curved blade, is in the Hoover Archives.

My squadron joined the Philippine Liberation Campaign at Luzon. In the spring of 1945, we moved from Morotai to Clark Field. To the Second Emergency Rescue Squadron, Clark Field was "luxury." Out of the mud at last! There were wood floors and tents like a real room. Roads replaced quagmires. The natives were civilized, light-skinned and spoke English and Spanish. They were puppy friendly and hung around the tents offering to wash our clothes for cigarettes. Their washing machine consisted of an entire family pounding rocks on clothes in stream beds.

The laundry service at Clark Field

Here we encountered Negritos and Hukbalahaps. Militant bands of unpleasant Filipinos were called Huks, short for Hukbalahap. These were communist guerrillas whose raison d'etre was violent overthrow of the government. They still operate in Luzon. Both groups would steal, Negritos stole food and Huks stole weapons. Negritos were strange looking pygmies, primitive and furtive, with black skin and hair as kinky as brillo. "Negritos" is Spanish for "small, black ones." They'd drift onto Clark Field begging for food. They were aboriginal in the Philippines, living as hunters in the dense rain forests of Luzon. Thus isolated, they didn't interface with "civilization" and looked like what they were—aborigines. We called them "abos." There were also occasional banditos who infiltrated our perimeter. Once we surprised one in our tent. He received political indoctrination in the Law West of the Pecos. No más!

Some of the local "Negritos"

The Army Air Corps in the Philippines was destroyed by Japanese bombing Clark Field after they hit Pearl Harbor. At high noon they found our B-17s and pursuit planes lined up on the runway. Clark Field was soon rubble, wrecked by bombs and by Zeros. I have yet to see an official report explaining why our planes were wiped out in one raid, coming several hours after Pearl Harbor.

Manila, "Pearl of the Orient," is the heart of the Philippines. Located on Luzon, it is the government, cultural and commercial center. The huge naval base at Cavite lies across Manila Bay. In 1941, Western Pacific Army headquarters were in the rock fortress of Corregidor guarding Manila Bay. Clark Field was headquarters of the Army Air Corps. Its long, wide runways were a joy to behold after the skinny, short jungle strips. It had permanent structures and was in range of Formosa, Okinawa and China. It was our main Pacific air base until the Pinatubu volcano buried it a few years ago, and the Air Force transplanted its Pacific headquarters to Guam.

Japan had settled a severe and oppressive occupation across these pleasant people. The Japanese would torture them on a whim. Any suspected of aiding Americans were shot. After three years of The Rising Sun, Filipinos were ecstatic to see it set.

Clark Field was about sixty kilometers from Manila. When off duty, the adventurous would con a jeep from the motor pool for a foray into Manila. Even though in rubble and ruin, coming from Morotai, it seemed civilization at its highest.

MacArthur declared Manila an "open city" in 1941, rather than have

Corregidor with Bataan in the background

it destroyed. Nor did Yamashita defend the city in 1945. He took his 200,000 man army north into the mountains of Luzon. But there were 17,000 Japanese Imperial Marines left in Manila over whom he had no authority. They were under the command of Admiral Iwabachi who ordered a fight to the death. The only urban battle of the Pacific War was in Manila, street by street, building by building, room by room. In weeks of murderous fighting, the Japanese died to the last man, but not before massacring 100,000 civilians in the Rape of Manila.

I saw Manila soon after it was captured. The city was a shambles. The university, hospital and residential districts had been destroyed. The Government Center was wiped out. The 400 year old Intramuros Walled City was rubble.

William Man-
chester in *Goodbye Darkness* described the destruction of Manila:

"*The devastation of Manila was one of the great tragedies of World War II. Of allied cities, only Warsaw suffered more.*

A war-torn Manila

Eighty percent of the residential district and 100 percent of the business district were razed. Nearly 100,000 Filipinos were murdered by the Japanese. Hospitals were set afire after their patients had been strapped to their beds. The corpses of males were mutilated, females of all ages were raped before they were slain, and babies eyeballs were gouged out and smeared on walls like jelly."

Other than the rubble-soaked landscape that was Manila of 1945, I remember that for the first time I

Manila after the Japanese occupation ended, 1945

saw USO and Red Cross girls. From them you received smiles and cof-

The USO and Red Cross in Manila

fee, welcome gifts. Feminine forces avoided jungle bases. At Clark Field there was a PX where you could buy film. My 98¢ Kodak Brownie became freshly impregnated and remained so for the rest of the war. My photo collection of Luzon, Bataan, Corregidor, Manila and Okinawa is in the Hoover Archives.

Command and Control.

Only two or three crews of our squadron were initially dispatched to Clark Field. It was at Clark that I rose rapidly in the Air Force command structure, my genius being recognized at last. By this time, I had thirty or forty missions under my belt and my advanced age, twenty-three, pro-

vided me more college time than the nineteen-year-olds. Thus, I promptly rose to ranking intelligence officer, meteorological officer, supply officer, history officer and whatever slot was vacant on the Table of
Organization. The important slots of Operations and Engineering were
filled by men of competence. As the manning tables legitimately filled, I
was stripped of authority, but for a spit of time, I commanded all I sur-
veyed. Then it was back to business over Okinawa, Formosa and China.

The navy base at Cavite on Luzon became operational and the submarine fleet began operating from there. The navy always enjoyed an
abundance of riches, e.g., fresh food, ice cream, cold beer and even sheets
and pillows. Since we were amphibious we often dropped in on Cavite
Bay for scrounging. I traded a parachute for a Navy .38 revolver to replace
my Army automatic .45 caliber in which I had lost confidence in Borneo.
We had deposited General Blamey with his command during the invasion of Brunei Bay and were parked on the strip talking to some Aussie
soldiers when a Japanese soldier charged out of the trees hollering "banzai" and heading straight for me. I snatched my .45 automatic from its
holster and began firing at the hostile presence. In fire arms training, we
were taught to aim, take a deep breath, exhale slowly and gently squeeze
the trigger. The immediacy of the situation replaced my breathing and
squeezing exercise with pointing and shooting. The .45 has an enormous
kick which jerked my shooting arm straight up shooting at the sky.
Fortunately, an Aussie raised his tommy gun and splattered the villain. I
determined to replace that .45 and the Navy base provided the opportunity. Even after returning home, like many vets, I slept with that .38 under
my pillow.

Missions to Remember.

From Clark Field we flew two memorable missions—the recapture
of Hong Kong and the General Yamashita snatch. After the Nagasaki
bomb, but before V-J Day, we were on patrol over the Hong Kong sector
of the China coast, lost an engine and, rather than fly back across the
South China Sea on one engine in typhoon weather, became uninten-
tionally the first Americans to set foot in Hong Kong since its surrender
on December 25, 1941 (discussed in the Chapter: Hong Kong, Milton
Friedman & Me).

The other memorable mission involved General Yamashita.
Yamashita led the Japanese Army in the capture of Singapore, the
"unconquerable bastion of the British Empire." He was Japan's most celebrated general. Instead of attacking Singapore, its six golf courses and

1,000 tennis courts from the front in the teeth of its massive fortifications, Yamashita saddled up his army on bicycles and paddled down the Malayan Peninsula, approaching Singapore from the rear. Without a fight, General Percival surrendered a numerically superior British Army to Yamashita, henceforth dubbed the "Tiger of Malaya." Yamashita bragged that he would give MacArthur the same lecture he gave General Percival at Singapore: "All I want to know from you is 'yes' or 'no'."

Even after our army captured Manila, the battle for Luzon was far from over. Yamashita slipped his Fourteenth Army north, past Clark field and into the mountains and jungles of northern Luzon which became one giant graveyard. There were no roads. Trails hugged the sides of mountains shrouded in fog, drenched in downpours or wrapped in stifling heat. It was a trackless wilderness infested with Japanese caves. On a mountain track called the "Villa Verde Trail," our infantry fought for every yard. The Japanese were dug in so well that our artillery had no effect on their spider holes which harbored soldiers huddled in dark, dank caves, waiting to rush out and attack. Like rats, they would dart out of their hole, shoot guns or toss grenades, then scurry back. These spider holes were Yamashita's brainchild. He could not defeat us, but he could bleed units that might soon invade Japan. Although little known, Luzon was the largest and costliest campaign in the Pacific. Our six divisions suffered 40,000 casualties, 2,000 from kamikazes alone. The closer to Japan, the more fierce the fighting. When our soldiers entered Bayombong, they found the Japanese hospital with all the patients still there, all dead. Rather than let their wounded be captured, they went through the hospital wards shooting their own people.

Yamashita was still fighting when war ended, even without planes, ships or tanks. Japan's Luzon casualties were six times greater than at Iwo Jima. Yamashita refused to surrender until ordered to do so by the Emperor himself.

The Yamashita Snatch.

Sometime around V-J Day, my crew was called to the Operations shack for briefing on a secret mission.

General Yamashita

We were to fly a couple of VIPs to a rendezvous on a lake in north Luzon. Our PBY5A Catalina was the weapon of choice, since it was amphibious. We were given maps showing a small lake, isolated deep in the mountains. We were to arrive at a specified time, land on the water and taxi to the north shore. A Japanese party would emerge from the jungle. We were to take them aboard and fly them out. We were sworn to secrecy and ordered not to discuss the mission.

Next day we took off, landing on the lake on schedule. Sure enough, out of the jungles strode a burly, swaggering Japanese officer, complete with ribbons, samurai sword and some of his staff. They were quickly put on board our plane. We were not introduced, but I'm confident it was Yamashita. I sneaked some pictures with my Brownie.

The gunner on our crew was Pete, a street-mean guy from Brooklyn, whose hatred of the enemy was rabid. He had been in the 41st Division (called "Butchers" by Japan because they took no prisoners) in the early New Guinea campaigns of 1943 around Buna Mission. The fighting there was deadly. No prisoners were taken by either side. Pete survived, returned home and was recycled to the Pacific, where he was assigned to our crew as gunner, manning .50 caliber machine guns mounted aft in each blister.

Escape Out the Blister.

After taking off from the lake, we were cruising along at 8,000 feet over the jungle when Pete sidled up and nudged me in apparent consternation. "Lieutenant, one them Japs escaped out the blister." Recognizing the dynamics of the situation, I growled: "Damn you Pete, you're going to get us all court martialed." I then inquired if anybody witnessed the departure. He responded reassuringly, "Oh, no sir!"

The minute we landed, the passengers were whisked away by a cadre of MPs without discussion. Like the Yamamoto shoot down mission, also flown by the 13th Air Force, no notes were taken and no debriefing occurred.

REFERENCES

Breren, Wm. B., *Retaking The Philippines*, N.Y. St. Martins Press, 1986
Falk, Stanley, *Liberation Of the Philippines*, N.Y., Ballantine, 1971
Flanigan, E.M., *Corregidor, The Rock Force Assault*, Novato, CA, Presidio Press, 1995

CHAPTER TWENTY-SEVEN

Hong Kong, Milton Friedman & Me

To the utter astonishment of my friends and accomplices, I am priv-ileged to enjoy a personal friendship with Milton Friedman. Many years ago we met during a seminar conducted by the Hoover Institution at Stanford University. Milton was lecturing the political leaders of Romania, Bulgaria and Czechoslovakia on the topic: "Taking Eastern Europe Out Of The Red." Also on the panel was another Nobel Laureate, Gary Becker, a Hoover Fellow from the University of Chicago. The setting at Hoover is informal and cordial. Both Friedman and Becker being ten-nis players, we enjoyed some good doubles games. Over the years we have maintained correspondence, sprinkled with personal visits at Hoover Institution meetings.

In February 1997, the *Wall Street Journal* reported the visit of Milton and Rose Friedman to Hong Kong, where his fame and respect exceeds even that in the U.S. He cites Hong Kong as a prime example of capital-ism, where a tiny island with no natural resources other than industrious people has become one of the wealthiest enclaves on earth. On reading the article, I wrote Milton:

"I see where you are again in Hong Kong, wallowing in celebrity status and doling out autographs. Well sir, I, too was once a Hong Kong celebrity, circa August 1945. Therefore, I'm a Really Old China Hand, with unique personal involvement. Involuntarily, I was the first American to set foot in Hong Kong since its surrender on Christmas Day, 1941.

"In early 1945, my Squadron of the 13th Air Force was moved up from Morotai to Luzon when Clark Field was recaptured. From there, we staged north to Okinawa and patrolled the South China Sea across to the Chinese mainland searching for Japanese ships and American air crews which might have ditched in the ocean. When one of our planes went down, every effort was made to rescue the crew. The Japanese were sadistically brutal to cap-tured American flyers, who were first tortured and then gleefully beheaded in a ceremonial undertaking. The Chinese, on the other hand, were very friend-ly. The Chinese people helped us at great risk to themselves. Many Americans owe their lives to the Chinese who protected those who were shot

down over China. The movie Thirty Seconds Over Tokyo is an accurate por-trayal of the warm friendship between American flyers and the Chinese peo-ple.

"*In early August 1945, after the Hiroshima bomb, but before VJ Day, we were patrolling the South China Sea when we lost an engine. Both sides were under a cease fire, but nobody knew what that meant. I faced a diffi-cult decision for Playmate 71, our call sign that day. I could either turn back through terrible/typhoon weather and try to reach Clark Field on one engine, or I could take a chance and land in Hong Kong, not knowing what we would encounter there. We flew on to Hong Kong and landed at Kai Tek Airport. The Japanese controlled the airport. When we landed they belliger-ently surrounded our plane, brandishing their rifles with those long bayonets. We had pulled our .50 calibers off their gun mounts and stowed them out of sight, trying to look innocent. We handed some cigarettes out the cockpit window and pointed to the feathered prop on the starboard engine. There was a lot of excited jabbering amongst the Japanese, which we couldn't understand, but I did not like the body language. They were large of size, so I think they were Imperial Marines or maybe Koreans. It was obvious they couldn't decide what to do.*

"*I told Flight Engineer Schultz to open the cockpit very slowly, crawl out on the wing and try to get the engine started. This dragged on. Gradually, a few Chinese people edged out on the airfield and approached the plane, which was obviously American. They were fearful of the Japanese whom they clearly hated. They kept walking closer. Finally, one old man came near the cockpit and held up a beautiful Chinese black silk robe with a golden dragon embroidered on the back. I offered him a pack of cigarettes for it. Trade with China had begun.*" (It's now among the World War II items I donated to the Hoover Archives.)

A reply was soon received from Milton Friedman:
"*I found your letter of February 24 absolutely fascinating. I yield prima-cy to you as having landed in Hong Kong ten years before I first did. However, your letter left me completely baffled. How did you get off Hong Kong? You say how you got on, but not how you got off.*"

Proud to have baffled him, I replied:
"*I'm the only humanoid ever to baffle Milton Friedman. I got off Hong Kong just like I got on—on a wing and a prayer.*"

CHAPTER TWENTY-EIGHT

Kamikazes

Those two suicide bombers which pulverized the World Trade Center were not America's first kamikaze experience. Pacific veterans encountered such demonic destruction in 1944 when we returned to the Philippines. What began as a rain of death never stopped. Instead it

A group of kamikaze pilots

increased as Japan's suicide arsenal expanded to suicide boats, guided bombs and human torpedoes. Our losses were staggering. The damage was so great Nimitz banned news releases about kamikazes to prevent Japan learning just how successful they were. We suffered 10,000 casualties and lost hundreds of ships at Okinawa alone from 1,900 kamikaze attacks. There was no absolute defense against suicidal fanatics determined to die. No matter how thick the walls of flak thrown up to barricade, some always got through. Trying to stop a diving kamikaze is like trying to hit a bullet with a bullet. MacArthur reported: "Suicide attacks are one of our greatest threats." Then it was a terrible weapon which shocked the world. It is the same today.

The term "kamikaze" means "divine wind," sent by the sun goddess to shatter the invasion fleet of Kubla Kahn in the 13th Century. Kamikazes became Japan's ultimate weapon to defend the homeland. Since they could not defeat the Americans, this was their weapon of choice. Seppuku (suicide) innate in Japanese culture, was converted into an offensive weapon. A double-edged sword, it boosted morale at home and would demoralize Americans who could not withstand Japan's fighting spirit (Yamatodamashii). Eager kamikaze pilots prepared with ritual prayer, farewell poems, and the "thousand stitch belt" (a strap of cloth that 1,000 women had sewn, uniting themselves with the pilots' sacrifice). They sent fingernails and hair home, and distributed personal effects to the squadron members. They wrote their last letter home in their own blood. Sake, a gift from the Emperor was drunk in special lacquer cups. Their commander told them: "You are already gods. I shall watch you to the end and report to the Emperor." They then wrapped the traditional "Hachimaki" sash around their head and took off between rows of cap-waving fanatics. Thousands of young men eagerly flew such missions, consumed with desire to die for the Emperor.

Pilots took a seven-day kamikaze course. Two days were used to practice take-offs, two days on flying and three days of tactics. They didn't practice landings since there was no need to. Once they took off, they had no idea where they were. Trained pilots, like Judas goats would guide kamikazes to their targets. Then the veterans would return and round up another herd. At first, kamikazes tried ramming our planes, but switched to ships as more profitable targets. High altitude attacks began about five miles from the target and went into a steep dive. Low level attacks approached on the deck, then climbed and dove straight in. They came singly and in waves. Worst were the Kikusui (floating chrysanthemums), wolf packs of fifty to a hundred kamikazes, impossible to protect against. They also exacted an unseen toll as men fighting exhaustion were kept under continuous alert by kamikaze planes which roared in and blew men into the sky like broken dolls.

During the Leyte invasion in 1944, Admiral Onishi discovered he could enhance his striking power by flyers committed to death, which became an enormous multiplier of force. "If we are prepared to sacrifice a million lives in a kamikaze effort, victory will be ours. Each fighter must carry a 500 pound bomb and crash on a carrier deck. Your mission involves certain death. Your bodies will be dead, but not your spirits." The dead would levitate to Yakasuni Shrine and be revered forever.

Their access to our Leyte landing forces was simplified when Admiral Halsey took the Japanese bait and withdrew the big carriers to chase

Ozawa's empty fleet north. The kamikaze was an instant hit. Great destructive power was unleashed with a minimum of explosives. We were attacked every day. At Leyte, the cruiser Nashville was wounded. One crashed on the carrier St. Lo which sank in twenty minutes. The USS Franklin was hit. Kamikazes rammed six other escort carriers—White Plains, Kitkun Bay, Kalinin Bay, Santee, Suwanee and Petrol Bay. At Lingayen, kamikazes destroyed the escort carriers Ommaney Bay and Manila Bay, damaged battleships New Mexico and California, and cruisers Louisville, Columbia and Australia, along with 25 other ships and destroyers. Their smashing success pleased the Emperor who praised "the magnificent efforts of the Shikishima Units."

Next came the Iwo Jima campaign in which kamikazes sank the carrier Bismarck Sea, damaged carriers Saratoga, Bunker Hill, Lunga Point, Randolph and several other ships. Then at Okinawa, the carriers Essex, Franklin, Wasp and Enterprise were damaged. The closer we came to Japan, the greater our losses. We suffered more casualties on Iwo than did Japan.

Not only individual pilots, but entire squadrons went suicidal. In July 1945, Japan's Squadron of Aces, including Sakai and Oshibushi with 25 kills each, was led by Captain Genda, who planned the Pearl Harbor attack, against Task Force 38. Genda's orders were: "Destroy the enemy and retreat like a bolt of lightning." The U.S. Pacific Fleet suffered twenty-six ships sunk and 164 damaged by kamikazes during six weeks in 1945.

The Pacific also held exclusive franchise to the Ohta bomb, stubby manned missiles dropped from a mother plane. Its guidance system was a pilot literally strapped to the bomb. That terminal tactic earned its nickname "Baka," meaning stupid. Kamikazes and Bakas were spectacular, but not the only suicide weapons. Human torpedoes were in the sea and human bombs were in the sky. We were further entertained by suicide boats, and by Fukuyuris, strong swimmers with mines strapped to their back. Suicide submarines (Kaiten) were large torpedoes steered by the pilot riding in a housing on top. Like kamikaze pilots, young men selected were instant heroes. After minimum training, they were given leave. Sake and geishas were theirs. They wrote heroic poems: "May my death be as sudden and clean as shattering crystal, like cherry blossoms let us fall pure and radiant." Prior to their mission, toasts would be drunk, and the Warriors Song sung. They strapped on martyr headbands, just as today's terrorists do.

Even battle-hardened Americans were stunned by kamikazes. These planes didn't evade. They rammed. They weren't experienced pilots, since there's no such thing as an experienced kamikaze pilot. But their attacks were terrifying. They believed that was their one-way ticket to Yakasuni shrine, where they would lie in constant revelry among surroundings that, restated in terms of today's Islamic kamikazes, equates to seventy virgins in green fields who never get sick or defecate. Murama Takaji, a twenty-year-old kamikaze pilot, bragged "it would be a great honor to crash into an American ship. I hear there are many pretty geishas in the next life."

Nimitz wanted the Army B-29s to strike air bases of the kamikazes. LeMay demurred, saying big bombers were not effective against concealed planes. Admiral King then suggested that if the army air forces were not willing to pitch in against the kamikazes, the navy might decide to stop delivering supplies to the bombers. B-29 raids on Kyushu continued, but they never stopped the kamikazes. Even so, at times ninety percent of Air Force missions were flown to protect the fleet.

Kamikaze tactics were used by the mighty Japanese battleships "Yamato," "Nagato" and "Haruna." With fuel for only a one-way voyage, Yamato sortied as a suicide weapon to beach on Okinawa and spend its last firepower on Americans. Orders were "to fire every gun of every ship until the ammunition was gone." Survivors were to join their land forces and fight to the end where they would "find glory." And thus they steamed out of the Inland Sea heading for Okinawa. The armada was intercepted by U.S. planes which bombed and torpedoed the Yamato for three hours before she was sunk along with her escorting ships. In the greatest naval suicide in history, six warships and thousands of sailors went to the bottom.

We saw up close planes, ships and soldiers determined to die. We witnessed mass military and civilian suicides on Saipan and Okinawa. We saw an entire nation committed to victory or death. They fought until they died. Japan was prepared to sacrifice a nation rather than surrender. Ten million people were homeless. Their cities were crematories, except for their sacred city of Kyoto, which we graciously spared. Their navy was destroyed. Their army in the islands was dead or dying. Kamikazes were their weapon, suicide was their strategy. 5,000 kamikaze planes had been carefully husbanded on the homeland. "They would sink the entire U.S. fleet in Tokyo Bay" was their boast. Farmers were armed with spears and women with sticks. Women who tossed their babies off cliffs and jumped after them are serious people. We will fight on "if we are forced to eat weeds, gnaw sand and sleep in the hills." People were issued two hand grenades. They would throw one at the Americans and blow themselves up with the last one.

At home, Japan husbanded 2,000,000 troops and thousands of kamikaze planes. The people thought of themselves as a national suicide unit. "The Japanese spirit is like mountain cherry blossoms, radiant in the morning sun. The shattering of the hundred million is like a beautiful jewel." Seeing a nation intent on national suicide whose final writhing could take down a million Americans, Truman, fearful of Japan's fanaticism decided to end the war in a decisive way, dropped our ultimate weapon, recording in his memoirs: "Let there be no mistake, the bomb was a military move, and I never had any doubt it must be used." Remember, the first atom bomb at Hiroshima did not stop the Japanese. Not until after the second bomb at Nagasaki did the Emperor decide to call it quits.

Although these were our first kamikazes, now we know they were not our last. They were conscious efforts of dedicated people whose calm acceptance of death demonstrates the impact of ideology. They were terrorists, pure and simple, invoking terror to demoralize. They cannot be reasoned with. We knew they were trying to kill us. We knew we must kill them first, swiftly as we could and decisively as we must. During America's long holiday from history, there has developed a notion that terrorists can be talked to tranquility, a misapprehension media magnified. Better we should study Clausewitz's Principles of War: "Draw on the wisdom of those who've gone before."

America forgets those kamikaze attacks at its peril. Today's terrorists are kamikazes, evil and evasive. These have no morality and know no borders. They are not site specific. Their time is endless. Their threat spans the planet. America is at risk, while others offer to hold our coat. Our sliver of land and slice of people is the custodian of human freedom. Terrorists abhor freedom.

In 1940, Winston Churchill, with his nation at risk, sagely forecast: "Long dark months of trials and tribulations lie before us. Not only great dangers, but many misfortunes, many mistakes, many disappointments will surely be our lot. Death and sorrow will be the companions of our journey; hardships our garment; valor our only shield. We must be united, we must be undaunted. Our qualities and our deeds must burn and glow until they become the beacon of our salvation."

Robert Conquest, the distinguished Hoover Institution scholar, wrote in Reflections on a Ravaged Century: "The Century's disasters have been due in a major way to ignorance of history."

REFERENCES

Coox, Alvin, Japan, *The Final Agony*, N.Y., Ballantine, 1971
Foster, Simon, *Okinawa, 1945*, London, Armour Press, 1995
Hallas, James, *Killing Ground On Okinawa*, London, Praeger, 1996
Mitsuru, Yoshida, *Requiem For Battleship Yamato*, Tokyo, Kodansha, 1985
Schultz, Duane, *The Last Battle Station*, N.Y., St. Martin's Press, 1985
Skatea, John Ray, *The Invasion of Japan*, Columbia, South Carolina, South Carolina University Press, 1994

CHAPTER TWENTY-NINE

V-J Day and Clare Boothe Luce

One day a "really old" guy showed up with his B-4 bag and dropped it on an empty cot in our tent at Clark Field. There wasn't any "Welcome Aboard" hubba hubba. Nobody pushed conversation. He was a disconnect, a guy forty plus amongst nineteens and twenties. Tent mates moved in and out. Sometimes, if a tent mate didn't return, somebody was ordered to collect their effects. A hated job that made your skin weep, bundling up letters and moldy clothes (they all reeked of jungle), and sending them to a family immersed in grief. After a few days, I began conversing with him. Captain David Boothe was engaging and worldly wise beyond our mien.

The intellectual horizon of our young crews was limited. Only a small fraction had been to college. Compared to today we were antediluvian. There were guys who had never driven cars, who had never spent a night away from home, who had never been outside their own county. Because of my vast intellectual horizons, college

Author David Witts with David Boothe

and FBI training, I became Boothe's tete a tete compadre. We talked a lot. He was reserved, never caroming into Manila for entertainment. We flew some missions together. He was also an L-5 pilot (a Piper Cub that flew low and slow, observing enemy lines). He had been an artillery spotter for an infantry division slogging along in New Guinea, but got transferred out of that dead end. I figured if I were checked out in a Piper Cub, I could buzz around kind of a one man Filipino Baedeker. So I asked Boothe to check me out in an L-5. (This will send P-38 Aces like Rex Barber, Bill Harris and George Chandler cackling). He agreed and, I must say, he was not a cowboy. He checked the wings, prop, aileron and rudder for nicks.

Then engine run-up, fuel check and controls. Only after checking all operating devices, would he take off. Even in a Piper Cub, he wasn't "get in and go."

Clare Boothe Luce, I learned, was his sister. I knew of her from Broadway plays, from TIME magazine published by her husband Henry Luce, and from her service on the House Armed Services Committee. Leaving a brilliant trajectory in her wake, she was a genuine celebrity at a time when there were few female celebrities. Beauty, brains, career and power, she had it all. Today, you find those talents fragmented in individuals, but I know none who has them all in combo She was a talented, balanced and beautiful "feminist." Eleanor Roosevelt and Frances Perkins were nationally prominent, but bereft of other qualifications.

Military orders reached our Squadron ordering personnel hither and yon. They were always signed by an Adjutant. One day an order for Boothe came in signed simply, MacArthur. I can still see those letters, so singularly empathic fifty years later. David Boothe had earned a rest leave in Australia and it was time to go. I never knew how red tape got short-circuited, but I was awed. Boothe was no dilettante or draft dodger as he might well have been. He was mean, tough, and combative. He survived the New Guinea graveyard.

V-J Day dawned on us at Clark Field. When word came the war was over, reactions were explosive, emotionally and ballistically. Shooting and shouting was everywhere. We emptied our .45s and carbines into the skies. Down at the flight line tracers laced the sky. Jeeps were doing wheelies around revetments. Sequestered booze materialized from our two-ounce ration, doled out after each mission and hoarded into a critical mass -- therapy enhanced by quantity. In all this frenetic madness, Boothe disappeared. Looking for him, I found him draped over the barbed wire, crying. I thought he had been shot during the revelry. Why are you crying? Without looking up he said, "We'll just have to do this all over again against the Russians." That was a scenario beyond my comprehension, having studied Economics from professors who taught that Communism is good, Capitalism is bad. Certainly a college professor could not be wrong, else why would he be a professor? I have since learned the difference between the two systems. Lots of professors have not.

Although we neither understood nor comprehended an atomic bomb, its repercussions spread far beyond the blast area. It saved the life of every prisoner of war who survived because Japan intended to kill all prisoners. Japan's home islands garrisoned 2,000,000 troops frenzied to die for the Emperor. 2,000 planes had been husbanded for kamikazes. The blood bath which would have washed across American soldiers would have exceeded any carnage in our history. The mass surrender of German armies in Europe would not be duplicated in the Pacific. When the guns of war fell silent, joy and relief were accompanied by a determination to punish those who had treacherously attacked us and then tortured, maimed and starved all who fell in their grasp. That determination was fueled by the pathetic condition of the surviving prisoners who, though scarred, diseased and emaciated, when freed struggled to stand erect to salute the American flag as tears blotted their eyes

After V-J Day, priority in returning home was determined by "points," which were earned by time overseas, missions flown, decorations, dependents and other mystic G.I. criteria. I completed my fiftieth mission about the time of Hiroshima, so I had sufficient points to make the return roster. Flyers were often given the option of flying a "war weary" plane or waiting for a ship billet. "War wearies" were planes lined up on the runways with no visible defects. It was pretty much climb in, grab some maps, gas up and head east. Lots of guys chose this exit strategy. Those distances were so daunting, those planes' health so problematical, I chose discretion over acceleration.

When my ship came in, I boarded it at Manila. The trip was blessedly uneventful. Men were stuffed and stacked like sardines, but officers had individual bunks and space to sit on the deck in chairs, a real luxury. There was ice on board which, after that stultifying heat, was angel's breath. It was hot when we left Manila, but cold caught up with us somewhere in the North Pacific. We had only GI khakis. Deep thinkers amongst us had jammed flight jackets in our B-4 bags and were comforted thereby. We sailed into San Francisco beneath the Golden Gate Bridge, where tradition demanded disposal of 'gook money'. Golden Gate Bridge became a Trevi Fountain of coins.

Japanese war currency

We didn't dock in San Francisco, but migrated up stream to Richmond. When I walked down the gang plank, I dropped to my hands and knees and feverishly kissed my own, my native land. Nor was I the only one to do so.

"Processed" there, we received orders for leave and travel. My orders levitated me back to Washington D.C. on a Pullman train with real berths and white sheets. I endowed the Red Cap (people who did service jobs on the trains) not to fold up my berth but leave it down. For three days and nights I decompressed in that cocoon, emerging fitfully for food and drink. Exhaustion overwhelmed. Once home, everybody's stated agenda was the same—the first year, sit in a rocking chair. Second year, rock.

You were discharged where you joined. Since I bailed out of the FBI to join the Air Corps, my exit was celebrated at Ft. Meade, near Washington, D.C., where I received little boxes with gold trim and some pay. The boxes were a nuisance. The pay was a blessing.

My first stop was at 3701 Ingomar in Chevy Chase, a large home where I roomed while working in Washington. It was a memorable return to Marilyn, a beauty from the Pennsylvania Poconos. She faithfully corresponded with me, engendering visions of sugar plum fairies on my return. My gratitude knew no bounds. Nor did my exuberance. I now understood what we were fighting for.

Before I shipped out of Clark Field, David Boothe wrote his sister Clare Boothe Luce in Congress, that I would be homing in at D.C., and would she treat me to the Blue Plate Special. He gave me the letter and asked that I mail it soon as I hit stateside. I called Clare Boothe Luce's office and was connected instanta. "Where was I and when could I come down?" Her warm response surprised me since I figured on nothing but a dutiful "welcome home." She insisted on sending a car for me. I scrubbed, donned clean khakis and headed for the Capitol. Meeting her

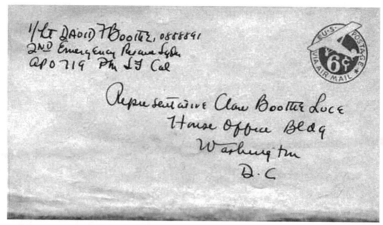

A letter posted to Clare Boothe Luce

was a dynamic experience. Beautiful, vivacious and electrifying, she insisted on showing me around. First she took me to Sam Rayburn's office, the House Speaker, where she introduced me as her friend and with political twist, telling him I was from his District. Then over to the Senate to meet the Majority Leader, and then the Vice President. She strode in every office without protocol. Whatever was going on took five when she pranced in. She and everybody else, treated me like somebody. The military was not loathed then.

She took me to Congress where I saw a debate I still remember. There was a little guy yapping who she identified in scurrilous tones as "that little communist son-of-a bitch Vito Marcantonio." Never in my life had I heard a lady curse. I was stunned. She explained "the strength of America lies in its heartland, not in the hands of these east coast wimps." That intelligence contradicted my depression era professors extolling the virtues of communism. That was my epiphany on communism. If Clare Boothe Luce said communism was evil, then it must be so. From that moment on, I became, and remain, a virulent anti-communist, knowing its depredations and seeing its ungodly evil. She talked about politics and religion. Clare had me chauffeured to her and Henry Luce's mansion in Connecticut, where I was bedazzled by Chinese art. Then to their plantation in South Carolina, Mepkin I think it was called, where I was exposed to gracious southern living, an event long overdue.

Boothe had told me of Clare's first marriage to a man named Brokaw (I think), who he said was a drunk that Clare subsequently ditched in a Reno drive-by. Their daughter Anne was the delight of Clare's life. She was in college when hit by a car. She was devastated. This was a sorrow from which she never recovered.

David told me of her marriage to Henry Luce, which as best I could tell was one of convenience. Luce, he told me, was an oddball. Raised in China by missionary parents, his was not an engaging personality. David disliked Luce and called him "that four flushing bastard" because he put a guilt trip on Clare, claiming she rendered him sexually impotent. For this "offense" Luce demanded a divorce. This was a terrible cross for her to bear since she adopted Catholicism in a heavy conversion. I recall she met with the Pope and with Bishop Fulton Sheen on her dilemma.

David didn't believe Luce's claims of Clare-induced impotence. When he returned to the U.S. from Clark Field, he set Luce up. To prove to Clare that Luce was lying, she packed for a weeks trip to Connecticut and departed. Quite unexpectedly, she returned to their apartment in the Waldorf. When she walked in, David said: "she caught the bastard in the hay with some broad."

David died like he lived, at full speed. He enjoyed a colorful life in pre-war Wall Street, as a running buddy of Bernard Baruch's son. Each day after the market closed, David and Baruch Jr. went to their club, played squash and refreshed for the evening's activities, consisting of "booze and broads" in his words. Variety was the order of the day, in partners and activities. I recall the name Peaches Browning, but the context is lost. Boothe also knew Damon Runyon whose philosophy he admired. He often quoted Runyon: "In life, it ain't all straights and flushes; if you're looking for a message in life, go to Western Union." He knew the guys with strange names from Runyon's books—*Harry the Horse, Spanish John, Big Nig* and *Guinea Mike.*

At that time movies were being made about the war. Clare offered to get David a job in Hollywood. He wasn't excited at the prospect, claiming Hollywood was full of "fags and phonies." But it was a soft-money job. He went to California from where he stayed in touch with me. One day I got a letter saying, "Things didn't work out between Sis and me, which is either very good or very bad. You'll be getting some money, which I want you to send to this girl who I promised money to get her teeth fixed."

A few days later an article appeared in the paper: *Brother of Clare Boothe Luce Killed.* "*David Boothe, while flying a single engine plane off the coast of Santa Monica, in clear weather plunged into the Pacific at high speed.*" Sure enough, sometime later a check came to me, which I arranged for delivery to a certain lady. David Boothe's correspondence with me is in the Hoover Archives, along with other war time correspondence.

When I got home, I had about a year of law school to finish. Enrolled at SMU, I was named editor-in-chief of the Law Review, founded the Barristers Society and hit the streets looking for a job, which were few and far between in 1948.

Section III

THE HIDDEN HOLOCAUST

The neglected subject of World War II is "hidden holocaust"—the story of bestial savagery inflicted on those who fell under the shadow of Japan's battle flag.

No act was beyond Japan. They shot our pilots in their parachutes. They transported captives to factories and mines in packed and suffocating hell ships. They starved and beat prisoners, beheaded, crucified, burned or buried them alive. Prisoners were nailed to trees and used for bayonet practice. Japan developed and implemented a vast germ warfare program whose doctors experimented on American flyers. Dragooning thousands of young women to service their soldiers on straw mats across Asia is a degeneracy without precedent.

None will ever know how many millions died from starvation and disease, slave labor and torture emanating from Japan's aggression.

This great tragedy of the Pacific war is compounded by its obscurity. History's darkest deeds lay buried, unreported by scribes and unseen by the world. Its perpetrators mostly avoided punishment for their crimes. Its victims, unorganized and inarticulate, without voice or champion, slowly fade away as they walk their last mile into the dark shadow of the setting sun.

CHAPTER THIRTY

Japan's Prisoner of War Camps

Japan's savagery was indiscriminate, unrepentant, unpunished and unknown, falling on men and women, soldiers and civilians, Asians and Caucasians. Japanese soldiers did not surrender. Their oath required "I will never suffer the disgrace of being taken alive." Japan had neither sympathy for prisoners, nor a system to contain them. At Manila, Hong Kong and Singapore, large scale surrenders forced Japan to establish prison camps. Their scorn of prisoners was so imbedded that even guarding prisoners was dishonorable, and many guards were misfits or insane. At Singapore with thousands of prisoners on hand, the Japanese commander inquired "what can I do with these dogs?"

American Prisoners of War in Luzon

The death rate at Japan's POW camps often approached extinction. The camp at Sandakan near Brunei Bay, held 3,000 prisoners—six survived. Stalag Luft 3 in Germany held 10,000 prisoners. All survived. Nazi crimes should not be trivialized. Japanese crimes should not be ignored.

When the war ended and prisoners were freed, people learned the death rate of American prisoners approached 50% and the torture rate 100%. Guilt was not punished. The Tokyo Trials dawdled with Japanese war criminals. Only seven Class A criminals were executed. Most others were never tried. Japanese war crimes trials were a joke in context of the intense, highly publicized Nuremberg trials in Germany, which brought justice not only to military, but also corporate officials, cabinet officers, national leaders and police like the SS and Gestapo. War criminals were tracked down all over the world, tried and sentenced by courts in countries where they had committed offenses, pursuant to the U.N. decree that "criminals will be pursued to all corners of the globe."

The International Military Tribunal's Tokyo trials were slow, fractious and marked by bickering. The prosecution took six months. The defense dawdled for eleven months, using more depositions than witnesses. Germans were meticulous record keepers, Japan destroyed all evidence and killed witnesses. Other than Tojo, the criminals were a nameless faceless collection unlike Herman Goering, Goebbels, Himmler and cronies that were front page news for years. Tokyo trials took place in the squat, ugly Sugamo prison which closed its doors in 1956, and set its inmates free. Only in the Philippines, where trials were conducted by MacArthur, were proceedings structured and decisive. Generals Yamashita and Homma were tried, their appeals heard by the U.S. Supreme Court and in time were duly executed. Japan's war criminals went on to Parliament and industry. Hirohito made a triumphant world tour and Japan's war crimes were forgotten and forgiven.

The only large scale capture of Americans occurred in the Philippines. MacArthur pleaded he was fighting a war "stony broke, reduced to slings and arrows." He sent frantic calls for help: "Just three planes so I can see," he begged. Philippine President Quezon cried out: "America writhes in anguish at the fate of a distant cousin Europe, while a daughter, the Philippines, is raped in the back room." Roosevelt sent Quezon a New Year's message: "I can assure you that every available vessel is bearing strength that will crush the enemy." Chief of Staff Marshall cabled MacArthur: "a stream of four-engine bombers is en route—another stream of bombers started today from Hawaii." MacArthur passed on the encouraging news: "Help is on the way." But no ship or soldier was ever sent, none was ever planned. MacArthur had been led to deceive his troops because Roosevelt would not confess to America the Philippines were abandoned. That deception plagued MacArthur throughout the war. Derisively he was called "Dugout Doug."

As the Japanese Empire exploded across the Pacific, only the Battling Bastards of Bataan resisted, and to the death as it were. Abandoned and starving, the Americans fought on. Talk of mile long relief convoys that never arrived added to the bitterness. Men scrounged for food, eating dogs, cats, lizards and monkeys. They ate their horses and mules. They gnawed on roots and leaves. Japan's timetable for conquest of the Philippines was one month. Yet that scrappy garrison held out for six months. Another supposedly easy conquest of the white man fell apart against the rock of Corregidor, described by MacArthur as "a barren war-torn rock, yet it symbolizes that priceless, deathless thing, the honor of a nation."

Impatient and frustrated, the Imperial General Staff ordered: "Overwhelmingly crush the island and exterminate its defenders." 16,000 shells struck Corregidor in twenty-four hours. That finished everything. General Wainwright, a gaunt figure with tears in his eyes spoke haltingly: "My brave men, you have fought a courageous fight against an enemy numerically superior. I wish that I could tell you that victory which you so richly deserve was within our grasp, but fate has not decreed it so. Today we must lower our beloved flag. It pains me deeply to tell you that we must swallow the bitter pill of defeat and further humiliate ourselves by yielding to the Japanese army. I ask you to conduct yourselves with dignity and respect becoming of the American soldier. LOWER THE FLAG, SERGEANT." As the honor guard lowered the Colors, all wept unashamedly; it was high noon, the 6th day of May, 1942.

"No army had ever done so much with so little" was the epitaph given by MacArthur. But their misery had just begun. It was the darkest chapter in American military history. The Battling Bastards of Bataan fell silent:

> We're the battling bastards of Bataan;
> No mama, no papa, no Uncle Sam;
> No aunts, no uncles, no nephews, no nieces;
> No pills, no planes, no artillery pieces
> ...and nobody gives a damn.

Abandoning the 140,000 American-Filipino Army was the most igno-minious defeat ever suffered by American armed forces. A scarecrow army was herded by bayonets of jeering guards in the Bataan Death March, during which 10,000 American and Filipino soldiers were mur-dered in a grisly sixty-five-mile trek of sadistic inhumanity. More than twice as many Americans died in prison camps in the two months fol-lowing the Death March than died during the march itself.

Washington simply wrote off the Philippines—the men, the nurses, the civilians. When the American flag was hauled down, it was spitefully trampled to shouts of "Banzai." A bloody curtain lowered across the

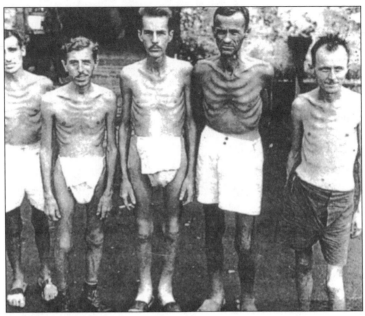

American Prisoners of War

Philippines during a four-year sentence of torture. Of the 23,000 soldiers, sailors, airmen and marines captured in the Philippines, less than half survived. Of those on the Death March, forty percent were dead in three months. They were stripped of watches, jewelry and even toothbrushes. One American officer who could not remove his Academy ring had the finger chopped off. Nurses were raped. Missionaries were massacred. Prisoners were used for bayonet practice.

Parade of the Dead, by Dr. John Bumgarner, a U.S. Army physician in the Philippines, tells of his experiences:

"Ninety people were crammed into each railroad car, so close we had to stand. The floors were deep with manure. The heat and stench became intolerable. When we arrived the Japanese began searching us for loot, but our watches and rings were already stolen. When it rained, Jack and I crawled under the schoolhouse to keep dry, but the ground under the building was covered with chicken excrement. We scooped away enough of the filth to try to sleep.

"I thought I had reached the end of human misery until we received Death March survivors from Camp O'Donnell. Their ribs were sunken grooves. Legs and arms looked like pipe stems. 3,000 POWs were in our hospital. We were having thirty deaths per day. Zero Ward was a place of zero medicine and zero hope. The men lay in pools of their own filth, dying. Filth

and flies produced terrible dysentery. Those who slept below a patient with dysentery found themselves covered with feces that dripped down between the bamboo strips. I remember two men lying on the ground and someone threw a cigarette down. Both men grabbed for the cigarette and fought over it, crazed like animals. Moments later the two men were dead, the shredded cigarette between them.

"A sick soldier was wobbling along when a Jap soldier threw him in front of a tank which ran over him, followed by other tanks. There was no way you could tell there had been a man there. His uniform was imbedded in the rocks. Officers were beaten and tied by the main gate. Col. Briggs was beaten so badly that one eye hung down over his cheek, both thighs were broken with bones protruding through the skin."

O'Donnell—Extermination Camp of American Hostages in the Philippines, by Colonel John Olson, an army doctor, describes their treatment:

"Tsuneyoshi, the camp commander expressed his implacable hatred: 'You are the eternal enemies of Japan. You are so much dirt.' They provided only two water spigots for 8,000 prisoners. Long lines of bony men would stand the whole day under the sun without getting to the spigot. Some prisoners were buried alive. Bayonet wielding Japs struck bodies as they feebly tried to raise up out of the grave... The bodies were skeletons with hide stretched over them except for holes where bones had worn through the hide."

A Thousand Cups of Rice, Surviving the Death Railway, was written by Kyle Thompson. I first met Kyle when he was press secretary to Governor John Connally in Austin and later to Senator John Tower in Washington. I recently spoke with him during a symposium on Japanese War Crimes at the Nimitz Foundation in Fredericksburg, Texas.

Kyle joined the national guard at sixteen for extra money. Transfer to the regular Army increased his pay to $21.00 per month. He was assigned to the 131st Field Artillery, and sent to Java in November 1941 to protect Dutch airfields. When he arrived, there were no airfields to protect. Under Dutch military command, these Americans were ordered to surrender. The Americans did not want to surrender, planning to escape to the mountains. The Dutch commander threatened to have them shot unless they surrendered.

Kyle, with others of the "lost battalion," were joined with survivors of the U.S.S. Houston, sunk during the Battle of Java Sea. They went as slave labor to build the Death Railway in Burma, where more than 100,000 workers perished. Kyle recalls the camp commander addressing the prisoners:

"You should weep with gratitude at the infinite favors of His Imperial Majesty. We will build the railroad over the white man's body. You will not see your homes again. Work cheerfully at my command."

He tells of Dr. Henri H. Hekking, a Dutch doctor in the prison camp who made medical history, of sorts, using maggots for medicinal purposes. He applied the maggots to wounds. The larvae ate the pus. When the pus was gone, the critters continued eating the flesh, until scraped off. The doctor used maggots as protein, putting them into the soup without the men knowing it.

In the *Odyssey of the Wake Island Prisoners,* by James W. Wensyel prisoners were told:

"'You gave up everything when you surrendered. You are our slaves.' Once when prisoners cheered a P-51 shooting down a Zero, furious guards bayoneted them. Some worked in a mine seven days a week, where conditions were so bad

Prisoners being tortured by the Japanese

prisoners would break their own arms to avoid work. Once, when guards were beating a prisoner, Marine Sgt. Bernard Kaz interfered. The guards beat him senseless, tying him to a pole. For two weeks he was beaten every day. His nose was broken and his eyes gouged out."

Don't Forget How They Starved Us, by Maj. Livingston P. Nell, Jr., Army Medical Corps:

"These facts about Japanese mass murder I set down because of a tendency here to forget, even forgive, the enormity of Japan's crimes. I do not want the American people to ever forget."

Of the men on Bataan, only one in seven was still alive ten years later. Those who survived were physically scarred for life by their captors and emotionally wounded by their government, which abandoned them during the war and turned its back on them thereafter. The Veterans Administration doesn't consider Japanese captivity as a service-connected disability. Disabled veterans are the only branch of federal government whose disability pay is deducted from retirement pay.

As shocking as the fifty percent death rate of POWs is, the fate of flyers captured is far worse. All airmen captured were tortured, few survived. Yet where is their story? These war crimes were neither punished nor publicized.

The Australian historian, Gavan Daws, in *Prisoners of the Japanese*, reports gruesome executions:

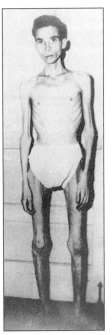

Another American Prisoner of War

- *Four flyers in Bicycle Camp in Batavia were shot standing alongside graves they were forced to dig.*
- *In Japan, B-29 crewmen were paraded through the city naked, and then beheaded.*
- *At Hankow, three flyers were burned alive. At Beo, four were bayoneted at a ceremonial parade.*
- *At Kendebo the Kempeitai chopped off the head of a fighter pilot. His body was cut up, fried and eaten by Japanese soldiers.*
- *On Chichi Jima, a Japanese general ordered captured airmen killed, then he ate their flesh. An admiral who was present put in a request for the liver of the next airman.*
- *Japanese civilians were told that any white man coming down in a parachute should be killed. One flyer who parachuted into a river was pulled out and beaten to death. Another was buried alive. One was tied in a schoolyard with a sign, WREAK YOUR VENGEANCE.*
- *In Niigata Prison flyers had their fingers broken. They were asked "do you need a manicure?" Their fingernails were then pulled off.*
- *At Fukuoka, flyers were used to train soldiers how to execute prisoners with swords.*
- *In Tokyo, a pilot was locked naked in a zoo's monkey cage for public amusement.*

- *Medical professors at Kyushu University cut up eight B-29 crewmen alive. They stopped blood flow in an artery near the heart, to see how long death took. They dug holes in the skull and stuck a knife into the living brain to observe the effect.*
- *On August 15, the last day of the war, ten flyers were executed in Fukuoka Prison in Tokyo to prevent their becoming witnesses.*

When Japan invaded Indonesia, they were initially welcomed as liberators, 400 years of Dutch colonialism having embittered the natives. Hatred of the white race spilled onto American flyers who came down in Indonesia. On missions over Java, Sumatra, Celebes and Borneo, we were briefed to avoid the Indonesian patrols, natives who turned flyers over to the Japanese for reward. I know of no American airman who survived Indonesian captivity.

Shobun—A Forgotten War Crime In the Pacific, by Michael J. Goodwin, tells of an American PBY crew imprisoned at Sandakan. All nine crewmen were executed. A Japanese officer described their fate: *"The executioner raised his samurai sword and brought it powerfully down on the prisoner's neck. The young American was beheaded amid great cheering and applause. His head fell into the grave. His body was then kicked into the grave. A number of soldiers began calling drunkenly for the other Americans so that they could kill them too."* Major Sueo Matoba commanded prisoners at Sandakan. A number of American airmen

The beheading of an American flyer by Japanese

fell into his hands. He used them for bayonet practice. Flesh was cut from their bodies while still alive. He cooked the pieces and fed the flesh to his subordinates as a big joke.

In *Hidden Horrors: Japanese War Crimes In World War II*, Yuki

Tanaka writes about the Sandakan camp on Borneo which held 3,000 allied prisoners, including many captured flyers. Six survived—a survival rate of 0.24 percent. Guards placed wet cloths over prisoners' mouths. To breathe the man had to pull air through the soaking fabric, filling his stomach with water until he was grossly distended. Guards threw the prisoner to the floor and jumped on him from a chair. Prisoners were force-fed dry rice. The guards ran a water hose down their throats. The rice expanded, causing excruciating pain.

Despite what I know and what I saw, this scene still shocks me sixty years later. "The Jap officer stood on a stool holding a hammer. He raised the prisoner's left arm, and, driving a nail through his hand, fixed it to the arm of the cross. He nailed the prisoner's right hand to the cross. He nailed both feet to a wooden board. He nailed his head to the cross by driving a large nail through his forehead. The officer then cut the prisoner's stomach and pulled out the intestines."

The *New York Times* reported December 15, 1996:

"Japanese War Criminals Honored as Heroes. Royal Family and Prime Minister pay Tribute at War Shrine: Japan's Royal Family along with Prime Minister Hashimoto and other government members, traveled to Yasukuni National Shrine to pay official tribute. They bestowed the status of national heroes upon 1000 war criminals enshrined at Yasukuni. Buried there is Prime Minister Tojo, who led Japan in World War II.

"The Liberal Democratic Party (Japan's ruling political party) requires the prime minister and cabinet ministers worship at Yasukuni every year. The Japanese government has systematically whitewashed its wartime record, dismissing all evidence of atrocities as propaganda. The Government refuses to apologize for its World War II crimes or compensate victims of those crimes, the 35 million deaths, the sexual slavery of 200,000 women, and the use of Allied prisoners of war in biological and chemical experiments. Their government thumbs its nose at the survivors, denying its responsibility and honoring the perpetrators. And the world remains silent."

Commander of the Prisoner Escort
Navy of the Great Japanese Empire

REGULATIONS FOR PRISONERS

1. The prisoners disobeying the following orders will be punished with immediate death.

    a Those disobeying orders and instructions.
    b Those showing a motion of antagonism and raising a sign of opposition.
    c. Those disordering the regulations by individualism, egoism, thinking only about yourself, rushing for your own goods.
    d Those talking without permission and raising loud voices
    e Those walking and moving without order
    f Those carrying unnecessary baggage in embarking
    g Those resisting mutually
    h Those touching the boat, materials, wires, electric lights, tools, switches, etc.
    i Those climbing ladder without order
    j Those showing action of running away from the room or boat
    k Those trying to take more meal than given to them
    l Those using more than two blankets

2. Since the boat is not well equipped and inside being narrow, food being scarce and poor you'll feel uncomfortable during the short time on the boat. Those losing patience and disordering the regulation will be heavily punished for the reason of not being able to escort

3. Be sure to finish your 'nature's call', evacuate the bowels and urine, before embarking.

4. Meal will be given twice a day. One plate only to one prisoner. The prisoners called by the guard will give out the meal quick as possible and honestly. The remaining prisoners will stay in their places quietly and wait for your plate. Those moving from their places reaching for your plate without order will be heavily punished. Same orders will be applied in handling plates after meal.

5. Toilet will be fixed at the four corners of the room. The buckets and cans will be placed. When filled up a guard will appoint a prisoner. The prisoner called will take the buckets to the center of the room. The buckets will be pulled up by the derrick and be thrown away. Toilet papers will be given. Everyone must cooperate to make the room sanitary. Those being careless will be punished.

6. Navy of the Great Japanese Empire will not try to punish you all with death. Those obeying all the rules and regulations, and believing the action and purpose of the Japanese Navy, cooperating with Japan in constructing the "New order of the Great Asia" which lead to the world's peace will be well treated.

The End.

Japanese POW regulations

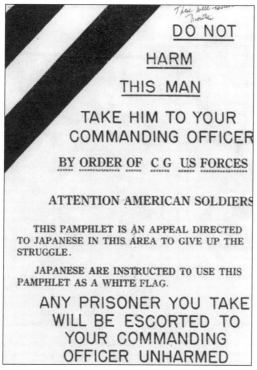

American Surrender Pamphlet

REFERENCES

Charles, Robert, *Last Man Out*, Austin, Tx, Eakin Press, 1999
Daws, Gavan, *Prisoners of the Japanese*, N.Y., Wm. Morrow, 1994
Goodwin, Michael J., *Shobun*, Mechanicsburg, Pa., Stockpole Books, 1995
Kerr, Bartlett E., *Surrender & Survival*, N.Y., Wm. Morrow, 1985
Martindale, Robert, *The 13th Mission*, Austin, Tx, Eakin Press, 1998

CHAPTER THIRTY-ONE

And I Was There

Japan's brutality to American airmen was unreported at the time and forgiven thereafter. Such is the guilty secret of the Pacific War. Much is known about flyers captured by Germany. Frank Sinatra engineered Von Ryan's Express. Hogan's Heroes is still playing. No information on prisoners leaked from behind Japanese lines and Red Cross visitation was denied, so the world did not see these atrocities. The treatment was so hideous, even now people recoil from the gruesome reality. Japan simply denies they occurred. Although never captured, thank God, I hold first hand experiences. Reporting these atrocities is not intended as polemic, but simply to pull back the curtain concealing the dark side of war in the Pacific.

Palawan Massacre.
American prisoners were herded into trenches, sprayed with gasoline and set afire. My involvement was reported in the book, *Bridge Across the Seas*, by Admiral Walter Innis, and discussed in the chapter "Palawan Massacre."

Balikpapan.
My plane was the first to land at Balikpapan after it was re-taken by the Aussies. There I saw natives who worked as slave labor in the refineries. Their achilles tendons had been cut so they could work, but hobbled, could not run away. Discussed in the chapter "Waltzing Matilda."

Brunei Bay.
My plane flew General Sir Thomas Blamey, commanding general of Australian armed forces into the invasion of Brunei Bay. There I witnessed Sikh prisoners who, when freed, turned on their captors (who had used them for bayonet practice). The surviving Sikhs lined up their newly acquired prisoners and ordered them to "count off," a meaningless Japanese daily ritual imposed on prisoners. At each miscue, the Sikhs smashed their captives in the mouth with rifle butts. This ritual is discussed in the chapter "General Blamey and The Sultan of Sarawak."

Manila.

One of the world's lovely cities, was known as the "Pearl of the Orient." I saw Manila, black, gutted and reeking, a hundred thousand civilians raped, bayoneted and burned. The Pearl was broken and dead.

The first American airmen to fall into Japanese hands were the army B-25 crews shot down in April 1942 during the Doolittle raid on Tokyo. Bombs fell near the Emperor's palace. Japan was stunned. The Emperor was insulted. How could this have happened? The Imperial General Staff had promised their holy soil would never be violated. The military was embarrassed and vengeful. American flyers were not to be treated as prisoners. They were designated "special war criminals" to be disposed of by the Kempeitai, Japan's gestapo—a group of sadistic thugs. That sealed our flyers' fate. Torture and execution awaited those captured during the next four years.

This heroic mission, known as "Thirty Seconds Over Tokyo," was led by Colonel Jimmy Doolittle. A legendary flyer who earned a Ph.D. in aeronautical engineering from M.I.T. and held nearly every flying trophy available. After the despair of Bataan, America needed to strike back. The only way to get near Japan was by a scheme never before tried—flying army bombers off a navy carrier. Doolittle trained his B-25 crews in short takeoffs. Sixteen planes were parked on the 800 foot carrier Hornet as it sailed under the Golden Gate Bridge, ostensibly ferrying planes to Hawaii. Approaching Japan, they were spotted by a patrol boat, forcing a launch twelve hours and 250 miles ahead of schedule. All planes struck their targets, but eight flyers were shot down and captured. They were stripped, paraded through the streets of Tokyo like animals and then beheaded. The Japanese press shrilled: "Our pure countrymen are urged to completely annihilate the Americans, whose bombing of Tokyo is an attempt to terrorize civilians through the most horrible means ever devised by a fiendish mind." (Contrast that with the Japanese press denouncing our defending Pearl Harbor: "They should have accepted our bombs as divine will.") Some planes flew on and landed in China. Japan fanned out search parties for the downed airmen who were concealed by the Chinese, infuriating the Japanese who unleashed their "Three all policy: loot all, kill all, burn all." Japan massacred entire villages suspected of hiding the Americans. A burning, bayoneting and raping savagery left a quarter million Chinese dead across hundreds of miles.

Japan hated American airmen. Unburdened by the Geneva Convention, any captured flyer was doomed. They were sure to be tortured, if not killed on the spot. Terrible things were done to them. There is no record of executions since Japan destroyed the evidence. Killings came to light, if ever, only when there were surviving witnesses. The Palawan Massacre is unknown. Bill Harris, the13th Air Force Ace, told me he never heard of it until he read of it in these chapters, despite his being stationed on Palawan.

William Dyess

Japanese savagery was first reported by Army Air Corps Captain William E. Dyess in his book *The Dyess Story*. Dyess escaped from a Japanese prison and incredibly made his way back to the U.S., where he wrote of his experiences. So shocking, it was banned by Roosevelt, who feared it would dampen his Europe-first strategy. When finally published, outrage was volcanic. Senator Bennett Champ Clark called for bombing Tokyo out of existence and hanging the Emperor.

The heroic career of Captain Bill Dyess was honored when Dyess Air Force Base at Abilene, Texas, home of our B-1 bombers, was named for him. Dyess was a star athlete at John Tarleton College. Enlisting in the Air Corps, he received training at Randolph Field, "The West Point of the Air." A natural pilot, neighbors in the west Texas cowtown of Albany recall his buzzing a P-40 down Main Street, banking around the courthouse and racing back up Main Street.

When war broke out, Dyess was a captain on Luzon. He strafed convoys, machine-gunned soldiers and shot down two planes. His squadron was down to four planes when he was ordered to a dirt strip on Bataan, where he rigged 500-pound bombs to his wings, sinking ships in Subic Bay. In January 1942 his pursuit squadron, with no planes, was assigned to the infantry. Dyess went from a fighter squadron commander to commanding a bunch of rifle-toting Air Corps guys fighting as infantrymen. In Bataan he came face to face with Japanese treachery. He wrote: *"The enemy would play dead until we went past them. Then the supposed corpses would rise up and shoot us in the back."* When Corregidor surrendered, he was forced into the Bataan Death March.

In October 1942, Dyess and others went to Mindanao, the southernmost Philippine island, as laborers. While on a work detail outside the prison, Dyess and nine others just kept on going. They struggled through a dense jungle until they met Colonel Fertig, an Army officer who had taken to the hills and led a guerrilla force. Fertig contacted MacArthur by radio, who arranged for the men to be picked up by a sub. They made it to Brisbane where MacArthur decorated Dyess and promoted him to major. When the men reached the U.S., they were anxious to tell their story, but were muzzled by Washington. Their escape leaked out and so did their story. His book, *The Dyess Story*, created a firestorm:

"Japanese guards formed a wall around us to forestall friendly Filipinos giving us food and water. The long hike to O'Donnell Prison Camp lay ahead, but a third of us never made it. We were fed only once and were never given water. No one was permitted to lag behind, or stop. Whoever fell by the wayside or tried to get water was bayoneted or shot. Many prisoners, crazed for lack of food and water, went insane and were shot. Prisoners were struck, beaten and spit upon by passing Japanese officers and soldiers.

"Exhausted and starving, the Japs lined us up and displayed ladles of sausages and rice. An officer shouted denunciations at us. 'We told you that you would eat. Now that is changed. You will have no food. You will march five miles to Orani.' By this time many had reached the end of their endurance and went down. I never can forget their trying to get up. I observed the Jap guards paid no attention to these. I wondered why. The explanation soon came. There was a sharp crack of rifle fire. Skulking along behind us came a clean-up squad of murdering Jap buzzards. Their victims sprawled on the road were easy targets. Their bodies were left where they lay. The guards enjoyed the sport! One who spoke a little English asked 'Sleepee? You want sleepee? Just lie down on road. You get good long sleep.'

"Lt. Col. Biggs, Lt. Col. Breitung and Lt. Gilbert, were caught trying to escape. The Japs stripped them, tied them to a post and forced passing Filipinos to beat them across the face with a board. These officers were kept in the blazing sun for two days without water. Col. Biggs was beheaded and the other two were shot."

Based on this information from Captain Dyess and others who escaped with him, Secretary of State Hull sent a protest to the Japanese government: "At Camp O'Donnell, conditions were so bad that 2,200 Americans and 20,000 Filipinos died in the first few months. Prisoners lay naked on the floor, too sick to move from their own excrement. Americans lay outside in the heat of the blazing sun. The American doctors in the camp were given no medicine, or water to wash the human waste from the bodies of the patients." Japan ignored Hull's protest. MacArthur did more than protest. He issued a warning to Japan that he would hold enemy leaders responsible for mistreating prisoners. And he did.

Lou Zamperini

Lou Zamperini is the only 13th Air Force member I'm aware of who was captured and lived to tell about it. A famous athlete, he broke the world record for the mile run while in high school in California. He was the youngest member of the U.S. Olympic team at the Berlin Olympics. When he was crowned Olympic Champion for winning the mile run, he scaled a flag pole and ripped down a Swastika flag. That picture brought him world fame.

He volunteered for the Army Air Corps, graduating as a bombardier second lieutenant. Assigned to the 13th Air Force, he was flying B-24s for the 307th Long Rangers when his plane ditched in the Pacific. He and two other crew members survived and crawled into a life raft. Forty-seven days they drifted, starving and parched. Chocolate bars and drinking water went the first two days. Three times search planes flew over but didn't spot the tiny raft. During six weeks, they caught two fish and some birds which landed on the raft. Lou once grabbed a small shark by the tail which they ripped open and ate raw. Every few days a rain squall doled out water which collected in the bottom of the raft. On the 27th day, a Japanese bomber spotted them and machine-gunned the raft. Forty-five bullet holes failed to sink it. On the 33rd day the youngest crew member whispered "How long will I last?" Being honest with the boy, Lou said: "I think you'll die tonight." The boy gasped: "I think you're right, lieutenant." That night, the boy moaned. Lou felt for his pulse. There was none. The young heart beat no more. At dawn, Lou recited the Lord's Prayer and gently slid the shrunken body into the sea.

Burned by sun and frozen by night, on the forty-seventh day they drifted into the Japanese held Marshall Islands. They were taken aboard a Japanese boat. Tying their hands, the Japs brandished bayonets across their throat as a joke. They were taken to Truk, Japan's huge base in the central Pacific. Ironically, Zamperini had recently bombed Truk on a seventeen-hour mission flown by his Long Rangers squadron.

Zamperini was recognized as the famous olympic athlete. He was asked: "Do you think Japan will win the war"? When Lou said "no," he was clubbed in the face, breaking his nose. Other Japanese cheered, awaiting their turn to beat the prisoners. Lou held his broken nose in place for weeks, hoping it would set. Later, a Japanese officer noticed his broken nose and clubbed it again. He was forced into races with Japanese. His 170 pound body, withered to ninety pounds, was easily bested by Japanese runners who taunted him.

He was transferred to Omori Prison in Japan, where he met Sgt. Watanabe, a sadistic son of a wealthy family. Watanabe was known as "the Bird" by the prisoners who were forbidden to speak his name.

Watanabe indulged in creative cruelty. He forced the Americans to do push ups over troughs used for toilets. If they did not collapse, guards would stomp their heads into the excrement. The lavatories were filthy with maggots crawling the floor. When the flyers stumbled out of those places, guards made them lick the soles of their shoes with their tongues.

The Bird had 103 American officers and men under his control. He hated officers and would call them to his office, showing letters mailed to them. He would then tear up the letters. One officer was shown three letters addressed to him and Watanabe threw the letters into the fire while the officer was forced to stand at attention and watch them burn. A pilot, Captain Martin, refused to work as an enlisted man. Watanabe beat him with a club, breaking his teeth and nose and knocking an eye out of its socket. Watanabe would line up the officers and make each enlisted man walk down the line hitting the officers in the face. If the man did not hit hard enough, he would club the enlisted man, forcing him to hit the officer again and again until Watanabe was satisfied. The officers spared themselves additional blows by telling their men to hit hard the first time and get it over with. Zamperini confessed, "we'd rather be struck by our own men than those dirty Japs. If I had to go through that again, I would kill myself."

After the surrender, the guards became very solicitous, saying "we will all soon be friends again." The Bird disappeared.

When Zamperini came home he was a celebrity, but was overtaken by alcohol. His wife took him to a tent meeting where he met a young evangelist named Billy Graham. That was the turning point of his life. He refocused on a love of God. He was in great demand as a speaker and shared his story with thousands across the country. He developed the Victory Boys Camp, which became the model for Outward Bound. He carried the torch of the gospel to the world. He was among those who carried the Olympic torch before the 1984 games in Los Angeles, the 1996 games in Atlanta, and the 1998 games in Japan. His book *Devil at My Heels* is being reissued with a foreword by Senator John McCain.

Fiske Hanley

My friend Fiske Hanley is the only flyer I personally know who was captured and lived to tell about it. He wrote *Accused American War Criminal...The Shocking Story of Captured Airmen Awaiting Trial and Execution*. His B-29 was shot down over Tokyo. I see Fiske at monthly meetings of the Happy Warriors at Wyatt's Cafeteria in Dallas. His explanation for survival is that with war nearing its end, the Japanese needed prisoners to hand over, and he was one. I was present when prisoners were freed at Balikpapan and at Brunei in Borneo. I spoke to those prisoners, but none knew of any captured American airman who was still alive.

Fiske Hanley writes:

"Shorty was our name for the official in charge of American prisoners at Kempei Tai Headquarters. We became well acquainted with this cruel, vicious, sadistic, inhuman, murderous little bastard. Shorty was the embodiment of Japanese cruelty and atrocities. He thrived on our misery. I could not then, nor can I now, imagine why anyone so vile should be allowed to live on this earth.

"Shorty informed us: 'This building is where two American criminals of Doolittle's B-25 raiders were executed. You are an accused war criminal. You will be imprisoned until you die or are executed.' One day Shorty entered my cell with a paper in Japanese and directed me to sign. I was told it confessed war crimes. I refused to sign. Shorty ordered the guards to beat me. Even though it appeared I wouldn't survive the beating, I didn't sign it, and I lived through the night. I was dragged to a dungeon where guards jabbed me with bayonets. I still have nightmares about this.

"We were walking skeletons. Our rice contained protein in worms and bugs and they tasted mighty good. Diarrhea was a death sentence. Prisoners with diarrhea received no food and were allowed to starve to death.

"Peterson's toes began to fall off. His cellmates begged for a knife to amputate his gangrenous toes. They were refused and beaten for their request.

"Fox was a P-51 pilot in good shape when taken prisoner. The Kempeis beat him almost to death. He went from 160 pounds to ninety pounds. He died in his cell in the arms of another pilot, Art O'Hara.

"Lester Morris' leg was cut almost in two when he bailed out. It was a terribly infected wound full of maggots. Deeb had rope burns on his neck after the Japs tried to hang him. Jones had bad flak wounds. Ring's leg was torn open in a wound eighteen inches long and two inches deep. Willis White was beaten and put on public display where he was stoned and beaten by civilians. My cellmates—Snellz and Jensen—were burned and then murdered by Japanese doctors.

"During air raids, we were left locked in burning wooden cells. Those who broke out were chopped to pieces with swords and bayonets. Others burned to death. Cells had twenty Americans packed inside the eight-by-ten-foot walls. One prisoner to every two square feet of floor space. They slept standing up. The Kempei Tai commander ordered the surviving fifty airmen

*beheaded immediately after the emperor's surrender speech, so there would be
no witnesses."*

Fiske Hanley can't explain his luck. On May 25, at the Tokyo military
prison there were 62 American flyers ranking from private to colonel. On
May 26, there was not one alive of those 62.

Last Man Out, a book by Robert Charles, a survivor of the Texas
National Guard Field Artillery Unit surrendered to Japan by the Dutch in
Java, tells about his experiences as a member of "The Lost Battalion." He
concludes with a searing question:

*"It is as unconscionable to forget what happened to Japanese POWs as
it is to forget the Holocaust. Every August, people of the United States are
supposed to take their annual guilt trip because they dropped those atomic
bombs. But didn't anyone know about the hundred thousand people the
Japanese starved to death, tortured and killed? Why not publicize that
annually too? If there was any logic in keeping alive the memory of gas
chambers and atomic bombs, then why wouldn't the same logic apply to
keeping alive the memory of what happened to the thousands of Americans
who were imprisoned, tortured and executed by Japan?"*

REFERENCES

Rutherford, Ward, *Fall of the Philippines*, N.Y., Ballantine, 1971

Morris, Eric, *Corregidor*, N.Y. Stein & Day, 1981

Lamont-Brown, Raymond, *Kempeitai, Japan's Dreaded Military Police*,
    Sutton Publishing, Gloucestershire, England, 1998

Hanley, Fiske, *Accused American War Criminal*, Eakin Press, Austin,
    Texas, 1997

CHAPTER THIRTY-TWO

The Palawan Massacre

Numerous atrocities committed by Japan are unknown. A couple like the Rape of Nanking and Bataan Death March leaked out. Most, such as Ambon, Banks Straits, Parit Sulong, Lae, Andaman, Peg Basket, Kalagon, Loa Kulu, Singapore, Palawan and Sandakan, have gone unreported.

My squadron played a role at Palawan, as related in the book, *Bridge Across The Seas* by Admiral Walter Innis:

"Lt. David Witts, USA, who was in the 2nd Emergency Air Sea Rescue Squadron, 13th Army Air Force, tells how Captain Clarence L. Solander in his squadron picked up seven persons. They were Corporals William J. Belches, USA; Alberto D. Pashee, USA; Rufus W. Smith, USMC; Edwin A. Petry, USA; Eugene Nielsen and one civilian, Thomas F. Loudon, all of whom had been prisoners for three years."

Three hundred Americans taken prisoner at Corregidor were moved to Palawan in the Philippines. Four who survived were rescued by our squadron. This is the story they told:

"In 1944, US bombers ranged over Palawan, bombing the airstrip. Them Japs had a mortal fear of our four engine bombers and they'd take it out on us each time they came over. It was pretty bad, I can tell you.

"On the 14th of December 1944, the Japanese herded all the prisoners into trenches. As soon as the prisoners were all in the trenches, trucks were driven in and gasoline was pumped over them and ignited.

"Some died quickly, others screaming in agony struggled to get out of the flaming trenches only to sink back to their death. A few who got out of the flames of the furnace, were mowed down by the machine guns. All had to be killed so none would be left to tell the tale."

By some miracle, a few escaped into the jungle:

"We went as fast as we could through that jungle. We had burns, but we didn't take no notice of them. God, it was awful! I'll never forget the screams and the smell of burning. Some tried to hide under bushes, but the Japs shot them. We were lucky. Our clothes were burned off and we had no protection

against the thorns and insects on those damn islands.

"I began to think the guys the Japs got were lucky. They went quick. Then, soon after it got light, we heard someone coming. It was old Louden from the Philippines! Well, that old guy, and he was seventy-five years old, heard the shots and come to take a look. He shared his water and food and led us up in the hills. Hell, I still can't talk of the old guy without breaking up. Well, he had an old patched up radio and he sent a message that fixed up the rendezvous at Brooks Point with the PBY.

"He said he'd guide us to Brooks Point as we'd never find our way over the mountains and through the jungle. Anyhow, he got us there and were we glad to see that plane. The PBY took us back to their base and we saw the good old Stars and Stripes. I'll never forget that sight and what it meant to all of us. When we was captured at Bataan our flag was in the dirt. All we could think of when we got off that PBY was to thank God that we lived to see it flying high above us.

"The crew of the plane, *Playmate 42*, of the 2nd Emergency Air Rescue Squadron, 13th Air Force, never forgot the pride of these men when they saw the hundreds of fighters and bombers assembled on the airbase at Morotai. Then they were sure that we'd soon have the Japs finished off."

Dennis Wrynn wrote about the Palawan Massacre in *World War II Magazine*:

"The Japanese unit in charge at Palawan was the 131st Airfield Battalion, under command of Captain Nagayoshi Kojima, who Americans called the 'Weasel.' Americans were tied to trees, whipped with wire and clubs. Guards beat them unconscious, sometimes breaking their arms with an iron bar. When Red Cross supplies were delivered, the Japs kept them.

"In October, 1944, Palawan came under attack by B-24s. The Japs allowed the Americans to paint 'American Prisoner of War' on the roof of their barracks. The Japs then stowed their own supplies under the POW barracks.

"December 14, 1944, POWs were ordered into air raid shelters by Lt. Yoshikazu Sato, the 'Buzzard.' Soldiers doused the wooden shelters with gasoline and set them afire. Then they hurled hand grenades into the flames. Screams of trapped Americans mingled with cheers and laughter of the Japanese soldiers. As burning men broke out of their fiery deathtraps, guards machine gunned, bayoneted and clubbed them to death. Several attempted to swim across the bay but were shot in the water.

"Eugene Nielsen of the 59th Coast Artillery said some Americans ran to the Japs and asked to be shot in the head. The Japs would laugh and bayo-

net them in the stomach. Nielson dived into the bay. When he surfaced, the Japs were shooting at him. He was hit in the leg, head and ribs, but finally reached the opposite shore."

Radioman Joseph Barta, reported:
"A Jap officer drew his saber and forced me in the shelter. I saw several men on fire being shot down by the Japs. So I and several others went under the fence. Just as I got outside, I looked back and saw a Jap throw a torch in our hole, and another threw in a bucket of gasoline. The slaughter continued until dark. August Evans of the 59th Coast Artillery, stood up and shouted, All right, you Jap bastards, here I am and don't miss me. He was shot and his body set afire.

"Glen McDole, witnessed five or six Japs jabbing a wounded American with bayonets. Another Jap came up with gasoline. I heard the American beg them to shoot him and not burn him. The Japs threw gasoline on his foot and lit it. The other Japs laughed and poked him with bayonets. Then they did the same thing to his other foot. When he collapsed, the Japs threw the bucket of gasoline over him. He burst into flames.

"Of 146 Americans in the Palawan prison camp, only 11 survived the massacre. Filipinos reported the Japanese officers held a celebration to commemorate the event the same night that it occurred."

After the war, Lieutenant Sho Yoshiwara and Captain Kojima, the prison camp commander, were not located. Many Japanese, knowing they would be held accountable, disappeared. Japanese documents were destroyed. The Allied War Crimes Tribunal accused the Japanese Demobilization Bureau of protecting war criminals. Those few Americans who survived captivity, never forgot nor forgave. It was forgotten… by the U.S. Government.

REFERENCES

Innis, Walter D., *Bridge Across The Seas*, Washington, D.C., Devon, 1995

CHAPTER THIRTY-THREE

The Rape of Nanking

Although not central to this book, this event depicts the enemy confronting 13th Air Force crews each time they rose to fight and the fate awaiting them if captured. It signaled that Japan was an enemy with no morality and no remorse.

The death toll at Nanking exceeded those at Hiroshima and Nagasaki combined. Japanese soldiers raped, tortured, and murdered 300,000 Chinese civilians. Its culprits never spent a day in court. For example, Masanobu Tsuji was a coldly brutal mass killer, so proud of his tortures he kept a diary. In 1950, he was elected to the Japanese Diet and became a member of the ruling LDP. Other war criminals insinuated themselves into commerce and politics. War criminals are today commemorated at Yasukuni Shrine.

This atrocity was obscured until 1997, when Iris Chang wrote *The Rape of Nanking.* The book is banned in Japan.

"Nanking should be remembered for its cruelty. Chinese men were used for bayonet practice. 80,000 Chinese women were raped, disemboweled, breasts sliced off, nailed alive to walls. Fathers were forced to rape their daughters, and sons their mothers. Babies were sliced not just in half but in thirds and fourths. Roasting people became routine. There were diabolical tortures such as hanging people by their tongues on iron hooks and burying people to the waists and watching them torn apart by German Shepherds."

The author identifies specific tortures:

Mutilation.
Japanese disemboweled, decapitated, and dismembered victims. They nailed prisoners to wooden boards and ran over them with tanks... eyes gouged out, noses and ears hacked off... stabbed by zhizi needles along their mouths, throats, and eyes... people with their penises cut off. Japanese believed eating them increased virility.

Death by Fire.
Pushed into a pit, sprayed with gasoline, ignited and exploded into flames.

Death by Ice.
Stripped naked, and driven into icy water. Their bodies hardened into floating targets that were riddled with Japanese bullets.

Rape.
Rape is embedded in Japanese military culture. Soldiers wear amulets made from pubic hair of victims, believing they possessed magical powers. Little girls were raped so brutally they could not walk. Girls under ten were raped and their vaginas sliced open. After gang rapes, Japanese soldiers slashed open pregnant women and ripped out the fetuses for amusement.

"I think I have said enough of these horrible cases—there are hundreds of thousands of them... so many of them makes the mind dulled."

After Nanking, Japan continued its murderous rampage of the Chinese countryside. No one knows how many million Chinese died. Their troops robbed buildings before setting them on fire. They raped women by the thousands. School girls were raped to death. Babies were bayoneted. Women not killed were hauled off to the barracks. Chinese were not worthy of the land which Japan wanted. They were bugs to be exterminated.

After the rape was over—Denial. Japan's ambassador to the U.S., Kunihiko Saito, criticized the *Rape of Nanking* as "inaccurate and biased." Japanese teachers deny Nanking ever occurred. Nanking was reported when it occurred by Sin Shun Pao, the Japanese newspaper, with a straight face: *"The harmonious atmosphere of Nanking develops enjoyably. The Imperial Army entered the city, put their bayonets into their sheaths, and stretched forth merciful hands, giving medical aid and food. Soldiers and the Chinese children are playing joyfully together in the play ground."*

The Rape of Nanking is the most outrageous crime in living memory. Although obscured by Pacific War fog, it was witnessed by many in real time. In 2002, the Japanese War Museum opened in Tokyo as the official portrayal of Japanese military history. As reported by Rick Shenkman,

Editor of HNN:

"I was unprepared for the wholesale fabrication of history including omission, bias and outright fraud. The Rape of Nanking is depicted as a glorious battle in which Japan's brave soldiers helped the suffering residents of Nanking to once again live their lives in peace..."

REFERENCES

Chang, Iris, *Rape Of Nanking*, N.Y., Basic Books, 1987
Fogel, Joshua, *The Nanjing Massacre*, Berkeley, CA, University of California Press, 2000

CHAPTER THIRTY-FOUR

Rising Sun and Dark Crimes

Our Pacific War was fought against a blood-thirsty enemy, often in stone-age hand to hand struggles. Violence was a cultural imperative to Japan's military. Gratuitous brutality pervaded its conduct, both in mass murder like the Palawan Massacre or individual crimes. Their unrelenting policy was "Three All—Burn All, Kill All, Loot All".

Germany's war crimes are discussed more today than when they occurred. German crimes were products of national genocide and bureaucratic planning. Concentration camps were mechanical and impersonal. They left survivors and a vigorous constituency. Japanese crimes were intensely personal, leaving few survivors and no history. Japanese enjoyed killing, laughing and joking as their victims died. Bestial acts were accompanied by celebrations, parading through streets with heads of American airmen impaled on poles. Time Magazine reported on February 7, 1944: "They shot pilots in their parachutes, starved, emasculated, decapitated, crucified, burned, buried alive, used for bayonet practice, and hung them from trees with severed genitals stuffed in their mouth." Considering rape a sport, their condoms were wrapped with a picture of a soldier charging with a bayonet. The label read "Totsugkei," or charge! They waxed poetic about death:

> Across the sea, corpses soak in the water
> Across the mountains, corpses heaped upon the grass
> One hundred thousand hearts beating as one
> One hundred thousand people as one bullet.

While blood was hot and memories fresh, our determination to punish the guilty was proclaimed by the New York Times VJ-Day editorial of September 6, 1945:

"As the smiling little Japanese people try to defuse our anger, we shall do well to keep constantly in mind the story of wanton and inhuman cruelty to American war prisoners. Our task is to punish those responsible for their atrocities."

Japanese boast of their genetic purity which they deem superior to "mongrelized races like in the U.S." Individually, Japanese are polite and self-effacing. Collectively, they transmogrify into aggressors, seeking to dominate, militarily or economically, all in their path. Japan emphasized military invincibility, racial superiority, and a destiny to purge the world of the white race expressed in the Tanaka Memorial. The emperor, a descendant of the Sun God, is considered the state. Japan is a world within a world. They speak of their two faces: "honne," the true face, and "tataeme," the facade. An ant colony cut off from the rest of the world, Japan has yet to make a lasting contribution to civilization. Historian William Henry Chamberlain explains: "Japan is great in small things and small in great things. They have produced no great philosophy, religion, science or literature. In war, the only weapon they invented was the kamikaze."

Samurai is the most revered class in a their class conscious society. Its code is death before defeat. Surrender was an unwashable disgrace. Consequently, prisoners were treated with scorn and torture. In Europe, the death rate of prisoners was one percent In the Pacific, it approached forty percent.

School days begin with pupils bowing toward the imperial palace and intoning "our dearest ambition is to die for the emperor." By the time they join the military, the brain has been thoroughly washed. The soldier's greatest service was to die for the emperor. Their military rescript had to be memorized: "Duty is weightier than a mountain, while death is lighter than a feather." The booklet issued soldiers contained such instructions as: "The imperial desire for peace requires rescuing Asia from white aggression. . . . If you discover a dangerous snake, kill it and swallow its liver raw as there is no better medicine. . . . Before you is the enemy whose death will lighten your heart. Westerners are cowards who fear dark and rain. Remember in 2,600 years Japan has never been defeated."

British General Slim fought the Japanese in Burma. He said that while many speak of fighting to the last man, only the Japanese really do it. To take a position manned by 1,000 Japanese, 999 of the defenders had to be killed, and the last one would kill himself. In Bougainville, this scene played out: "We came across a raft with four live Japs in it. As our destroyer came close the Japs opened up with a machine gun on the destroyer. The Jap officer than put the gun in each man's mouth and fired, blowing out each man's skull. The officer was the last to die. He blew his brains out."

A rare glimpse of their senjinkun, or battle ethics (an oxymoron if ever there was one), was captured by marines who recovered General Saito's last message to his men on Saipan: "Since the American devils landed, our officers and men have fought well and bravely for the honor and glory of the imperial forces. But now we have no materials and our artillery has been destroyed. The barbarous attack of the enemy continues. Whether we attack or stay where we are, there is only death. However, in death there is life. I will advance with those who remain to deliver another blow to the American devils and calmly rejoice as I offer up the courage of my soul for the eternal life of the Emperor."

In addition to operational problems bedeviling Pacific flyers, there was an omnipresent antagonist—ethereal, formidable, intangible. It was the spirit of the samurai. A fighting spirit was considered their most devastating weapon. Faith in their invincibility made them fearless, unafraid to die. As a matter of fact, they seemed to look forward to it, thereby insuring immortality. The samurai's spirit became a religious mantle, investing their soldiers with the fatal hubris of invincibility.

We encountered this ancient tradition in the field. When we joined our 13th Air Force operational unit on Morotai, we met our c.o., Captain "Jungle Jim" Jarnigan, an appropriate nickname. He had been in the Pacific so long his skin was yellow as a lemon. His orientation talk told us the highest honor for a Japanese soldier is to die for the emperor. "Your orders," he said "are to help him achieve that honor."

The sword was the samurai status symbol. It embodied mystical qualities and, like other Japanese traditions, much is theater. Crafting the sword was done by artisans, forging layer upon layer of steel to produce an ultimate weapon. When samurai spirit merged with steel, they became one. Although guns were introduced by Portuguese traders in the 14th century, they were spurned by samurais because their blow was not personally delivered.

The samurai sword was designed to behead with a great sweeping stroke. The enemy's severed head was proof of victory in battle. It perpetuated as the traditional weapon of Japanese officers. Some pilots carried them in planes, as can be seen in the photo of kamikaze pilots on page 179. When Yamamoto was found in the Bougainville jungle, Japan reverently reported: "He wore white gloves, his left hand grasped his sword, and his right hand rested lightly on it."

Survivors of Japanese prison camps tell of officers who demonstrated skill by cutting the neck in a single blow without severing it, leaving it attached to the body by skin. The swordsman then scornfully kicked the head off.

Pacific airmen encountered the samurai sword in their very first flight over Japan, when some of Doolittle's Army B-25 crews fell into Japanese hands. The captured Americans were ceremoniously and publicly beheaded by the slashing samurai sword. Roosevelt branded the Japanese "barbarous, uncivilized, inhuman and depraved". Beheadings continued to the last day of the war when many of our flyers were beheaded in Tokyo.

My commercial interfacing with the Japanese after the war required I learn something of Japan's history, of which they are intensely proud. The samurai warriors originated as tax collectors. That figures. They were mean and trained to shake down taxpayers. They became professional warriors doing the dirty work for the shoguns who did the ruling. Their spectacular regalia was designed to intimidate. They didn't joust, they fought to the death. Death was honorable; defeat a disgrace. Traditionally, when a samurai warrior was wounded in battle, his head was cut off and hidden so it would not fall into enemy hands. If a samurai warrior failed, he redeemed himself by hari-kari, belly splitting in which the dagger is plunged into the stomach and then ripped sideways to insure a slow, painful death. No Japanese general officer was ever captured alive. Soldiers finished off their wounded to avoid captivity.

From a Japanese diary in New Guinea:

"I glanced at the young airman and he seems prepared. He gazes at the clear sky and green mountains as the sword fell. The severed head rolled on the grass like a white doll. Another soldier who disemboweled the decapitated flyer exclaimed: 'these white bastards are thick bellied too.'"

Bataan: March of Death, by Falk, tells of the Balanga murders in Luzon, where 400 Filipino soldiers were hacked to death in a frenzy of slashing swords. The enlisted man's bayonet was his counterpart to the sword, which they wantonly plunged into prisoners, sometimes for torture, sometimes for practice, sometimes for fun. Samurai swords were a prized souvenir, but one was too long for my footlocker. Instead, I brought home one of those long, mean bayonets, now idling in the Hoover Archives.

The enduring shame and horror inflicted on thousands of young women as sex slaves was official Japanese policy. In the grand tableaux of that war it was the unforgivable crime. Young women were rounded up wherever the hinomaru battle flag was hoisted. From Korea, China,

Philippines, Hong Kong, Singapore, Indonesia and Malaya helpless Asian and Caucasian women were dragooned to service Japan's garrisons. Ignored by the world, there were no prosecutions, no books written, no stories published.

These women had their youth wrenched from them on straw mats in military barracks. They were disposables of the Pacific War. Those that died were the lucky ones. Suicide was their only escape. The cadaverous survivors were sick and syphilitic. Vilified for their disgrace, there was neither home nor family to return to. Having nothing left, they hide in dark shame, having already died so many times.

As this book is written, occasional reports of comfort slaves surface. They strike a match which flames for a second, then dies out. Why, I ask, in this world of maudlin humanitarians and bristling feminists, where no sparrow falls from a tree unlamented, does the greatest pillage of women in the twentieth century repose in tranquility?

I've never seen a book about comfort slaves. However, Yuki Tanaka in *Hidden Horrors: Japanese War Crimes in World War II*, mentions them:

"When Hong Kong was invaded, British doctors in the hospitals were shot and grenades thrown into the wards. The Japanese then gang-raped the British and Chinese nurses throughout the night.

"'In the Sandakan Camp in Borneo, we were virgins. A Japanese officer stood in front of me laughing. He paid a lot of money for opening night... he threw me on the bed... pinned me under his heavy body. The tears were streaming down my face as he raped me... it was worse than dying... They stripped my self-esteem, my dignity, my freedom... they ruined my young life. Each woman was given a daily quota: twenty enlisted men in the morning, two NCOs in the afternoon, and senior officers at night. Even after fifty years, I still experience total fear burning me up.'"

Occasionally a story appears such as this one from Manila in March 2002, interviewing Lola Rosa, a young Filipino girl who was forced to be a sex slave when she was fifteen: *"There were seven of us taken to their garrison. We were kept in small rooms with a curtain for a door, and the only furniture was a bamboo bed. We were raped by ten to thirty soldiers every day. After we were rescued it was two months before I regained consciousness. I wanted to speak, but no words came from my mouth. I could not eat. My mother spoon fed me. I could not stand or walk. I crawled like a baby. I hid in dark corners. When I tried to speak, I drooled, saliva dripping from my mouth like a dog."*

REFERENCES

Dower, John W., *War Without Mercy*, Pantheon Books, NY, 1986

Harris, Merion & Susan, *Soldiers of the Sun, The Rise & Fall of the Imperial Japanese Army*, Random House, NY, 1991

Edgerton, Robert, *Warriors of the Rising Sun*, Pathfinder Publishing, Ventura, CA, 1991

Wygle, Peter, *Surviving a Japanese POW Camp*, Pathfinder Publishing, Ventura, CA, 1991

CHAPTER THIRTY-FIVE

Rising Sun Shines on Propaganda

Truth is sparse in Japan's military lexicon. Their army and navy competed for favor. They falsified reports and institutionalized deceit. The Battle of Midway was described as "a great victory." Their navy didn't tell the army about its losses at Midway, reporting it as "a calamitous defeat for the U.S.". The army described retreats at MacArthur's hands as troops "marching elsewhere." The Emperor, however, was fully informed, receiving daily reports from both army and navy.

I've witnessed first hand their sanitizing of savagery. In 1945 during the Luzon campaign I liberated an official Japanese picture album from its owner who had no further need of it. It is now in the Hoover Archives. It contains syrupy editorials and staged photos of Japan's Philippines conquest. The spelling and grammar of these excerpts are directly from the album:

Liberated portrait of Japanese soldier

"*The Asiatic Fortress of America has been crushed and their inimical designs for aggression have been checked. The spiritualism of Japan subdued the materialistic civilization of America. Note the expressions of our warriors faces bear the image of the SAMURAI. The Filipinos have finally awakened from their long years of blind devotion to the Americans and the past is now just like a passing storm. Proud to be under the leadership of Japan, the inhabitants are starving to create a NEW PHILIPPINE. The unfurling of the Japanese RISING SUN over the heads of the multitude drowned the people in a sea of exultation. Military songs such as AIKOKU KOSHINKYOKU and KOKOMIN SHINGUNKA are rapidly becoming popular among the Filipinos. General HOMA entered MANILA amidst fervent welcome offered by its populace.*

"While still at BATAAN, we advised the enemy not to attempt futile resistance. They were amazed at our true strength before even realizing how weak they were.

"These Indian soldiers have volunteered their services in cooperation with the Imperial Army during the Singapore operation, and are mighty warriors fighting for ASIA.

"Girls are seen hulling rice in the cool shed of a KAIMITO tree. True, these girls are not beautiful when judge by EUROPEAN standard; but on the other hand the bashful simile, and lips that tacitly speak of joy of living. The implicit trust they have in the Imperial Army has made them immune of fear.

"Constant effort is exerted to pacify newly conquered populace and bring them under the reign of the Emperor.

"But now that the people here, who have their homes burnt and provisions stolen, have received kind treatment form the Japanese Army, they realize that they were mislead by false propaganda. Extreme hatred of Americans is arising.

"Laughter has returned to every town and the people are jubilant. The people have come to realize the vial importance of Japanese language in the movement to save EAST ASIA and the lips that once spoke ENGLISH now speak JAPANESE.

"In the past their mother country had repeatedly insulted our sacred JAPAN. They attempted to forestall the survival and progress of our nation. Such dastard act will not be left disregarded: Just look at the hopeless expressions and destitute smells of those American prisoners sitting in the dust.

"SANTO TOMAS University enemy alien internment center at MANILA. Here are the people of the impertinent countries that attempted to abuse us. These are the people who only yesterday arrogantly walked the sidewalks of MANILA absolutely unaware of the superior character of the Asistics.

"This is an enemy freighter bombed by our many planes and sprawled on its side. The day when its homeland will experience the same fate is not very far off.

"Our braves press firmly on the Samurai songs, Wherever our men go, the battlefield is theirs, Their sings voices solence enemy guns. Flowers line the roads, birds sing in the air. Fair are our soldiers, mighty the Empire's

arm. *The multitude of people rejoice over new establishment of righteousness. From the happy smiles on the faces of these maidens, we can perceive the new happiness brought to Asia. Our loudspeakers explain the spirit of Greater Asia Co-prosperity to the enemy, reveal dishonesty of the Americans.*

Americans and English, who had arrogantly walked the streets of MANILA till the day before, were shattered when the Imperial army entered the city. The Tyrone Powers, Claudette Colberts, and Jackie Coogans were all interned as a mixture of personalities at SANTO TOMAS UNIVERSITY. However, the treatments accorded the internees was so GENEROUS that it cause a Japanese, who also had undergone the same experience, to ream that their life was comparable to that in heaven. American and British Internees are profoundly grateful for the treatment they are receiving.

"The soldiers are magnificent. Their hearts are pure and their pose stalwart. The sailors at sea and the soldiers on land all have our firm determination—to die for our country. On the land, on the sea, and in the air, we are the victor. We have won the respect of the conquered people. This is the beginning of prosperity for our nation.

CHAPTER THIRTY-SIX

Hell Ships, Slave Labor and Death Factories

Japan conscripted slave labor wherever their troops set foot. So did Germany. Japan's slave labor legions, however, included thousands of Americans scooped up in the Philippines, Wake Island and Indonesia. Those that didn't get tickets on the Burma Railway were shipped to Japan on "Hell Ships." Japan recorded the total number of POWs sent to Japan as 70,000. Barely half survived the hellish travel conditions to get there.

"Voyage of Infamy," a symposium at the Nimitz Museum convened survivors of "Hell Ships." The ships were so named because of the inhumane conditions. Japan's large corporations imported slave labor and operated the transport ships, being paid by the number of POWs transported—thereby incentivizing mass packing. A radio message in September 1942 reported: *"Due to serious labor shortage, more POWs are earnestly required. Send POWs by every returning ship."* Conditions were so bad many arrived dead or crippled. Records show untold thousands were lost at sea. Roy Bodine was on the Enuri Maru where 1,426 out of 1,600 perished. Morris Shoss was on the Shingo Moru where only eighty-two out of 750 prisoners survived.

"When it was nearly full, guards came down and with whips beat us farther back into the ship's hold until it looked as if no more men could get in. Yet, more and more were coming. The ceilings were low, only about five feet high, but we were made to stand. We were crammed so tightly if a man fainted he could not fall to the floor. He remained packed. Men began screaming and fighting. They tore at each other, fought and pushed. Their screams were terrible things. Suddenly, there was more room. The fainting and the dead were sliding down until men littered the floor underneath our feet. We had more room to move in. But under our feet were the bodies of men."

Major McMinn testified before the War Crimes Tribunal:
"Hell Ships carried prisoners to Japan to work in factories and mines.

Thousands died at sea. We were shoveled below decks. This Jap hit me with the shovel as I went down. He hit several others, injuring some seriously. Our group of 800 had no room to sit. They then nailed boards over the hatch, leaving only a crack for air. Commander Portz asked the Japs to remove the boards so we could breathe. Wada told him to keep quiet or the hatch would be closed completely. Within an hour several men became insane. Within two hours many died. Several who drank urine died immediately. Sixty more died during the night."

Fall of Corregidor, by Otis H. King: *"We boarded a Hell Ship. Japan never marked them as having POWs aboard. The Japs herded us into a small hold and covered the hatch. There was no room to lay down. Men had to lay on top of one another. There were no toilet facilities. Two weeks underway, we docked at Formosa. The Japanese marched us through the streets to show off. In November 1942, we were put aboard another freighter to Yokohama. We were marched through the streets like zoo animals. Numbered in groups of ten, we were admonished if one escaped the other nine would be executed. Thus began two years where we toiled as slave laborers in Yokohama shipyards operated by Mitsubishi, maker of many automobiles found on American highways today."*

One "hell ship" voyage transporting American prisoners from the Philippines to Mitsui coal mines and Mitsubishi factories in Japan was documented by George Weller of the *Chicago Daily News*, who wrote *Voyage of the Death Ship*. This voyage of the Orokyu Maru lasted forty-nine days and, of the 1,600 Americans who boarded at Manila, only 300 survived. They were survivors of Bataan and Corregidor. The men, starving and thirst crazy, began going insane and attacking each other. The Japanese refused to send down benjos for waste. They wallowed in their filth. The temperature in the holds was 130°. Without water, men tried to scrape moisture off the bulkheads to drink. They sat naked like galley slaves between each other's legs. Jammed into the airless, filthy pits, all were naked, thirsty, hungry and sick. Denied water, some slashed their wrists and drank blood, others drank urine. They began to die.

At sea, American bombers strafed the ship, which ran aground. Major Longwith Berry describes: *"The man ahead of me on the ladder was hit. He fell dead back in my arms. I fell back into this dark hold. There were two men on each side of me who seemed to be asleep. I touched them. They were cold and dead. There was another flash. I looked up at the lieutenant. He was so full of holes he looked like a pepper shaker. Capt. Ted Parker* made a rush for the ladder. A sentry shot him twice through the body, once through the head."

The prisoners who survived the bombing were taken off the burning ship. They endured four days with no water. Many died of suffocation or were driven insane. Ashore, they were herded onto concrete tennis courts as their prison. 1,300 men were forced to sit with knees drawn to chin. After all day in the sun, they were desperate for water. Water was rationed to four teaspoonfuls per man per day. As the sun went down, men burnt red during the day began to chill. Some were naked. Six men died the first night. There was rice and water nearby, but the Japs denied access to them.

After several days, the water ration was fiendishly increased to four tablespoonfuls. A ship arrived and they were rushed aboard, the guards slapping them with swords and yelling "speedo." They were on a freighter which carried horses. It was like a barn, full of manure and flies. Horse feed was scattered in cracks. They scraped the leavings. A man died every hour. As they went north, it got cold. Men who had broiled, now shivered night and day. They reached Formosa where they were bombed again. The hold "resembled a butcher shop." More than 200 were killed. The Japs would not allow them to remove the bodies. They laid with their mangled dead for two more days, while in Formosa, 350 more died.

Two weeks later some 800 wounded and sick skeletons boarded another ship for Japan. Some had to be carried. Capt. Walter Donaldson crawled on his elbows and knees up the ladder. Fourteen died and were tossed in the water.

This ship was small. The survivors were jammed together—forty-seven more died the first day. "The Japs would call the roll, standing like little gods at the top of the hatch. It grew colder. They huddled together as bitter cold sucked through a ventilator. Colonel Beecher pleaded to close the ventilator. They refused. This wind of death brought pneumonia. Rain and snow fell through the open hatch on the bodies beneath. On a ship with water tanks full, they were given only four spoons daily. If you forgave them every-thing else, we would not forgive them denying us water all the way from Manila to Japan. Some starved, some suffocated, some were shot, some died of sunstroke, some of cold, but everybody was deliberately kept thirsty all the time."

On January 30, 1945, they reached Japan. Although it was freezing, the Japanese lined them up on deck and ordered them to strip naked. The last muster was called. It showed 300 men out of 1600 still alive. They went to work as slave labor.

The single ship death record is held by the Junyo Maru. Reported by

Robert Barr Smith in *Tragic Voyage*, of 1,700 Allied POWs, only 96 survived. Japan refused to identify ships ferrying prisoners with the Red Cross symbol, so tragedy was compounded by death delivered from American planes and subs unaware those ships carried prisoners. As this ship was sinking, Japanese crew members boarded life boats. As floundering prisoners sought to hang on to the sides of the boats, guards chopped off their hands as they slid into the ocean.

A sketch of American POWs mining

Germ Warfare

Japan's vast germ warfare program was secret during its operation and concealed thereafter. Remotely located in Manchuria, Japan's own planes were restricted from the site, an area so vast it covered two square miles. After the war, Japan denied its existence. Washington fell silent. As with other atrocities, paucity of survivors facilitated secrecy. American soldiers victimized by this death factory were officially ordered not to discuss their experiences. With the declassification of thousands of pages of documents relating to Unit 731, the frightening story is finally being revealed.

Japan's scientists believed an atomic bomb was possible. The enormous industrial effort was too taxing for Japan's insular economy, whereas germ warfare was a cheap means of mass destruction. Emperor Hirohito, a biologist, understood biological warfare. On his orders the Imperial Prevention and Water Supply Unit of the Kwantung Army was established at Pingfan in Manchuria. Biological warfare experiments were conducted and actually deployed. Germ warfare is nothing new. In the 1300s, Tartars catapulted dead bodies over fortified city walls to bring bubonic plague to their enemies. Today it's a poor man's nuclear arsenal. Microbes and toxins are cheap, easy to make and easy to hide. A grain of anthrax can kill a person. Fifty years later, those germs and toxins produced by Japan remain in remission. Neither the emperor nor the scientists were ever questioned.

Japan's Biological Warfare & The American Cover-Up, by Sheldon

Harris (1995) reported on Unit 731 in Mukden, the site for germ warfare experiments. An enormous project, it occupied 150 buildings. Chinese, British and Americans were victims. Live people were guinea pigs. Called "marutas" or logs, they were infected with cholera, typhoid, anthrax and syphilis. They were dissected live, electrocuted, frozen and boiled. To study gangrene, prisoners were shot. Human blood was replaced with horse blood. Some were spun to death in centrifuges, or put in compartments where pressure was raised until their eyes popped out.

A strain of bubonic plague was developed that could be transmitted by fleas. But there was no flea delivery service. A "Cherry Blossom" bomb with a flea canister was designed for delivery to California by submarines and balloons. No public records are available on this effort. However, it is known that in 1942, incendiaries from Japanese balloons blew across the Pacific and ignited forest fires on the west coast.

Doolittle's Army Air Force raid on Tokyo inadvertently gave rise to an enormous human laboratory. Some of these planes landed in China. When Japan was unable to find the Americans, in vengeful fury, Japan attacked entire areas. Planes sprayed plague germs. Cholera and anthrax germs were tossed into rivers. 250,000 people were killed. The experiments were so successful that parts of China remain infected today. The Emperor awarded Dr. Ishii, the project director, a medal.

British journalists, Peter Williams and David Wallace, report in their book *Unit 731*, that Dr. Ishii's human experiments with anthrax were horrendous. Women and children "were tied to stakes and protected with helmets, but their legs and buttocks were bared and exposed to shrapnel from anthrax bombs." Humans were fed food laced with anthrax and then monitored to measure death.

After the American survivors were set free, they were ordered "not to talk about their experiences." When pressed for information, the army reported "all records related to Japan's germ warfare activities had been returned to Japan."

Congressional hearings held in Washington in 1986 revealed American POWs were among experimental subjects. Said Montana Congressman Pat Williams at the end of the hearings: "*These men are victims of a terrible secret. This has been the longest kept secret of World War II, denied by Japan and concealed by the U.S. Government.*"

Professor Yoshiaki Yoshimi at Chuo University analyzed the report on Japanese chemical warfare by the U.S. Army in May 1946. Japan produced 1,646,326 units of chemical weapons, and had a stockpile of 91,371 units at the end of the war. Although Japan signed the Chemical Weapons Convention, it has not cleaned up its poison dumps. 700,000 units were stored in China. The Chemical Weapons Convention required disposal of such weapons. Japan is still discussing the situation.

On May 28, 2001, the *South China Morning Post* reported: *"Half a century later, atrocities still resonate. One cannot pick up an Asian newspaper without reference to Japanese war crimes and Japan's adamant refusal to compensate victims. Unit 731's physicians would experiment in bitter weather. Guards would strip a victim, tie him outdoors and freeze his arm to the elbow with water. Once the lower limb was frozen, doctors would test their frostbite treatment and amputate part of the arm. They would then repeat the process on the upper arm. After the arms were gone, doctors moved on to the legs. When the prisoner was reduced to head and torso, he would be used for bubonic plague experiments."*

When the Soviets entered Manchuria, they discovered the program and removed data and microbes to Sverdslosk where they then established their own germ program. They prosecuted Japan, and the author Russell Woking reported: *"In the 1930s, the Emperor established Unit 731 in Manchuria, known as Epidemic Prevention and Water Supply Unit, headed by Ishii Shiro, a military physician. This war crimes trial revealed Japan's chemical-warfare is estimated to have killed 250,000 people. Most of Unit 731 war criminals went on to respectable careers. Lt. Col. Ryoichi Naito founded Japan Blood Bank. Gen. Ishii Shiro lived in peace until his death. Japanese tourists often come here… they think it's funny."*

In February 2002, Oneta McNaught in the *London Times* reported: *"Away from the eyes of the world, Japan conducted the largest biological warfare program in history. Japanese military scientists killed twelve times the number of civilians as did the Nazi's under Dr. Josef Mengele. The Association to Reveal Historical Fact of Germ Warfare by Japan, numbering 108 survivors, filed suit against the government."* But Japan had destroyed the evidence. When the war ended, Dr. Ishii machine-gunned all the workers. The human guinea pigs were "stuffed into incinerators in piles so big they did not burn." No Japanese ever went to trial. Americans who survived were sworn to secrecy and threatened with loss of pension if they ever discussed their experiences. These atrocities are intensely topical in view of germ warfare programs underway in nations hostile to the U.S.

REFERENCES

Daws, Gavan, *Prisoners of the Japanese*, Wm. Morrow, NY, 1994

Edwards, Barnard, Blood & Bushido, *Japanese Atrocities at Sea*, Brick Tower Press, NY, 1997

Lamant-Brown, Raymond, Kempitai, *Japan's Dreaded Military Police*, Sutton Publications, Sydney, Australia, 1998

Tanaka, Yuki, *Hidden Horrors, Japanese War Crimes*, Westview Press, Boulder, CO, 1996

Section IV

FORGIVEN GUILT

There is a smoldering, festering resentment among those Pacific war veterans who, in fighting the Japanese, encountered their savagery in combat or capture. The dimensions of the silence that settled so soon and so pervasively over Pacific war crimes once the war drums fell silent puzzles and perturbs. I've seen it with my own eyes. I've heard it from the lips of survivors with trembling words and cracked voices. Why has this guilt been forgiven?

The depth of those feelings was vented by Richard Gordon in his book *Horyo, Memoirs of an America POW*. He wrote the memoir for his children but it sat on the family bookshelf until a friend persuaded him to publish and share his experiences with the insulated world. Ordered to surrender in Bataan, Gordon survived the Death March, prison camps, hell ships and slave labor in Japan. By the time V-J Day came he had been reduced to a diseased skeleton covered by skin. Although most of his fellow soldiers died from hunger, thirst, torture and sadistic beatings, his belief in God and country invested him with the will to live. He writes:

"I have yet to see an account that conveys my feelings. No one, including myself, can ever adequately describe those conditions. It would have been better to die than live as a slave of the Japanese Imperial Army. Germany had the courage to admit their guilt, but Japan lacks that courage. We must continue to remind them of their responsibility. We, their victims, can never forgive nor forget what they have done."

CHAPTER THIRTY-SEVEN

Deception, Denial and Double Standard

The unchanging nature of war is blood and violence. To ignore history is moronic. To falsify it is worse. It dishonors those young Americans who were rushed across the Pacific to confront the marauding tiger, who never flinched, who whipped the beast back into its cage, and returned to those who owed them so much, only to encounter ears that were deaf and eyes that were blind.

History will remember the twentieth century for the long bloody war which engulfed our nation and cut short so many young lives. We fought two mighty enemies through to unconditional surrender. What won't be remembered is the double standard by which war criminals were treated.

In Germany, in addition to the Nuremberg trials, U.S. military courts prosecuted Nazi lawyers, doctors, industrialists, diplomats and administrative officials. More than 600,000 people were punished, by 25,000 property confiscations, 22,000 banishments from public office, 9,000 imprisonments, 481 executions and 500,000 monetary penalties.

In 1979, the U.S. Department of Justice established the Office of Special Investigations to "prosecute German war criminals and collaborators." It has deported fifty-seven defendants, stripped citizenship from seventy-one residents, and has thirty more cases in process. The only publicity I've seen is that of John Demjanuk, the eighty-two-year-old Cleveland resident whose citizenship was recently revoked on archival evidence that sixty years ago he was a prison guard in a concentration camp.

Class action litigation here forced Germany to put five billion dollars in a fund for slave laborers. Switzerland ponied up another billion dollars for money taken from bank accounts. Clinton applauded such payments and sponsored legislation decreeing such payments immune from taxation. Another class action suit has recently been filed because "those payments weren't enough."

The U.S. is the only nation among the Allies in World War II that refused to make payments to its citizens brutalized by Japan. The State Department actively interceded to block compensation to prisoners forced into slave labor by Japanese companies. Au contraire, it supported such payments by Germany.

Recent books have peeled back kimonos, exposing ugly truths. One is Linda Goetz Holmes' *Unjust Enrichment: How Japanese Companies Built Postwar Fortunes Using American POWs.* She reports that exploitation of POWs was official government policy. Thirty-six thousand U.S. prisoners labored as slaves in factories and mines of Japan's industrial giants, e.g., Mitsui, Mitsubishi, Nippon Steel and Kawasaki. Many were worked to death. After interviewing over 400 POWs, Linda Goetz Holmes concludes: *"The miraculous recovery of Japan's industries began on the backs of our POWs. They came home to a lifetime of medical problems and permanent injuries caused by that labor."*

These companies profited, yet refused to pay for their "unjust enrichment," even though legally obligated to do so by Japanese law. The legal claim is for wages, not "reparations." 11,532 American prisoners perished in Japanese captivity. No company, no executive has ever been held accountable. U.S. intelligence officers ordered returning POWs <u>NOT</u> to talk about their treatment by Japan, threatening them with loss of pensions.

At the fiftieth anniversary of the 1951 Treaty of San Francisco ending the Pacific War, Japan managed to side step the slave labor issue with their eternal tea ceremony. Money was pumped into organizations "celebrating" that anniversary. When Tom Foley was Clinton's Ambassador to Japan, he officially resisted those claims. Sumitomo hired Foley's wife as a "consultant." Now in a Washington law firm, Foley's retainer continues, only this time cutting out the middle woman.

The slave labor story surfaced nationally in the recent article by Peter Maas in *Parade Magazine*: "They Should Have Their Day in Court." The author revealed how Americans were forced into slave labor by Japan's biggest corporations. Prisoners were sent to a Mitsui coal mine, so dangerous that Japanese miners refused to work it. Others were sent to Mitsubishi copper mines, clad only in gunnysacks. The POWs trudged through 10-foot-high snowdrifts in bitter winter cold.

Lester Tenney is an amazing man, who, on returning home, successfully pursued a Ph.D. Speaking personally with him is inspirational. His book, *My Hitch in Hell*, tells how American POWs were tortured. Almost fifty percent of POWs died in Japanese prison camps. Those living today bear medical and emotional scars. Americans who survived and came home were awarded $1.00 a day for each day's captivity, which payment was then given an IRS hair cut.

Legislation passed in California in 1999 authorized 5,000 slave labor victims still living to file compensation claims. Similar legislation was passed in New York, West Virginia, Pennsylvania, New Mexico, New Jersey and Nebraska. In California, seventeen suits were filed in state courts seeking compensation. They were cut off at the pass by Washington. The cases were consolidated in federal court in San Francisco. Judge Walker, Federal District Judge in California, not only complied with the U.S. State Department's request to dismiss their claims, he went out of his way to demean the veterans, ruling: "*While compensation in the economic sense is denied these former prisoners, the immeasurable bounty of life for themselves and their posterity in a free society and more peaceful world services the debt.*"

The veterans then ran an end-around to state legislatures to authorize their claims. The rising sons geared down to state level. Japan sent letters warning those states of economic reprisals. Signed by the Japanese ambassador, the letters stated:

"*Japanese firms are one of the largest foreign investors in your state as well as the second largest market for your state's exports... I bring to your attention your Legislature's Resolution. I am concerned by the adverse affect this resolution may have on the bilateral relations between your state and Japan, as well as future action.*"

Outraged over the U.S. State Department's mugging U.S. citizens, on March 22, 2001, Republican Congressmen Dana Rohrabacher and Democrat Mike Honda introduced HR1198. The "Justice For United States Prisoners of War Act of 2001" to preserve actions against Japanese companies brought by our military personnel held as prisoners of war, seeking compensation for wages. It directs the State Department and Justice Department "to allow claims against private Japanese companies without obstruction." It withholds funding from federal attempts to deny such rights. That bill passed overwhelmingly. It became part of the annual spending bill. However, in the conference committee, Michael Armacost and Thomas Foley, former Japanese ambassadors, and former Democratic Vice President Mondale, lobbied against the bill. The provision disappeared from the bill before it was signed.

For half a century a hoax has been perpetrated on these veterans. The U.S. State Department glibly announced that the peace treaty eliminated private claims against Japan, but it failed to disclose a secret amendment to the treaty automatically invoking the "most favored nation" clause. Article twenty-six states: "*Should Japan make any settlement granting greater advantage, those same advantages shall extend to all parties to this treaty.*" That language is obligatory: "*those same advantages shall extend.*" Japan secretly made favorable settlements with eleven other nations— Burma, Switzerland, Philippines, Netherlands, Soviet Union, Sweden,

Spain, Indonesia, Vietnam, Denmark and Korea. The U.S. Government kept those settlements secret.

The secret agreement signed by John Foster Dulles and Prime Minister Yoshida in 1951 was declassified in April 2000. It reveals the calumny. One day before treaty signing, the Netherlands decided to join Korea, Russia, China and India in refusing to sign. Since a Dutch walkout could lead the United Kingdom, Australia and New Zealand to also drop out, the morning of the signing John Foster Dulles negotiated a secret agreement between the Netherlands and Japan preserving rights of Dutch citizens to pursue reparations.

Thus we now know our State Department negotiated a treaty permitting victims of Japanese companies to pursue claims, but kept it secret from American victims. After the declassification, most people entitled to payments were dead.

Another untold Pacific war story is the treatment of American civilians and their families who lived in the pre-war Philippines. Unlike military families who were hustled home in the months preceding Pearl Harbor, civilians were denied passports to return to the U.S. Like tethered goats, they were staked out to assure the Filipinos the U.S. was committed to defending their homeland. When the Japanese stormed ashore, the status of 20,000 American civilians switched from pawns to prisoners.

Men, women and children were herded into POW camps where they languished and died in miserable conditions during 3-1/2 years. In those miserable camps starvation and disease ran rampant. Hundreds died as they were reduced to eating cats, dogs, rats and weeds to survive. Red Cross packages sent them were confiscated by their captors. As with our military, their condition was unknown at the time and covered up later. Information on this condition was reported in the Congressional Record years later when Francis B. Sayre, high commissioner of the Philippines, Dr. Claude Buss, adviser to the high commissioner, and Ervin Ross, passport agent, told about the State Department's denying civilians permission to leave. What goaded them to go public was the gift of $20,000 to every Japanese who claimed to have been interned in the U.S. The Americans received neither income nor compensation for their agonizing internment. They lost all their possessions and, in many cases, their health. The survivors have sought recompense akin to that given the Japanese, but Washington stonewalled.

The civilian prisoner outrage was flushed into public view in July 2002 by a lawsuit filed in Washington, D.C. by Marcia Achenbach who was four years of age when interned. Recently declassified documents reveal that Washington denied passports to thousands of American citizens in the Philippines while simultaneously rushing evacuations of Americans from Japan's path in China and Southeast Asia.

Japan's Holocaust is hidden. Why? The only rationale offered is a shrug of the shoulders. However, an obscure crack has appeared in the wall of silence. On July 26, 2002, California Congressman Michael Honda, in commemorating the opening of the American Museum of Asian Holocaust in Falls Creek, Pennsylvania remarked in the Congressional Record:

"Mr. Speaker, I rise to congratulate Eugene Wei for having the foresight to create such an important learning institution... The museum will display exhibits of the Asian Holocaust of World War II perpetrated by Japan in China, Korea, the Philippines, Singapore, Indonesia and Malaysia... It will tell of the American POWs who were forced to work for Japanese companies as slave laborers in mines, shipyards and steel mills, and their horrible experiences on hell ships... Exhibits on the Rape of Nanking, Comfort Women and Japanese biological and chemical warfare will be on display as well... This is not an easy history to tell, but it must be told!"

Quandary? Half a century of personal dealings with the Japanese, from both sides of those .50 calibers, provides perspective. In the '60s, as Japanese auto companies began marketing in the U.S., I assisted the distribution process of one such company. That led to interfacing with Japanese companies and individuals, both here and in Japan. Many personal friendships developed, particularly with those who credit the U.S. Army for saving them from starvation in the grim post-war years. Therein lies my quandary. I personally know them to be unfailingly polite and gracious. I also personally have known them to be unspeakably bestial. Which face is the "true" (honnae); which is the "facade" (tatemae)? No westerner can break that code. However, of this I am absolutely positive: The history of one of our Air Forces is missing, and the guilt of its enemy has been forgiven.

REFERENCES

Dower, John W., *War Without Mercy*, N.Y., Pantheon Books, 1986

Edgerton, Robert, *Warriors Of The Rising Sun*, N.Y., W.D. Norton, 1997

Tanaka, Yaki, *Hidden Horrors, Japanese War Crimes*, Boulder, Colo., Westview Press, 1996

CHAPTER THIRTY-EIGHT

Remember Pearl Harbor— Forget the Movie

The movie *Pearl Harbor* symbolizes the unique characteristics of that war—deceit and distance. Hollywood, hoping to piggy-back on a cash cow named *Saving Private Ryan*, suddenly remembered there was also a war in the Pacific. Here was a golden opportunity to educate young Americans about the color-blind values of duty, honor and country. Instead, the purveyors of "entertainment" opted for a sugary and inaccurate script. Rewriting history and pandering to Japanese movie-goers brought forth a turkey. Box office omnia vincit.

Veiling Japan's aggression, inferring that we bore responsibility, and lacing the Pacific air war with romance, are clear and present insults to those 100,000 Americans who paid the butcher's bill. The guilt of those who gave orders to those who enthusiastically carried them out can never be sensed by those who "experience war" eating hot buttered popcorn. Writer Suzanne Fields calls the movie "a tale told by an idiot, full of sound and fury and signifying nothing." Michelle Malkin says it's "a bad script conceived in ignorance and enhanced by pyrotechnics."

Real-time reaction to Pearl Harbor was expressed in the 1944 film *Purple Heart*, by a Doolittle flyer about to be executed in Tokyo:

"We Americans don't know very much about you Japanese and never did, and you know even less about us. You can kill us, but, if you think that's going to put fear into the United States and stop them from sending other fliers to bomb you, you're wrong—dead wrong. They'll blacken your skies, burn your cities to the ground, and make you get down on your knees and beg for mercy. This is your war—you wanted it—you asked for it. And now you're going to get it—and it won't be finished until your dirty little empire is wiped off the face of the earth."

The president of the Japanese American Citizens League complained about the Pearl Harbor movie: "We keep getting dragged back to

December 7." Who drags hordes of Japanese tourists to the watery grave of the USS Arizona in Pearl Harbor, where that great ship still bleeds oil from the tomb of a thousand American sailors? Who drags those sons of Nippon across this memorial, giggling and posing for photos? Why are Japanese tourists magnetized to this particular site? Why do Japanese, normally polite, become noisily irreverent on our sacred memorial? Hoping the "Day That Lives In Infamy" will not become the "Day That Lives In Amnesia" is why this little book was written.

CHAPTER THIRTY-NINE

After the Ball Was Over

A thousand years of Bushido erupted at Pearl Harbor where Japan sought to smash the last barrier to their conquering Asia. Other Pacific powers had been eliminated: China by conquest, Holland and France by surrender, Great Britain by other engagements. That left only the soft Americans, a tethered goat at Pearl Harbor helpless before the marauding tiger. Surprise! The professional samurais were felled by amateurs. The mighty shogun empire, which had never known defeat in its 2,000 year history, was crushed and cremated—not by invading armies, but by a rain of fire from above. Its fleet was sunk, its army defeated, its planes shot out of the skies and its cities incinerated into open crematoria. For the first time, a mighty empire was vanquished without conquering soldiers setting foot to home soil.

Like all Americans, I presumed "unconditional surrender" for which we had spent four years fighting, had been achieved. Euphoria erupted on V-J Day. Clark Field looked like a Fourth of July fireworks extravaganza. We were assured by MacArthur from the deck of the USS Missouri, "the

Tokyo on VJ-Day

holy mission has now been completed."

In the Japanese mind defeat is inconceivable. When the Emperor addressed his nation ending the war in a collection of strange and obscure phrases, the words "surrender" or "defeat" were not spoken. He simply observed the war "did not turn in Japan's favor." Denying responsibility, he said the war began to "ensure the survival of Japan and the liberation of East Asia." He condemned America, saying "the enemy has for the first time used cruel bombs to kill and maim extremely large numbers of the innocent and the heavy casualties are beyond measure. To continue the war could lead to the destruction of civilization."

Neither press nor politicians accepted their defeat. *Asahi*, Japan's premier newspaper, wrote its editorial on the surrender by "affirming the superiority of our race." Prime Minister Yoshida pronounced that "history has many examples of nations losing wars and winning the peace." Although the imperial army and navy were abolished, the imperial nation-state remained. Its citizens continue to refer to themselves as shido menzoku, "the leading race of the world."

People today have no frame of reference for the grim Pacific air war. Japanese obsession with slaughter, unsated in four years of uncensored depravity, continued to the very last day of the war when eight American airmen were hastily dragged from their Tokyo prison cells and beheaded.

The day the shooting stopped, denials began. Being stripped of their guns encouraged good conduct. Once they became prisoners, ferocity melted into mildness. Mantra falling from polite mouths was "very sorry," meaning, in their context, "too bad." Today Japan remains in denial, nurturing collective amnesia. Attempts to report history accurately are branded "blasphemy." Since the Emperor was never criticized, and the Emperor is the state, that proves they did nothing wrong. It's as though Japan's history ended in 1937, and didn't return for many years, during which time, for reasons they can't figure out, Americans started dropping bombs on them. Many in Japan don't even know there was a war. Lack of history facilitates ignorance. A decade of aggression vanished like a puff of smoke. Smiles replaced swords, bows replaced bombs.

The bone-chilling book *Rape of Nanking* is banned. Politicians deny Nanking ever happened. School books are sanitized. Their conquest of Korea was "annexation supported by western powers." Invading China, fourteen years and ten million casualties, is called the "China Incident." Their germ warfare program has been scrubbed out. Historic erasures fall on a receptive public, and in younger generations, an ignorant one.

Herbert W. Bix in his Pulitzer Prize winning book *Hirohito and the*

Making of Modern Japan, tracks Japan's aggression as driven by Hirohito. MacArthur, as supreme commander of allied occupation powers, used the Emperor to convert a military oligarchy into a democracy, although there is some doubt as to who manipulated who. Bix writes: *"The Tokyo war crimes trials were not straight adversary proceedings. The imperial family regularly socialized with the Americans at parties and 'duck hunts.' War leaders denied criminal liability and received back salaries and pensions. Many rose to political power. Japan, concentrating on economic development, has never acknowledged responsibility."*

The day Japan surrendered, the skies over Tokyo were black from documents going up in smoke. Records that survived fire-bombing did not survive the cease fire. On August 15, 1945, the Ministry of War ordered a massive destruction of documents in anticipation of war crime trials, but destruction was to be "with a sense of worship." The Emperor dismounted from his white horse, shed his uniform and was re-deified as the man of peace. A nation of 70 million people dropped its samurai sword and donned its kabuki mask. Elegant presents seduced round eyes bent on revenge. In reshuffling the global deck following V-J Day in 1945, Allies became enemies and enemies became allies. Russia and China changed roles. Japan was not subjected to reparations imposed on Germany. Guilt vaporized.

The war ended. Deceit did not! A bamboo curtain descended. Japan hid its war crimes behind a fig leaf peace treaty. Japan's corruption pyramid has most crime at the top and little at street level. The big combines insulate their nest with rich contributions. They maintain they don't owe anybody anything—not even an apology. This brings to mind the William Butler Yeats poem:

> *For how can you compete*
> *Being honor-bred, with one who*
> *Were it proved he lies*
> *Were neither ashamed in his own*
> *nor in his neighbor's eyes?*

After the atomic cloud cleared, the military metamorphosed. The venue for conquest became economic. The warrior samurai transmogrified into the economic samurai. The nation built an economic war machine, dispatching its soldiers to every corner of the earth. Their export offensive attacked targets, picking them off one by one, their thirst for domination salted by their galling defeat. Defending their insular economy with pathological protectionism, profit was subordinated to market domination

Characteristics defining Japan's warfare—meticulous planning, complex strategies, and total dedication are manifest in their economy. In wartime, they gloated over victories. Their economic victories in the sixties buried America's electronic industry and overtook its auto industry. In peace, Japan achieved what eluded it in war. American consumers subsidized Japan's factories. Their banks bulged, their tourists swarmed abroad. They gobbled up properties at any price. "Japan, Inc." was the model of the future, according to Harvard. Not quite. A funny thing happened. The Kremlin collapsed and technology arose. The West adapted; Japan did not. Unwilling to shift gears, the "Teahouse of the August Moon" cratered. Japan is mired in its worst ever depression. Banks are awash with unpayable debt. Their credit rating is lower than Botswana's; their business ethics are situational; reality remains in denial. The energy fueling their post war economy might well be the millions of corpses walled up in the foundation of their state. It bound them during the war. It still binds them today—their war forgotten and their guilt forgiven.

References

Keegan, John, *The Second World War*, Penguin Books, NY, 1989

Epilogue

When Japan attacked America at Pearl Harbor, we rushed to battle. We lied about our age to enlist. A generation of fierce patriotism was followed by a generation of self-indulgence. Doing one's own thing became the mantra for those who never did. Military service was avoided through foreign flight. Many of those who had no idea how freedom was won, nor at what cost, became the hands on our wheel, the voices in our ears. Fewer and fewer people share our values, who understand that there are things worth dying for, and yes, worth killing for. We thought those who followed in our footsteps would know our history and retain our values. Now we ponder the searing question posed by philosopher William Auden:

> *To save your world, you asked this man to die.*
> *Would this man, could he see you now, ask why?*

I am baffled by the paradox in which today's generation contemplates death. Fascinated by death, they play Nintendo games in kindergarten, take guns to school, and main-line on it in movies. Au contraire, military death is shunned and spurned. This phobia cost us dearly in Iraq. We spent a year gearing up for the Persian Gulf War, four days fighting it, and one hour seeing death. That one hour was our final hour. The war halted. Saddam is still there, still armed, cowing his neighbors, supporting terrorists, and guffawing at Clinton's impeachment wars. "Allies" returned to café society. Europe became a province of Islam, leaving us alone to absorb the hatred of Islam's fanatics.

My heart goes out to our wonderful military, so proficient they stood down a massive and aggressive communist military for fifty years. They reduced the fourth largest army in the world to the second largest army in Iraq in four days. To salvage a morbid presidency, they were scattered aimlessly over the world—grocery boys in Somalia; traffic cops in Haiti. Ordered into the Balkan morass to wag the dog and be home by Christmas. Four years later we're still there. Political loathing and media hostility have taken their toll. Men and equipment are worn out, service women pregnant, families broken, pilots resigning, pensions shriveled. Forces which are a genuine threat to America gathered strength while we stuck out our tongue.

Military's function is to take land and kill people. General LeMay said when you kill enough of 'em, they stop fighting. Trotsky's mordant words resonate: "You may not be interested in war, but war is interested in you." Only the dead have seen the end of war. The military machines of Caesar and Napoleon were trained to kill, not placate. Now training is for "cooperation" in a "permissive environment." Training is social as the intercourse that follows. Secretary of Navy John Dalton pronounced "pregnancy and parenthood are compatible with navy carriers." The training worked. Female sailors achieve a twenty percent pregnancy rate.

In 1776, the year of America's Declaration of Independence, Edward Gibbon wrote *The Decline and Fall of the Roman Empire*. Rome dominated the ancient world for centuries, because its military was strong and its leaders honorable. The Roman Empire extended from Spain, England and France on the west, through Africa, Greece and the Mid-East, encompassing: *"The fairest portion of the earth, the most civilized portion of mankind. It would not have lasted as long or been as great without its leaders being men of honor and its citizens imbued with virtues."*

Our founding fathers crafted the Constitution around Roman traits of freedom and citizen responsibility. The ordained function of government was to protect people and property. The founders knew that when Roman Emperors indulged their satyric desires, their degeneracy sapped morality from the citizens. Emperor Commodus indulged his sensual appetites in a seraglio of women. Outraged, the "senate decreed his name stripped from monuments, his statues toppled, his body dragged with a hook to satiate the public fury." But it was too late. The barbarians were at the gate.

Charles Hill of the Hoover Institution capsules: *"The self-sacrificing determination and national unity of the Wold War II years and the buoyant optimism of the post war period gave way to a hedonistic timorousness in a transformation not unlike that which changed the Roman character of old. The traits of decency faded to indulging in every desire."* True to form, the American Nero diddled for eight years while the world burned.

Most Americans are decent, moral and patriotic. But children are not born with these virtues. Aristotle said moral education must occur during youth. It can be learned from books or taught by parents. Children can learn America's virtues from our World War II stories, when American virtues were a beacon to the world. Better they should know our history than adulate rappers loose in the land.

The popularity of films like *Saving Private Ryan* and *Band of Brothers* reveals a hunger for heroes. Peter Gibbon's book, *Nil Admirari—Media and the Loss of Heroes*, recounts the Roman phrase "nil admirari" meaning "nothing to admire." Today's media culture finds crime and scandal newsworthy, but not history or valor. Our youth are dazzled with sleazy sights and sated with raunchy sounds. With nothing to admire, America's destiny, like the glory of Greece and grandeur of Rome, could pass prematurely into history.

We can't hide immoral acts and scandals from our children, but we shouldn't validate them. By failing to instruct our children, we commit the sin of moral disarmament. The moment of moral clarity has arrived for America.

THE DOGS OF WAR RETURN

After four years of study and contemplation, the last words of this book are written. Once again America is at war, not of its choosing, nor of its doing. So preoccupied with the "peace process" and the U.N.'s rhetorical baggage, we overlooked the one ingredient without which puffery and posturing has no value. Morality! Without morality there can be no peace. Peace, or rather the interim absence of war, rests not on words and promises, but on the morality and intent of those who speak them.

France, endemically envious and in fevered pursuit of commerce with Iraq, has selfishly ripped the flimsy fabric of the U.N., just as it once did to the League of Nations. When Hitler marched into the Rhineland, the French sat on their hands and the League crumbled into irrelevancy. To entrust our safety to a melange of hostile nations and dictatorships is to be tied down by Lilliputians. The decision of war or peace for America is not for Cameroon or Guinea, and certainly not for France. When peace involves walking on your knees, it's no longer peace, its suicide.

Living in two centuries as I have, provides olympian perspective. Robert Conquest, the famed historian at the Hoover Institution, says events do not cease to be significant because they belong to the past! America now represents the culture of the west; Islam represents the rest. This is not new. A thousand years ago cultures clashed. Now they clash again; only the weapons have changed. War or peace is not always our choice. Ernest Hemingway said: *"There are things worse than war, and they all begin with defeat."*

The suicide attacks of September 11, 2001, are spoken of as a new phenomenon. Suicidal zealots are nothing new to Pacific veterans. We encountered them. We fought them. They killed us. We killed them. We called them kamikazes. They caused more damage than any other weapon. At Okinawa alone 10,000 kamikaze casualties rendered it the bloodiest naval battle in U.S. history. Easy to train and nearly impossible to stop, suicide pilots dove across bristling war ships through curtains of lead, on a joy ride to eternal sake and sakura. Murama Takaji, a kamikaze pilot, boasted: "It would be a great honor to crash into an American ship. There are many pretty geishas in the next life." Today's suicide bombers go to "paradise where await seventy beautiful maidens with lustrous eyes who do not sleep, get pregnant, spit or defecate."

Today's fanatical enemies lack the military mass of soldiers who goose-stepped across Europe and overran the Pacific screaming "banzai." It took five years and fifty million deaths to bury them in the rubble of the Reichstag and the crematories of Tokyo. But there's no end game with today's enemy. This war broke out on a landscape forever altered in a world economically and electronically entangled. Continents and oceans have shrunk as space is squeezed and time compressed. This enemy has no homeland, no forts or factories. He can be anywhere in the world, hiding, scheming and mutating. He may have no face we can see nor address we can find. He found us.

The "hate America first" crowd, coddled and condoned, has graduated to mass murder. Assassins sortie from safe harbors in rogue nations, "states of concern," in politically correct lingo. First our barracks in Beirut, then World Trade Center Bombing I, then our embassies, then our navy, each progressively killing more Americans. Each time we backed off. Manhattan, the mental mecca of political correctness and Washington, its political protector, have been brutally introduced to terrorism. Those scars should remind us that terrorism, like Ebola virus, is invisible, contagious and lethal. It feeds on appeasement. Its habitat must be destroyed wherever it exists. Feet-on-the-ground intelligence must patrol its breeding grounds. This kind of war can't be won by clean air and pure thoughts. The threat is unique, but so is the moment.

There can be no reasoning with terrorists. Hiding and lurking, their targets are civilians, fear is their weapon. This is their war and America is their battlefield.

The first shots of a war are never the most destructive. Three kamikaze planes wreaked the only damage ever to strike our homeland, inconsequential perhaps to what might lay ahead. Today's generation, whose most vexing experience has been looking for a parking place and whose greatest concern is global warming, now finds itself the generation for whom the bells toll. Seeing in real time the vaporizing of the World Trade Center, symbol of American capitalism, and the Pentagon, symbol of American power has scripted what John Foster Dulles called "an agonizing reappraisal." I sense a resurgence of respect for our brave military, whose present Commander-in-Chief has restored honor and dignity to the Presidency and patriotism to the nation.

Casualties cannot be avoided. Real war is not a video game for politicians or stimulated protesters who demonstrate, not against Saddam or bin Laden, but their own President! In 1941, peace marchers boycotted the White House, but they never disparaged President Roosevelt in deference to Hitler or Hirohito. The twentieth century's soft last half lulled us into forgetting the only rule of war that matters—MacArthur's: *"In war there is no substitute for victory."*

Those of us who fought the fanatic Japanese warriors now leave this farewell. You have seen the face of evil. You have felt the hand of evil from "martyrs" who welcome death. The kamikaze pilots we faced were also eager for suicide missions. To die for their emperor made them martyrs. And so they did. They never surrendered. They never retreated. They never negotiated. Each battle was to the death. We never understood their cruelty—we simply killed them wherever we found them. We won! They lost!

Bibliography

Bergerud, Eric, *Fire in the Sky*, Westview Press, Boulder, Colorado, 1999

Bix, Herbert P., *Hirohito*, Harper Collins, New York, 2000

Boeman, John, *Morotai*, Sunflower Press, Manhattan, Kansas, 1989

Braddon, Russell, *Japan Against the World 1941-2041*, Stein & Day, New York, 1983

Bradley, James, *Flags of Our Fathers*, Bantam, New York, 2000

Brewer, Wm. B., *Retaking the Philippines*, St. Martins Press, New York, 1986

Brown, Richard F., *Lightning Strikes Four Times*, Bradley Printers, Phoenix, Arizona, 1996

Bumgarner, John, *Parade of the Dead*, McFarland Co., London, 1995

Caidin, Martin, *Fork-Tailed Devil: The P-38*, Ballantine Books, New York, 1971

Carter, Kit C., *The Army Air Forces in World War II: Combat Chronology*, Office of Air Force History, Washington, D.C., 1974

Chang, Iris, *Rape of Nanking*, Basic Books, New York, 1997

Charles, Robert, *Last Man Out*, Eakin Press, Austin, Texas, 1999

Cohen, Stan, *East Wind Rain*, Pictorial Histories, Missoula, Montana, 1981

Congdon, Don, *Combat, The War with Japan*, Dell, New York, 1962

Coox, Alvin, Japan, *The Final Agony*, Ballantine, New York, 1971

Costello, John, *The Pacific War*, Rawson, Wade, New York, 1981

Craven, Frank & Cate, James, *The Army Air Force in World War II*, 7 Vols., Office of Air Force History, Washington, D.C., 1973

Daws, Gavan, *Prisoners of the Japanese*, Wm. Morrow, New York, 1994

Dower, John W., *War Without Mercy*, Pantheon Books, New York, 1986

_____, *Embracing Defeat*, W.W. Norton, New York, 1999

Edgerton, Robert, *Warriors of the Rising Sun*, W.W. Norton, New York, 1997

Edwards, Barnard, *Blood and Bushido Japanese Atrocities at Sea*, Brick Tower Press, New York, 1997

Evans & Peattie, *Kaigun*, Naval Institute Press, Annapolis, Maryland, 1997

Fagel, Joshua, *The Nanjing Massacre*, University of California Press, Berkeley, California, 2000

Falk, Stanley, *Liberation of the Philippines*, Ballantine, New York, 1971

Flanagan, E.M., *Corregidor, The Rock Force Assault*, Presidio Press, Novato, CA, 1995

Foster, Simon, *Okinawa 1945*, Arms & Armour Press, London, 1995

Gailey, Harry, *War In The Pacific*, Presidio Press, Novato, CA, 1995

Gaskill, Wm., *Fighter Pilot in the South Pacific*, Sunflower Press, Manhattan, Kansas, 1997

Glines, C.V., *The Doolittle Raid*, Orion Books, New York, 1988; *Attack on Yamamoto*, Schiffer History, Atzlen, PA, 1993

Goodwin, Michael J., *Shobun*, Stackpole Books, Mechanicsburg, PA, 1995

Greene, Bob, *Duty*, Wm. Morrow, New York, 1985

Hallas, James, *Killing Ground on Okinawa*, Praeger, London, 1996

Hanley, Fiske, *Accused American War Criminal*, Eakin Press, Austin, Texas, 1997

Harris, Brooklyn, *Bill, A Pilot's Story*, Graphic Press, Klamath Falls, Oregon, 1995

Harris, Meiron & Susan, *Soldiers of the Sun, The Rise & Fall Of The Imperial Japanese Army*, Random House, New York, 1991

Hoyt, Edwin P., *Closing the Circle*, Reinhold Company, New York, 1982
_____, *Guadalcanal*, Jove Books, New York, 1982

Hunt, Frazier, *Untold Story of General MacArthur*, Devin Adair, New York, 1954

Innis, Walter D., *Bridge Across the Seas*, Devon, Washington, D.C., 1995

Jablonski, Edward, *Air War*, Doubleday, New York, 1971
_____, *Pictorial History of World War II*, Doubleday, New York, 1977

Kerr, Bartlett E., *Surrender and Survival*, Wm. Morrow, New York, 1985

Knott, Richard, *Black Cat Raiders*, Nautical Aviation Publishing Co., Annapolis, MD, 1981

Lamont-Brown, Raymond, *Kempeitai, Japan's Dreaded Military Police*, Sutton Publications, Sydney, Australia, 1998

Layton, Edwin T, *And I Was There*, Wm. Morrow, New York, 1985

Lippincott, Ben E., *From Fiji Through the Philippines*, Washington, D.C. 1946

Manchester, Wm., *Goodbye Darkness*, Little, Brown, Boston, MA,1979

Martindale, Robert, *The 13th Mission*, Eakin Press, Austin, TX, 1998

Mayer, S. L., *MacArthur*, Ballantine, New York, 1971

McBride. Wm., *America In The Air War*, Time-Life Books, Alexandria, VA, 1982

McBride, William M., *Goodnight Officially*, Westview Press, Boulder, Colorado, 1994

Miller, Francis T., MacArthur, *Fighter for Freedom*, Winston Co., Chicago, Illinois, 1942

Miller, Thomas G., *Cactus Air Force*, Harper, New York, 1969

Mitsuru, Yoshida, *Requiem For Battleship Yamato*, Kodansha, Ltd., Tokyo, 1985

Morris, Eric, *Corregidor*, Stein & Day, New York, 1981

Olson, John E., *O'Donnell, Andersonville Of The Pacific*, 1985

Pranz, Gordon W., *At Dawn We Slept*, McGraw-Hill, New York, 1981

Rutherford, Ward, *Fall of the Philippines*, Ballantine, New York, 1971

Sakaida, Henry, *The Siege of Rabaul*, Phalanx, St. Paul, Minnesota, 1996

Schultz, Duane, *The Last Battle Station*, St. Martins Press, New York, 1985

Skates, John Ray, *The Invasion of Japan*, South Carolina University Press, Columbia, SC, 1994

Smurthwaite, David, *Pacific War Atlas*, Mirabel Books, New York, 1995

Sommers, Stan, *The Japanese Story*, Marshfield, Wisconsin, 1980

Starke, Wm. H., *Vampire Squadron*, Documation, Eau Claire, Wisconsin, 1999

Stevens, Paul F., *Low Level Liberators*, Nashville, Tennessee, 1997

Stinnett, Robert, *Day of Deceit*, Free Press, New York, 2000

Sulzberger, C. L., *Picture History of World War II*, Bonanza Books, New York, 1966

Tanaka, Yuki, *Hidden Horrors, Japanese War Crimes*, Westview Press, Boulder, CO, 1996

Thompson, Kyle, *A Thousand Cups of Rice*, Eakin Press, Austin, Texas, 1994

Toland, John, *But Not In Shame*, Random House, New York, 1961

_____, *Infamy*, Doubleday, New York, 1982

Tsouras, Peter, *Rising Sun Victorious*, Stackpole Books, Mechanicsburg, PA, 2001

Wheeler, Keith, *The Road to Tokyo*, Time-Life Books, Richmond, Virginia, 1979

Winslow, W.G., *The Fleet the Gods Forgot*, Naval Institute Press, Annapolis, MD, 1982

Winton, John, *War in the Pacific*, Mayflower Books, New York, 1978

World War II Encyclopedia, Vol. 10, 17, Vol. 18, Vol. 19, Vol. 20, Orbis

Publishing, USA, 1972

Wygle, Peter, *Surviving a Japanese POW Camp*, Pathfinder Publishing, Ventura, CA, 1991

Youngblood, Wm., *Red Sun Setting*, Naval Institute Press, Annapolis, MD, 1981